T0331032

Generations
in the World of Work

Generations in the World of Work provides invaluable data-informed insights into the intergenerational dynamics in today's workplaces.

Generational experts and authors of *Generation Z: A Century in the Making*, Corey Seemiller and Meghan Grace present the perceptions, motivations, and preferences of various generational cohorts and share how those shape individual behaviors, communication and collaboration, as well as wider organizational structures and norms. They offer guidance for how to maximize productivity and relationships to navigate dynamics across generational cohorts.

Generations in the World of Work offers employees, managers, and organizational leaders guidance for maximizing productivity, relationships, well-being, and engagement across generational differences in order to create thriving workplaces that value and leverage each person's strengths.

Corey Seemiller is an award-winning professor in the Department of Leadership Studies in Education and Organizations at Wright State University. Her highly popular TED Talk on Generation Z at TEDxDayton showcased how Generation Z is making a difference in the world. Her work has been featured on National Public Radio (NPR) and in the *New York Times*, *Time Magazine*, and *Newsweek*, as well as in several other news publications. She has also been interviewed for podcasts as well as TV and radio shows worldwide.

Meghan Grace is a generational researcher, international speaker, consultant, and host of the podcast *#GenZ*. She is a research expert who co-leads the Institute for Generational Research and Education and has a background in organizational development, strategy, and learning.

Generations in the World of Work

COREY SEEMILLER AND MEGHAN GRACE

Routledge
Taylor & Francis Group

LONDON AND NEW YORK

Designed cover image: Conceptual design: Meghan Grace;
Technical design: Marilyn Rodriguez

First published 2025
by Routledge
4 Park Square, Milton Park, Abingdon, Oxon OX14 4RN

and by Routledge
605 Third Avenue, New York, NY 10158

Routledge is an imprint of the Taylor & Francis Group, an informa business

British Library Cataloguing-in-Publication Data
A catalogue record for this book is available from the British Library

Library of Congress Cataloging-in-Publication Data
Names: Seemiller, Corey, author. | Grace, Meghan, author.
Title: Generations in the world of work / Corey Seemiller and Meghan Grace.
Description: Abingdon, Oxon ; New York, NY : Routledge, 2025. |
Includes bibliographical references and index.
Identifiers: LCCN 2024037682 (print) | LCCN 2024037683 (ebook) |
ISBN 9781032890609 (hardback) | ISBN 9781032877853 (paperback) |
ISBN 9781003541035 (ebook)
Subjects: LCSH: Conflict of generations in the workplace. |
Intergenerational relations. | Intergenerational communication. | Diversity in the workplace.
Classification: LCC HF5549.5.C75 S44 2025 (print) | LCC HF5549.5.C75 (ebook) |
DDC 658.30084/2–dc23/eng/20241024
LC record available at https://lccn.loc.gov/2024037682
LC ebook record available at https://lccn.loc.gov/2024037683

ISBN: 978-1-032-89060-9 (hbk)
ISBN: 978-1-032-87785-3 (pbk)
ISBN: 978-1-003-54103-5 (ebk)

DOI: 10.4324/9781003541035

Typeset in Dante and Avenir
by Newgen Publishing UK

Contents

Acknowledgments

Thank you to the Board of Directors from the Institute for Generational Research and Education, the many researchers who worked tirelessly on the studies we referenced, the participants who completed our Generations in the Workplace survey, and our friends, families, and colleagues who provided guidance and support while on this journey.

Understanding Generations 1

"What do you want to be when you grow up?" From an early age, the concept of work, whether its value or the exploration of various types of professions, is introduced as an important aspect of our identities as humans.

After entering adulthood, the question of what we want to be shifts to: *"So, what do you do?"* For some, work is central to their purpose and calling in life. Others find work enjoyable, but a means to an end. And, others only work for a paycheck, but would gladly leave their jobs if they could afford to do so.

Aside from the internal reasons as to why someone works, there are also external ones. For one, our professions reflect how society views us – as a particular job title or as part of an industry. These identifiers can shape the way we see the world, reflecting deep value systems fostered through our career choices. For example, retail work might reflect the value of interpersonal interaction, whereas teaching might be akin to having a mindset of transforming others' lives. And, certainly, people would make assumptions about who we are by what we do.

Along with work, another lens that influences how we interact with the world is the generational cohort to which we belong. The workforce has always included multiple generations operating alongside and in collaboration with one another. Each generation has its own set of perspectives, values, and behaviors shaped by events and experiences during their upbringing.

The primary focus of this book is to explore the intersection of work and generations. How different generational cohorts perceive and navigate the

DOI: 10.4324/9781003541035-1

world can be crucial in leveraging each generation's strengths, as well as foster intergenerational collaboration in today's workplaces.

About Generations

A generation is a group of people born during a similar time in history who develop a shared set of values, behaviors, perspectives, and preferences in response to the societal events and experiences that occur during their formative adolescent and young adult years.[1] This is often referred to as peer personality or cohort culture, and is a relatively stable measure, despite demographic diversity, like race, gender, and socioeconomic status, within each generation.[2] By developing an understanding of each cohort's peer personality, we are more likely to succeed in recognizing, appreciating, and navigating differences between generations, which can elevate collaboration, productivity, and overall success.[3]

Lifecycle, Period, and Cohort Effects

The Lifecycle Effect, Period Effect, and Cohort Effect can assist us in better understanding the development of peer personalities of different generational cohorts.

Lifecycle Effect

The Lifecycle Effect refers to the relatively predictable nature of people engaging in various behaviors based on their stage of human development.[4] One can expect members of a generational cohort to "age into" behaviors, or act in a specific way, based on what we know about how people develop through their life spans. In essence, the Lifecycle Effect asserts, for example, that "teens will be teens" regardless of the time in history they were born into.

Erik Erikson's Theory of Psychosocial Development is helpful in understanding the Lifecycle Effect.[5] The theory posits that humans develop over the span of their lifetimes through a series of stages, with relationships and interactions with others playing a critical role in how they progress. These stages of development present a time of malleability as individuals shift from being in a smaller family unit or community to being in a larger, broader one in which they can create their own set of values. Within each stage, people go through points of conflict where the resolution of one stage allows them to move to the next stage of development. For example, in looking at Erikson's life stages during the working years, young adults may grapple with developing healthy relationships and thus may need to focus on forging collegial work connections as well as expanding professional networks. Middle age is the time period marked by feeling a sense of accomplishment and contribution, which in the workforce may appear as the desire to leave a legacy. Finally, older adults may be striving for a sense of completeness, which could manifest as succession planning and ultimate retirement.

The needs that individuals generally try to fulfill in a certain phase of life can almost be equated to the hard wiring that exists within humans. Knowing this progression can help in predicting growth and change as people age. For example, voting has been a long-standing example of the Lifecycle Effect. Decades of voter participation data show that younger people are less likely to vote than those who are older, but that as individuals age through their lifecycle, they are more likely to vote.[2]

Period Effect

The Period Effect describes the widespread influence of an event or movement within society that impacts members of all generations, regardless of life stage, often during a specific period.[4] Societal influences can include the following:

- Technological – How individuals use equipment or tools to gather information, complete tasks, and navigate their environment (i.e., the invention of the automobile).
- Economic – How consumers manage finances, including how individuals conduct work and engage in the workforce (i.e., the shift from a manufacturing to a service economy).
- Social – How people connect with one another and the issues and points of conversation that showcase the priorities of society (i.e., the declining nature of neighborhood communities).
- Political – How the actions and policies of government shape the lives of citizens (i.e., the Civil Rights Act).

These areas do not exist as independent spheres because they often overlap and intersect. For example, technological advancements, such as growth in video-based platforms, have shaping effects on the economy through the form of work interactions and structures. Similarly, advances in technology, such as social media, influence how interpersonal connections are built and fostered, as well as how information related to societal concerns is disseminated.

An example of the Period Effect is the terrorist attack on September 11, 2001. Regardless of age, most people who were alive that day have a conscious memory of the event or experienced its aftermath in some way. Even those born afterward have lived in a world shaped by the events on that day, for instance, greater safety measures at airports, increased spending on national security, contending with contradicting viewpoints on the subsequent War in Iraq, and navigating the varied political choices made by the government to combat terrorism. While each generation experienced September 11th in different ways based on their life stage, its impact cut across cohorts and will likely be there for years to come.

Cohort Effect

The Cohort Effect helps explain the varied impacts of a societal event on different generational cohorts based on the developmental stage they are in during its occurrence.[4] Further, if it took place during a cohort's formative years of adolescence or young adulthood, the impact may be more salient and long-lasting given that the cohort's values and worldviews are still being shaped.[1] Essentially, the Cohort Effect blends the developmental life stage approach of the Lifecycle Effect with the emergent influences of the Period Effect, resulting in an exploration of how certain events impact different generations during the same life stage.

The example of the COVID-19 pandemic can be used to examine the Cohort Effect across generational cohorts. While the pandemic impacted nearly every human around the world, members of each generation experienced the monumental shifts created by it in very different ways. For many Gen Zers (born 1995–2010), for instance, the pandemic occurred during their adolescent and young adult years in which they might have been completing high school or college and preparing for the next phase of life in their careers. Based on Erikson's theory, this stage of life is marked by the developmental outcomes of exploring identity, creating relationships, and learning to navigate the world.[5] When a global pandemic requires atypical schooling or an altered early career experience, it can have longer-term impacts on interpersonal relationships and perspectives on work because it happened during the years of life in which many individuals were exploring their personal and professional identities.

Using Data to Understand Generations

Before diving into an exploration of different generations in the world of work, first addressing the various data points used when studying generational cohorts is important. When discussions about generations happen, it's not unusual to hear comments like "That is very [fill in the blank with the name of the generation]." These are often driven by the recognition of a changing culture or moment of dissonance in observing that things are different between generations. While it's important to steer away from stereotyping, recognizing anything that might help create a fuller picture of a cohort culture or peer personality can be informative. For example, patterns over time observed repeatedly and triangulated through multiple angles of inquiry can help validate the key components of what ultimately reflect a generational cohort's peer personality.

Many data points in this book have been derived from our "Generations in the Workplace" study, which engaged more than 1,350 employees in the United States. Participants included 347 Baby Boomers, 304 Gen Xers, 340 Millennials, and 390 Gen Zers.[6] We recognize the importance of triangulating these findings with insights generated across multiple studies and data sources. Thus, other definitions, theories, and studies are integrated to help tell the story of the peer personalities of generational cohorts in the workplace.

Who Are the Generations in the World of Work?

There are four predominant adult generations in the workplace today. These include Baby Boomers, Gen Xers, Millennials, and Gen Zers. While some in the Silent Generation (born 1925–1945) may still be working, the very oldest are nearly 100 years old and the youngest are approaching their 80s, likely making most of the cohort retired. And, very few in the oldest living generation, the GI Generation (1901–1924), are alive today.

Table 1.1 *Overview of Generations in the World of Work*

	Baby Boomers	Gen Xers	Millennials	Gen Zers
Birth Years	1946–1964	1965–1980	1981–1994	1995–2010
Current Life Stages	Middle age and older adulthood	Middle age	Young adulthood	Teenage and young adulthood
Current Professional Stages	Senior leadership and retirement	Mid-career and senior leadership	Mid-career	Early career

While this book will go into much greater detail about the perspectives and experiences of each generation in later chapters, let's start by taking a 35,000-foot look at who they are. In our Generations in the Workplace study, participants rated 35 different characteristics based on the extent to which they believe each described them.[6] The following table presents the top three characteristics for each cohort.

Table 1.2 *Top Characteristics Identified by Each Generational Cohort*

	Baby Boomers	Gen Xers	Millennials	Gen Zers
1	Responsible	Responsible	Responsible	Loyal
2	Loyal	Authentic	Loyal	Unique
3	Authentic	Loyal	Confident	Compassionate

It is clear that leaders can expect loyalty from members across all generations, whether to the organization, profession, or both. Yet, days of promises of advancement, rewards, pensions, and organizational loyalty to the employee have come and gone in a lot of workplaces, leading some workers to question giving their loyalty in return.

Baby Boomers and Gen Xers have the same top three characteristics, highlighting the importance of older workers taking responsibility for the work they do and a desire to be their authentic selves. Millennials share two of the three, but also emerge with a sense of confidence, whereas Gen Zers identify as unique and compassionate.

Conclusion

In the coming chapters, we will explore the similarities and differences among generational cohorts in how they navigate the world of work. Each chapter will focus on presenting insights related to a workplace topic, highlight attitudinal and behavioral trends of each cohort, and offer strategies for working across generations.

Notes

1 Mannheim, K. (1952). The problem of generations. In: P. Kecskemeti (Ed.), *Karl Mannheim: Essays*. Routledge.
2 Seemiller, C., & Grace, M. (2019). *Generation Z: A century in the making*. Routledge.
3 Indeed. (2023). *The benefits of diverse teams in the workplace*. www.indeed.com/career-advice/career-development/diverse-team-benefits
4 Pew Research Center. (2015). *The whys and hows of generational research*. www.pewresearch.org/politics/2015/09/03/the-whys-and-hows-of-generations-research
5 Erikson, E. H. (1993). *Childhood and society*. WW Norton & Company.
6 Seemiller, C., & Grace, M. (2023). *Generations in the workplace*. Unpublished dataset.

The Landscape of the World of Work

2

The workplace is ever evolving. Sometimes, that evolution is linear – for example, technology that revolutionizes the way we work or the development of entirely new industries. In other cases, it is cyclical, as in moving from handcrafted work to mass production and back to handcrafted work, with both types of production offering value to consumers.

During this workplace evolution, however, society is still grappling with many of the same issues that were present over the last 100 years – industrialization, employees' working conditions and pay, recruitment and retention of employees, industry-specific labor shortages, training and development, pressure to innovate, and the proliferation of technology. While many of these issues are not unique to a particular era in history, how they are addressed seems to be continuously changing with each passing decade. Older generations that have been in the workplace for a substantial amount of time have witnessed this evolution, creating a contrast between "the way it's always been done" and "what needs to be done today." Younger generations, though, only know the workplace in its current state. Thus, the world of work, while appearing the same for all, can be interpreted and navigated differently depending on one's generational lens.

Exploring the factors that influence the landscape of the world of work in the twenty-first century helps to better understand each generational cohort's experience. Let's take a look at some critical issues and their impacts on employees across generations.

DOI: 10.4324/9781003541035-2

Rediscovering Career Trajectories

The process of reflecting on one's career path is nothing new in the modern era. People have been switching occupations and industries throughout history – often moving to a job that pays more, has better working conditions, is in closer proximity to home, or is in an emerging industry with promise for the future. Certain events, however, can spur this process on a mass level, leading to swaths of individuals rethinking and reevaluating their careers, particularly regarding where they were situated in history when they entered the workforce. Many Baby Boomers began their professional lives during a shifting economic landscape in which the growing desire for capitalism and merit-based reward systems were seeping into culture and laws. This ultimately led to the yuppie movement in the 1980s when making money and "Keeping up with the Joneses" was the key to prosperity. From this, many Baby Boomers developed a workaholic mentality to effectively compete in the elusive rat race to get their fair share.

For Gen Xers, the advent of the Internet and the proliferation of technology opened up new jobs and new industries, as well as re-conceptualized existing ones. Armed with tech savviness, this young generation possessed critical skills that were valuable in a rapidly changing workplace and could seek careers vastly different from what their parents did and what they imagined doing when they grew up.

For Millennials, the 2008–2009 Great Recession sent them into a financial tailspin as they lost jobs and opportunities promised to them by society, particularly those who earned a costly college degree. Some were able to persist in their careers, often with a downgraded wage, whereas others were laid off and ended up looking for recession-proof jobs.

For Gen Zers, the COVID-19 pandemic made their entry into the workforce challenging. Many didn't retain their jobs because businesses were forced to close or downsize. Some were left with little choice but to leave their front-line jobs requiring an in-person presence to move home to live with their parents. Having invested very little time in a professional field at their age, their ability to pivot to a new career path was far more viable than it was for older generations more deeply embedded in their professions.

While these critical events occurred during each generation's emergence into the professional world, older generations were not immune to their effects further in their own career lifecycles. For example, many Baby Boomers spiraled into questioning how they would retire after being saddled with losses during the Great Recession, and Millennials had to try to play catch-up with their pay wages yet again during the pandemic.

What all these events have in common is that they propelled many individuals into new occupations or even industries through layoffs and downsizing. And, some events provided enough of a shock that workers were prompted to deeply reflect on the question, "Is this what I really want to do with my life?"

This can be evidenced in how Gen Xers and Gen Zers navigated the working world during the COVID-19 pandemic. During that time, Gen Xers had to balance caring for their aging parents and supporting their children by assisting with remote education or opening their empty nests for them to return home to live. Working in inflexible jobs or doing work that didn't feel as though it added value to society in lieu of caretaking for their loved ones put a lot of Gen Xers on notice. On the other hand, many Gen Zers were highly in tune with their mental and emotional needs, prompting them to consider the long-term prioritization of occupations that embrace well-being.

Another question that often comes from experiencing critical societal events is, "Why am I staying in a place that doesn't value me, treats me poorly, or is just toxic?" Millennials haven't been shy about changing jobs, particularly in trying to play wage catch-up from the Great Recession, and thus, are three times more likely to change jobs than non-Millennials.[1] But, other generations, those that have typically been loyalists since their entry into the workforce, such as Boomers and Gen Xers, have also questioned remaining in a workplace that isn't satisfying. While they are more rooted in their careers and closer to retirement, they, too, are not averse to exploring other options when affecting events occur. This reflection process has spurred three significant phenomena in the workplace: the Great Resignation, rage applying, and quiet quitting.

The Great Resignation

The Great Resignation began shortly after the start of the pandemic when people realized that sacrificing their happiness or well-being for the benefit of the workplace was not a desirable nor sustainable way to live. Employees in industries on the frontlines, who were tapped from overworking and putting themselves at risk of illness during the early days of the pandemic, were tired of working in places that were short-staffed, paying low wages, and had limited flexibility. Entire businesses and even industries, such as food service, were shrinking by the minute as people quit their jobs. While individuals across generations participated in the Great Resignation, research has found that walkouts were primarily by Millennials and Gen Zers who opted to change workplaces, occupations, and career fields to seek better working conditions, even if that meant being self-employed.[2]

Rage Applying

Rage applying occurs when employees are upset or resentful of their employer for their working conditions and pay. Rather than quitting and trying to find a job, they apply for as many jobs as possible, creating both an actual path out of the situation as well as a mental relief that any interest they get from other employers would validate their value. While rage applying is not a new construct, the ability to apply to multiple positions online in a short amount of time makes the reach far wider than the days before the Internet. In some cases, rage applying can help someone land a better job with a higher salary. But, in others, individuals apply for jobs they aren't qualified for and end up with mass rejections, which can be particularly difficult for Millennials and Gen Zers, who are newer to the workforce, to accept.[3] And young workers are less likely to speak up about their concerns out of fear that their supervisors believe a voice in the workplace is earned over time.[4] This may result in greater amounts of rage applying as an exit strategy to a problematic work environment.

Quiet Quitting

Quiet quitting involves staying in one's job but only doing exactly what is listed in the job description. Many employees take on additional tasks or simply go over and above to help the organization. Quiet quitting means that employees scale back their non-contracted work, doing the minimum required of them in the hope that the employer becomes aware of how much more the employees were doing and adequately compensates them for their work or at least brings attention to the disparity.

Gallup has reported that around 50 percent of the workforce is comprised of potential quiet quitters, as they connect the phenomenon to a lack of employee engagement.[5] With younger workers less engaged than they were pre-pandemic, a surge of possible Generation Z and Millennial quiet quitters may be on the horizon. Given inflation has made it challenging for young people, in particular, to afford housing and basic necessities, the conditions are ripe, particularly if they are situated in an expensive geographic area where leaving is not an option. For older workers, quiet quitting may be a safer option than quitting altogether because they don't have to leave a job where they have become reliant on the sustained income to support the lifestyles of themselves and their families.

As the landscape of work continues to evolve and societal events emerge, workers across all age groups will be taking stock of their career choices. What is clear is that employees have much to weigh when making decisions about their work lives – paycheck, flexibility, well-being, and workplace engagement, some playing more prominent roles for each of the different generational cohorts. Thus, employers may want to take note before their workers depart for better opportunities.

Remote Work

Mostly spurred by the sudden onset of the pandemic, there have been mass changes both structurally and philosophically around where and when people work. While some industries require in-person labor, such as first responders, maintenance workers, store clerks, or restaurant servers, many office jobs can have flexibility in work location. Prior to the pandemic, some were already remote due to employee requests, streamlining of an organization's overhead costs, or employing a geographically dispersed workforce. But, with stay-at-home orders imposed by state and local governments, almost everyone except critical workers shifted to remote work. Teachers instructed their students through videos, fitness trainers led workout classes online, and even doctors delivered care through telehealth when possible.

But, as the pandemic wound down and most workplaces opened up again, many people continued working remotely. Prior to the pandemic, 43 percent of employees who could do their jobs remotely sometimes or always worked from home; two years later, that number was at 59 percent, despite onsite work starting up again.[6] The main reason employees noted for continuing with remote work was simply personal choice. The desire for remote work is so strong for some that a callback by Dell CEO gave employees two choices: work in a hybrid capacity or from home but fully remote work would mean relinquishing any opportunity for promotion. Nearly half of employees opted for fully remote.[7]

While remote work was designed to be a stopgap to keep the economy moving during the pandemic, there are empirical benefits to working from home. For example, remote workers tend to be happier and more productive working from home[8] and find they can more easily get their work done and meet deadlines.[6]

The Great Resistance

Once restrictions were lifted as the pandemic subsided and the shift to normalcy began, many CEOs started calling workers back to the office, arguing that doing so would increase collaboration and camaraderie as well as help employees better navigate organizational culture. While some were eager to come in person to minimize working with distractions in their homes or to have social interaction, others favored the flexibility of their remote workspaces provided.

Unsurprisingly, the summon from CEOs to return to in-person work led to the Great Resistance, which resulted in many workers quitting their jobs altogether or coming to the office less than their employers expected.[9] For many, the resistance came from their desire to work from home, seeing the call back to the office as a perk that was removed.[10] For others, it appeared that there was no logical rationale other than for their employers to be able to monitor their work more closely. The question that remained unanswered was, "If productivity was high while working from home, why do I need to come back?"

This push and pull between predominantly Baby Boomer employers who wanted to curb remote work and employees who sought to retain it was very much generational. Many older employees who had spent much of their work lives in an office setting have been more eager to get back to normal, where they could generate ideas simply by bumping into colleagues at the coffee machine.[11] Gen Xers and Millennials, who had gotten used to toggling between digital and analog worlds, were not as eager, mostly citing coming back to the office as exacerbating workplace inequities. For one, they were more likely to have children than their older counterparts, and working onsite necessitated childcare – a time-consuming and costly expense. And, for those who made less money, the cost of commuting was a heavier burden.

Presenteeism

For many in Generation Z, returning to the workplace has its benefits. Being onsite means, they can receive informal mentorship from seasoned colleagues when they see them in the halls and in the lunchroom and develop interpersonal connections in a field in which they have few networks. And since many are more likely to live near their workplaces rather than in the suburbs with their families, their commute is less cumbersome.[12]

However, presenteeism is at play with Gen Zers. This involves the perception, and perhaps reality, that being in the office where there are more touchpoints with leaders can result in more opportunities for advancement and more favorability with those in charge. Gen Zers may need that advantage at the beginning of their careers in ways that Boomers, Gen Xers, and Millennials who have worked onsite for much of their working lives do not. However, the burden of being present all the time can put undue stress on these young employees who may have side hustles to tend to and burgeoning personal lives, leading them to develop unhealthy workaholic behaviors.

This push–pull scenario around onsite work is one that will continue to prevail. With many organizational leaders requiring workers in the office, not only is there a disconnect with some employees who see this as an issue of mistrust and lack of value, but the reward systems built into presenteeism put undue pressure on Gen Zers, in particular, to overwork.

Balancing Personal and Professional Lives

The proliferation of technology, particularly after the advent of the Internet and smartphones, has made it easier than ever for people to have more blended personal and professional lives. Thus, working outside of office hours has become a daily way of life for many employees, out of expectation, to combat the feeling of needing to catch up due to a heavy workload or to make an impression on upper management.

Blurred Lines

In one sense, the pandemic helped to blur the lines between work and personal lives even more so, particularly for those who transitioned to working from home after having previously worked onsite. People created makeshift office spaces in their bedrooms, wore informal "Zoom attire," which often included only wearing professional dress from the waist up, and shared their spaces with family, children, and pets. Seeing a puppy jump on a coworker's lap during a video meeting or hearing a baby cry in the background while talking with a customer service representative became an everyday occurrence. However, research has found that while this arrangement offers the opportunity to work while taking care of kids, doing laundry, or being available for a package delivery, the distractions for many were high, and some struggled to find sufficient spaces to work at home.[13] Despite most not having children, Gen Zers, in particular, have struggled with finding adequate home office space. Often, living in tight quarters or with roommates, working in a quiet, secluded environment may not be an option.

Overburdened Workloads

One's professional balance is also influenced by their workload. Today, it's not unusual for employees to respond to messages from their manager after hours, use their personal laptops at home to finish projects they started on their office computers, and check emails while on official paid time off. This may be pronounced in organizations that have had layoffs or chronically unfilled positions, which can shift heavy workloads to remaining employees. Feeling pressure to stay in good graces with management or the need to get caught up with projects outside of work time creates real dilemmas for many, creating an unbalanced professional life.

Further, toxic productivity, which is the obsession with always being productive, can take a toll on one's work–life balance. In the workplace, "going the extra mile" to get ahead or impress the boss can cause exhaustion, stress, and even guilt if one does not accomplish as much as was intended.[14] As workplaces tighten their belts, there may be continued pressure for employees to lean into a toxic productivity mindset to survive in an effort to keep one's job or compete for promotions. This burden may fall more so on younger employees as they try to showcase their contributions for future advancement opportunities.

Intentional Balance

The Internet is filled with suggestions for maintaining balance while working from home. These include creating a workspace only for work, getting dressed every day as if one were going to an office, setting clear work hours and holding to them, developing a routine, and planning activities at the end of the workday so there is a definitive reason to stop working. These suggestions align with the concept of professional detachment, a term coined by Laurie Ruettimann,[15] in which employees focus on separating their job roles from their personal identities, setting clear boundaries, and tending to self-care.

For those who do engage in professional detachment, working from home actually provides more flexibility to spend time with loved ones, integrate fitness into one's schedule, and even complete household chores during the day. Unsurprisingly, remote workers have higher rates of satisfaction with their work–life balance and lower levels of stress than their hybrid or fully in-person counterparts.[16] Further, on average, the more hours an employee spends working remotely, the higher the level of happiness.[17] And these findings do have some generational differences. Millennials were found to have greater increases in happiness than other generations by adding just one additional remote workday.

While work–life balance is all the rage, with websites, programs, and entire organizations committed to offering a balanced, whole-person, supportive experience for employees, there are many workplace practices that inherently don't support balance. For instance, the expectations of being "on" all the time, even for shift work when managers expect to be able to text or call after hours, or "being a team player" by having to take on extra unpaid duties or mandatory overtime in a short-staffed unit, can easily create an imbalance.

Diversity, Equity, and Inclusion

Together, diversity, equity, and inclusion (DEI) are critical in creating workplaces that foster a sense of welcoming and belonging. And, a whopping 81 percent of workers "would seriously consider quitting their jobs if the company failed to demonstrate a true commitment to DEI."[18] Many companies have realized that DEI is not just good for people; it's good for business. Happily retained employees cost companies less in hiring and training costs, and turnover increases brain drain, where excellent ideas and organizational wisdom leave with those employees who resign.

Diversity

According to the American Psychological Association, diversity "refers to the representation or composition of various social identity groups in a work group, organization, or community."[19] Social identity groups may include those related to race, gender and gender identity, socioeconomic status, neurodiversity and physical ability, sexual orientation, age, and religion. It can also include veteran status, political affiliation, and other groupings.

There are many social benefits of diversity in the workplace. For one, having diverse perspectives can foster creativity when solving problems and engaging in innovation. The more ideas, the more options to explore. In addition, underrepresented people who work among others with similar identities may feel a sense of camaraderie or connection, prompting them to continue working in the organization. Further, diverse organizations that reflect the makeup of the communities they serve draw in and keep new customers and employees because of their ability to understand and connect with them.

Millennial and Gen Z workers not only represent a more diverse workforce, but they also want a commitment from employers to embrace that diversity.[20] And, a higher percentage of Millennials and Gen Zers, when compared to Baby Boomers and Gen Xers, believe that the increasing numbers of racial and ethnic "diversity in the U.S. is good for society."[17]

Equity

Unlike diversity, which focuses solely on representation, the American Psychological Association defines equity as "providing resources according to the need to help diverse populations achieve their highest state of health and other functioning."[18] This includes incorporating nondiscriminatory policies and processes, offering fair pay, and affording all employees with pathways for advancement. To differentiate from equality, which involves offering the same resources and opportunities to everyone in similar positions, equity ensures more goes to those who need it the most, even if it isn't equally spread across everyone. This may include providing upskilling training or professional development to ensure everyone is adequately prepared to thrive in their jobs. Some employees may already have the requisite skills and not need additional training, whereas others might need substantial training.

The issue of inequity took center stage in 2020 after the deaths of George Floyd, Ahmaud Arbery, and Breonna Taylor spurred racial justice movements across the country. Institutions and corporations scrambled to respond quickly with new policies to ensure equitable treatment for all employees. Although the conversation may have led to some changes, including the hiring of diversity directors, drafting DEI policies, or instituting mandatory anti-bias training, racism persisted. Within a few years, many state governments started passing laws curbing curriculum and programs, language use, and the availability of books and resources aimed at enhancing DEI initiatives and understanding. While private workplaces could make their own choices to some extent, those working in the public education sector were restricted in what they could teach and offer regarding DEI. Nevertheless, a tapestry of commitment and resources offered to enhance equity around these identities remains, driving those who can choose a workplace or geographic residence away from places that have limited equity. But others without that mobility are forced to stay.

Although inequities cut across race, gender, and sexual orientation, for example, it is also evident with age. A report from New America highlights the inequities that have developed between generations regarding pay.[21] The authors refer to it as "generational fairness," and discuss the importance of each generation having enough assets to manage their societal obligations. They share that since the 1990s, financial burdens previously held by employers (e.g., pensions) and the government (e.g., cost of higher education) have shifted to individuals. Because of this, younger generations are at a severe disadvantage in reaching financial security when compared with their older counterparts. For example, New America points out that Millennials earn 20 percent less than Baby Boomers did when they were in the same life stage. Add in inflation, the cost of housing, higher education debt, and expensive health insurance, and young people end up struggling more financially compared to older employees when they entered the workforce.

While organizations haven't been jumping at the chance to pay younger employees more, some have incorporated opportunities to level the playing field financially. For one, corporate partnerships with colleges and universities that offer workers free or reduced tuition for degree attainment can eliminate higher education debt for young people who enter the workforce without a college degree. Other benefits include student loan repayment assistance, parental leave, and clear opportunities for career advancement.

Inclusion

According to the American Psychological Association, inclusion "strives for an environment that offers affirmation, celebration, and appreciation of different approaches, styles, perspectives, and experiences."[18] Employees who feel like they belong, can be their authentic selves, and feel like they are treated respectfully have considerably higher levels of employee engagement.[22] However, this may be easier said than done. A study by recruiting firm, Glassdoor, found that 34 percent of workers have experienced or witnessed ageism; 33 percent, gender discrimination; 30 percent, racism; and 24 percent, LGBTQ discrimination. In total, 61 percent of workers "experienced or witnessed discrimination based on age, race, … [or] gender."[23]

But inclusion is more than just avoiding discriminatory behavior. It involves creating a welcoming environment where everyone can express their authentic selves in a safe place. Doing so allows people to work at their full capacities and leverage their strengths. There are many ways organizations are able to embrace an inclusive culture. For one, they can reconsider any limiting dress code policies, offer mentoring programs, provide opportunities for employee resource groups that offer social support for people with specific identities (e.g., women in engineering, and LGBTQ employees), upskill workers, and create formalized pipelines for employees at any level to share concerns as well as innovative ideas with those in leadership roles. And, while some, like insurance agency, Progressive, and financial company, TIAA, ranked in the top two spots on Forbes' 2024 ranking of best employers for diversity,[24] commitment to DEI can vary across organizations.

Intersectionality

Understanding different generations' experiences, particularly those who have one or more marginalized identities, is imperative for understanding the complexity of DEI. For example, it is important to consider how a gay Baby Boomer, who has worked for a particular organization the majority of their working life, might persist and cope under new management that is less open-minded and embracing of authenticity. Or, understanding Gen X women who may be more prone to workaholism than Gen X men after having adopted overworking habits for decades to combat the added pressure many felt in needing to prove themselves. Or, a Millennial person of color who does not ask for feedback, which is so critical for many in that generation, due to fear of having their competence questioned. Then, there is the Gen Zer, who may be terrified about financial security and ends up taking the first job offered, even if the pay is low, worried they won't receive another offer and not having a financial safety net to wait for a better one. These are just some of the complexities that organizations must consider when fostering a workplace that is diverse, equitable, and inclusive.

As it has been for decades, DEI will be an important issue that organizations will grapple with. Leaders will continue to be confronted with how they can embrace DEI to draw in the most talented people, leverage each person's strengths, and retain employees in a welcoming and supportive environment. And, if they don't, young workers, in particular, will likely go somewhere else.

The Economy

The economy is a powerful force in people's professional lives. It can determine the trajectory, and sometimes fate, of workers as wages, job opportunities, and emergent industries ebb and flow. Further, the economic conditions at the time of entry into the job market can impact career advancement and retirement decisions of workers as they move through their career lifecycles – essentially, what happens in the early years of one's career can affect them in the long-term.

The Great Recession

The Great Recession in 2008 and 2009 had a profound impact on individuals, organizations, and entire nations. The housing bubble popped, leading borrowers to foreclose on their home loans. Many banks shut down, and the stock market plunged. International trade nearly came to a halt, and global unemployment increased by 3 percent.[25] On a more individual level, retirement portfolios took a hit, particularly affecting Baby Boomers. Many property owners, who were mostly Baby Boomers and Gen Xers, lost their homes. And masses of Boomers, Gen Xers, and Millennials lost jobs.

The job loss was particularly pronounced for those Millennials who were graduating from college around the time of the Great Recession. The promise of plentiful high-paying positions that would offset exorbitant college loans did not quite come to fruition, at least initially. Many ended up entering a receding workforce, never fully recovering from accepting a position with a lower ranking and pay than they had hoped for. Millennials have been playing career catch-up ever since, as the United States has experienced the slowest economic growth during their working years than any other generation before them.[26] Further, Millennials lost, on average, 13 percent of their earnings in a 12-year period in the early 2000s because of the Great Recession, mostly given that many took lower-wage jobs, which set the baseline for future earnings.[27]

Student Debt

Despite any assertions that Millennials have indeed caught up, one-third of that entire generation is saddled with student debt,[28] which can influence their choice of career or industry because of the pressure to work a less satisfying job that brings in a higher paycheck or consistently seek opportunities for advancement. While Generation X holds nearly 39 percent of the nation's entire pool of student loan debt, the highest of any generation, it's Millennials that have the highest rate of individuals with student debt at 43 percent compared to 21 percent of Gen Xers.[29]

The Pandemic

Like the impact of the Great Recession on newly graduated Millennials, many Gen Zers starting careers during the COVID-19 pandemic may end up behind later on as their circumstances were similar to Millennials and the Great Recession. For example, during the peak of the pandemic, Gen Zers were disproportionately laid off, particularly because they were often the newest and least seasoned employees. And, some had to take pay cuts or accept positions not commensurate with their education levels to make ends meet. Although older generations certainly faced economic hardship, they were not as likely to have lost their jobs when compared to younger workers. During the first two months of the pandemic, one-third of Gen Zers who were looking for jobs remained unemployed, which was more than double the general unemployment rate.[30]

Further, while certain industries have bounced back to pre-pandemic levels of employment, such as management, engineering, and health care (more so professional occupations), others have not, such as administrative support, services, and construction (more technical and vocational occupations).[31] Due to a lack of experience and perhaps, education, it makes sense that those in younger generations wouldn't have the same types of opportunities to step into the sectors of the workforce experiencing the most growth.

Housing

On top of lower earnings, Gen Zers also entered adulthood in the early 2020s when housing costs and mortgage rates were high, making home ownership far more inaccessible than it had been in previous years. But it isn't just Gen Zers struggling with purchasing property. Forty-year-old Millennials have lower rates of homeownership when compared to Baby Boomers and Gen Xers when they were 40 years old.[32] On the one hand, those who rent might not be tied to a specific geographic area for work, giving them greater career mobility. On the other hand, those who were fortunate enough to have bought property might then be limited to a certain radius due to the difficulty of acquiring a new residence in a different location.

Retirement

Working Baby Boomers, while likely better situated with their housing and job tenure, are also confronted with more imminent effects of economic fluctuation. For instance, some Baby Boomers saw their retirement portfolios continuously rise and fall over the years, including during the Great Recession and pandemic. While some experienced a financial ebb and flow in their savings, making future planning more difficult, 27 percent of Baby Boomers hadn't even set aside any money for retirement.[33] This instability has prompted many to continue working later in life than intended.

Gen Xers also have a great deal of pressure to save for retirement, particularly because they have witnessed the disappearance of pensions, experienced volatility in employer-funded stock retirement plans, and are privy to the looming threat of the absence of social security set to take place right when they retire. In addition, Gen Xers find their salary split between many priorities, such as setting aside money for their children's expenses, including contributing to their college funds, and costs related to caring for their aging parents. These forces may prompt Gen Xers to make career decisions based on income potential in ways that could be different from those in other generations who may not be financially responsible for the caretaking of others.

Hysteresis

While the state of the economy can vary throughout one's lifetime, its level of solvency upon entry into the workforce can have long-lasting effects. Economists use the term hysteresis to posit that even after a situation has changed, its impact can continue. For example, Millennials and Gen Zers starting their careers in a down or recessed economy can lead them to accept and, ultimately, stay in jobs that have less ideal working conditions. They may opt for two jobs to make up for lost income, impacting other areas of their lives, such as going back to school or gaining professional skills. They may also have adopted physical and psychological behaviors that are less than healthy, such as not spending time on exercise, investing in a gym membership, or making healthy eating choices. Although the economy may rebound after a recession, habits can form, leaving generational cohorts at a disadvantage in the long-term.

Beyond salary, other factors such as how much student debt might need to be accrued to be credentialed for a specific occupation, the amount of money that can be saved for retirement, opportunities for advancement, and cost of living in certain geographic areas play a significant role in one's career choices.

Artificial Intelligence

Artificial intelligence (AI) involves the use of machines to mimic human behavior. These machines can complete automated tasks, and go so far as to make decisions, lessening the necessity for humans to take on those responsibilities. AI has already changed the nature of work because it has caused some job roles and entire industries to be phased out. For instance, many customer service representatives have been replaced by automated chatbots, and travel agents have been swapped out with online travel booking sites. While AI has been around since the mid-twentieth century,[34] its acceleration in recent years, particularly during COVID-19 pandemic, has affected the landscape of work.[35]

Efficiency and Productivity

One positive effect of AI is that it has the capacity to increase efficiency and productivity in the workplace, such as on a factory line where an automated system can yield higher output than a human doing the job. AI also operates 24 hours a day, 7 days a week, without the need to receive the typical, and often required, breaks or lunch hour that actual employees would get. And, because the machine itself removes the human element, there is less of a need to be concerned about making mistakes because there is little possibility of a robot exhibiting human error or having a bad day on the job. And, in the event of a malfunction, the problem can typically be quickly identified and corrected.

Efficiency and productivity are not limited to internal organizational functioning. Integrating AI into external processes can help customers and consumers. For instance, being able to deposit a check through a mobile app saves time and resources for the bank as well as for the consumer, who saves a trip to the branch to make the deposit. While only 48 percent of Baby Boomers trust banking apps, a whopping 86 percent of Millennials do,[36] indicating a greater proliferation of use by younger individuals.

Younger generations' greater acceptance of AI is also apparent around chatbots. For example, 96 percent of Baby Boomers, 91 percent of Gen Xers, 86 percent of Millennials, and 83 percent of Gen Zers specify that they prefer a live agent over a chatbot.[37] Although most people across all generations would rather talk to a human, the disparity between cohorts is telling.

Safer and Better Working Conditions

As the development of AI continues, more jobs will move away from manual work. For instance, warehouse stockers can be replaced by an employee who is able to work from an office or from home, programming and operating robots to stock shelves. These types of jobs can allow aging employees to stay in their industries longer because they do not need to do the labor-intensive work themselves.

AI also removes repetitive tasks that can lead to injury, such as eye strain or carpal tunnel syndrome. In addition, machines can take over dangerous jobs like mining, factory work, and construction or those that need to be done in extreme conditions, including in heat or underwater, eliminating the risk of putting a human in harm's way. This, too, allows for older employers to continue in industries they may have had to previously retire from due to the stress and impact of these jobs on the body.

Loss of Old Jobs, Gain of New Ones

Because AI isn't salaried or paid a wage, and doesn't require training and development, health insurance, or other benefits, it can easily replace human workers in a cost-effective manner. Thus, the fear of being replaced by a robot in the workplace is real for employees across all generations. However, this concern is more pronounced among older cohorts. For example, the percentage of Baby Boomers and Gen Xers who believe AI will put jobs at risk are 70 percent and 63 percent, respectively, whereas 57 percent of Millennials and younger agree with this statement.[38]

The World Economic Forum estimates that 83 million forward-facing roles, including bank tellers, clerks, and secretaries, will eventually be eliminated. However, it projects that those jobs will be replaced to the tune of 69 million new jobs, such as machine learning and sustainability specialists, business intelligence and information security analysts, fintech and robotics engineers, and data scientists.[39] In addition, occupations that might not have been conceptualized 20 years ago are emerging, such as a prompt engineer who serves as the brains behind the AI, programming exactly what questions to ask the machine to get the intended results.

With this labor market shift, employees working in waning industries need to upskill or reskill entirely to stay in the workforce. However, the cost to both individuals and organizations to prepare for an upskill shift is high and requires commitment, time, and money, potentially necessitating modifications to higher education vocational training programs and in-house professional development programs. Those in younger generations may be drawn to jobs that develop, build, and maintain AI because of its cutting-edge nature and the opportunities for growth. Or, those who do not want to engage in AI work could opt for a recession-proof career path that is not slated to become obsolete in the near future. Occupations such as law enforcement, child development, and teaching may be more difficult for AI to do and are always needed by society.

Ethics

The integration of AI and machine learning have brought to light many issues related to ethics. On the one hand, programming a set algorithm into a decision-making tree or process can ensure that everyone completing that procedure is treated in an unbiased way, particularly when humans aren't involved in making subjective decisions. However, people on the backend who program that decision tree may have their own biases, even unknowingly, that proliferate into the programming. In addition, by having a process tied to an algorithm, there may be no room for exceptions. This might even happen when humans use machines, for example, such as when a customer service agent attempts to provide an insurance quote using a built-in system that only allows for certain selections, none of which can be overridden.

The ethics of algorithms and programming built into digital processes aren't the only aspects that pose challenges; what AI can do may be deemed questionably unethical. For example, the emergence of ChatGPT, which aggregates content from the Internet and develops a written piece on any topic, is making it easy for students to "write" papers and authors to "publish" literary works. Research has found that 29 percent of employees who have used ChatGPT did so without their employer's knowledge, with 11 percent noting they faced disciplinary sanctions when they were discovered using it.[40] The use of ChatGPT is predominant across all generations, but the highest usage comes from younger cohorts. Fifty-four percent of Baby Boomers, 51 percent of Gen Xers, 55 percent of Millennials, and 61 percent of Gen Zers report using the tool at least several times a month.[36]

While machines can be more consistent and sustain work for longer hours, AI still lacks the ability to deal with ambiguity or complexity that warrants a change of course, meaning robots won't likely take over for humans entirely any time soon. But, to consistently improve machine learning, many jobs will emerge to tackle this challenge, and those across generations will have to assess their part in that evolution.

Entrepreneurship and Freelancing

Entrepreneurship and freelancing have always been hallmarks of the land-scape of the world of work, whether that is merchants and artisans peddling their wares or technicians selling their services. The essence of both is the ability to work for oneself, controlling when, where, and how business is done.

Entrepreneurship

Entrepreneurship, specifically, involves creating a business that sells one or more services or products and may involve overseeing employees and developing a standard operating procedure. Sometimes people become entrepreneurs from desire (wanting to do specific work or not work for someone else), necessity (losing one's job or to bring in more income), clari-fying passions (going out on one's own after reflection about priorities), or filling a market niche (noticing an opportunity to fill a gap).

Entrepreneurship can be traced back much further than the last 75 years; however, its presence throughout recent history has looked somewhat different for each generation as they emerged into the work-force. For example, young Baby Boomers are credited with jumpstarting retail and fast-food industries during a time in which convenience was the market niche.[41] Gen Xers capitalized on an era of technology disruption with some prominent Xers going on to later start up Google, Amazon, and Tesla. Millennials launched businesses such as Facebook, Pinterest, and Instagram, launching and leveraging the social media boom. And Gen Zers are engaging in entrepreneurial initiatives across a variety of industries aimed at challenging the status quo with regard to what organizations sell and how they do business, particularly around sustainability and human rights.

When it comes to entrepreneurial spirit, all generations have rela-tively similar rates. Millennials rank the highest with 36 percent. They are followed by Generation X at 33 percent, Generation Z at 29 percent, and Baby Boomers at 25 percent.[42] The middle two generations may be better poised to engage in entrepreneurship based on their position in their career lifecycles, just enough experience and wisdom but still ample time on the career clock. It isn't surprising then that the average age of entrepreneurs of the fastest-growing ventures is 45 years old.[43]

Freelancing

Entrepreneurship is often used as the blanket term for starting a business venture, whereas freelancing is one method of doing so and involves selling one's own services or products without being employed by another or employing others. Like entrepreneurship, freelancing can occur in any number of industries. Some more common jobs include reselling, crypto investing, influencing, coaching and consulting, writing, photography, massage therapy, ride-share driving, taking surveys, and live streaming or creating how-to recordings, videogame playing, or any other DIY service.

About 40 percent of freelancers are full-time workers.[44] The other 60 percent do it part-time out of interest, time, opportunity, or as a safeguard in that their primary form of income might be too variable and inconsistent. While all freelancers can be referred to as independent contractors and gig economy workers, those who freelance part-time in addition to other work are said to have a side hustle.

Freelancers are often able to work remotely with a flexible schedule, or at least one they control; have a say over their earning potential, since more marketing on their part can lead to more business; be their own boss; and do work that is meaningful to them. And, many simply need to capitalize on their skills and talents to bring in extra money – everything from selling homemade crafts to designing websites.

Freelancing has been growing at a steady pace.[45] Around 60 million people in the United States engage in freelancing,[41] with the highest rates coming from Generation Z, and declining with each subsequent older cohort.[46] Given its growth trajectory, and Generation Z's participation, this trend of freelancing will likely only continue to expand.

Conclusion

Regardless of generation, people will continue to grapple with the same questions: What factors are important to me in terms of selecting or even persisting within a specific career field? What does work–life balance mean to me, and what priority will it take? How essential is inclusion and belonging in my workplace? With evident trends in the world of work creating a nuanced time in history, members of each generation will have to weigh how and where they fit in its landscape.

Notes

1 Gallup. (2016). *How Millennials want to work and live*. www.gallup.com/workpl ace/238073/millennials-work-live.aspx?thank-you-report-form=1

2 Smith, M. (2023). Gen Z and millennials are leading 'the big quit' in 2023—why nearly 70% plan to leave their jobs. *CNBC*. www.cnbc.com/2023/01/18/70perc ent-of-gen-z-and-millennials-are-considering-leaving-their-jobs-soon.html

3 Joblist. (2022). *Almost half of job seekers lost confidence from receiving rejection letters*. www.joblist.com/trends/almost-half-of-job-seekers-lost-confidence-from-receiving-rejection-letters

4 Kobie, N. (2022). Can younger workers speak up without managers bristling? *BBC*. www.bbc.com/worklife/article/20221206-can-younger-workers-speak-up-without-managers-bristling

5 Herway, J. (2022). Need an answer to quiet quitting? Start with your culture. *Gallup*. www.gallup.com/workplace/403598/need-answer-quiet-quitting-start-culture.aspx

6 Parker, K., Horowitz, J. M., & Minkin, R. (2022). *COVID-19 pandemic continues to reshape work in America*. Pew Research Center. www.pewresearch.org/soc ial-trends/2022/02/16/covid-19-pandemic-continues-to-reshape-work-in-amer ica/#:~:text=Looking%20to%20the%20future%2C%2060,said%20the%20s ame%20in%202020

7 Thompson, P. (2024). *Almost half of Dell's full-time US workforce has rejected the company's return-to-office push*. www.businessinsider.com/us-dell-workers-reject-return-to-office-hybrid-work-2024-6

8 Owl Labs. (2021). *State of remote work 2021*. https://owllabs.com/state-of-rem ote-work/2021/

9 Bloom, N. (2022). *The Great Resistance: Getting employees back to the office*. Stanford Institute for Economic Policy Research. https://siepr.stanford.edu/publicati ons/work/great-resistance-getting-employees-back-office

10 O'Connor, B. (2021). The workers pushing back on the return to office. *BBC*. www.bbc.com/worklife/article/20210618-the-workers-pushing-back-on-the-return-to-the-office

11 Boyle, M. (2022). Older and younger bosses disagree on remote work. *Bloomberg*. www.bloomberg.com/news/articles/2022-07-20/remote-work-has-created-a-generational-divide-between-older-and-younger-bosses#xj4y7vzkg

12 Ito, A. (2022). Gen Z actually hates working from home. *Business Insider*. www.businessinsider.com/gen-z-hates-remote-work-office-jobs-work-from-home-2022-7

13 Shirmohammadi, M., Au, W. C., & Beigi, M. (2022). Remote work and work-life balance: Lessons learned from the COVID-19 pandemic and suggestions for HRD practitioners. *Human Resource Development International*, *25*(2), 163–181.

14 Wong, B. (2021). What is toxic productivity? Here's how to spot the damaging behavior. *Huffington Post*. www.huffpost.com/entry/toxic-productivity-work_l_606655e7c5b6aa24bc60a566

15 Ruettimann, L. (2019). *How to detach from work*. https://laurieruettimann.com/how-to-detach-from-work/

16 Future Forum. (2022). *Future Forum Pulse Summer Snapshot*. https://futurefo rum.com/wp-content/uploads/2022/07/Future-Forum-Pulse-Report-Sum mer-2022.pdf

17 Tracking Happiness. (2023). *Remote work is linked to happiness: Study of 12,455 respondents*. www.trackinghappiness.com/remote-work-leads-to-happiness-study/#remote-work-increases-happiness

18 GoodHire. (2022). *Most employees would quit over lack of company commitment to DE&I efforts, says new GoodHire survey*. www.goodhire.com/press-releases/most-employees-would-quit-over-lack-of-company-dei-efforts

19 American Psychological Association. (n.d.). *Equity, diversity, and inclusion*. www.apa.org/topics/equity-diversity-inclusion

20 Fry, R., & Parker, K. (2018). *Early benchmarks show 'Post-Millennials' on track to be most diverse, best-educated generation yet*. Pew Research Center. www.pewresea rch.org/social-trends/2018/11/15/early-benchmarks-show-post-millennials-on-track-to-be-most-diverse-best-educated-generation-yet/

21 Cramer, R., Addo, F. R., Campbell, C., Choi, J., Cohen, B. J., Cohen, C., Emmons, W. R., Fowler, M., Garon, T., Hancock, C., Hipple, L., Hodgson, J., Kent, A. H., McKernan, S. M., Medinica, V. E., Melford, G., Miller, B., Rademacher, I., Ratcliffe, C. … Zhang, Y. (2019). The emerging Millennial wealth gap. *New America*. www.newamerica.org/millennials/reports/emerging-millennial-wea lth-gap

22 Gallup. (2022). *Advancing DEI initiatives: A guide for organizational leaders*. www.gallup.com/workplace/395615/dei-perspective-paper.aspx?thank-you-report-form=1

23 Glassdoor. (2019). *Diversity & inclusion study 2019*. https://qnotescarolinas.com/wp-content/uploads/2019/11/Glassdoor-Diversity-Survey-Supplement-1.pdf

24 Rabkin Peachman, R. (2024). *America's best employers for diversity*. www.forbes.com/lists/best-employers-diversity/?sh=16220ef46468

25 Chen, W., Mrkaic, M., & Nabar, M. (2018). *Lasting effects: The global economic recovery 10 years after the crisis*. International Monetary Fund. www.imf.org/en/Blogs/Articles/2018/10/03/blog-lasting-effects-the-global-economic-recovery-10-years-after-the-crisis

26 Van Dam, A. (2020). The unluckiest generation in U.S. history. *Washington Post*. www.washingtonpost.com/business/2020/05/27/millennial-recession-covid/

27 Rinz, K. (2019). *Did timing matter? Life cycle differences in effects of exposure to the Great Recession.* U.S. Census Bureau. https://kevinrinz.github.io/recession.pdf

28 Hanson, M. (2023). *Student load debt by generation.* Education Data Initiative. https://educationdata.org/student-loan-debt-by-generation

29 Bareham, H. (2023). Which generation has the most student loan debt? *Bankrate.* www.bankrate.com/loans/student-loans/student-loan-debt-by-generation/

30 Jeong, A. (2021). *Gen Z most stressed by coronavirus, citing pandemic toll on careers, education and relationships, poll says.* www.washingtonpost.com/health/2021/12/07/gen-z-covid-pandemic-stress-mental-health/

31 DeLuca, M., & Pinheiro, R. B. (2023). *US labor market after COVID-19: An interim report.* Federal Reserve Bank of Cleveland, Economic Commentary 2023–04. https://doi.org/10.26509/frbc-ec-202304

32 Anderson, D., & Bokhari, S. (2023). The race to home ownership: Gen Z tracking ahead of their parents' generation, Millennials tracking behind. *Redfin News.* www.redfin.com/news/gen-z-millennial-homeownership-rate-home-purchases/

33 Credit Karma. (2023). *Americans have a net worth problem, and it's not positive.* www.creditkarma.com/about/commentary/americans-have-a-net-worth-problem-and-its-not-positive

34 Britannica. (n.d.) *Alan Turing and the beginning of AI.* www.britannica.com/technology/artificial-intelligence/Connectionism

35 McKendrick, J. (2021). AI adoption skyrocketed over the last 18 months. *Harvard Business Review.* https://hbr.org/2021/09/ai-adoption-skyrocketed-over-the-last-18-months

36 UserTesting. (2023). *UserTesting's global survey reveals that when it comes to banking & finance, people across all generations prefer a human touch.* www.usertesting.com/company/newsroom/press-releases/usertestings-global-survey-reveals-when-it-comes-banking-finance

37 Nice inContact. (2019). *Customer experience (CX) transformation benchmark.* https://get.niceincontact.com/CX-Transformation-Benchmark.html?utm_source=businesswire.com&utm_medium=referral&utm_content=usa-press-release&utm_campaign=NL_Q419_191868_CX-Transformation-Benchmark-eBook_EN

38 Tsai, P. (2023). The AI generation gap: Millennials embrace AI; Boomers are skeptical. *PC Magazine.* www.pcmag.com/news/the-ai-generation-gap-millennials-embrace-ai-boomers-are-skeptical

39 World Economic Forum. (2020). *Don't fear AI. It will lead to long-term job growth.* www.weforum.org/agenda/2020/10/dont-fear-ai-it-will-lead-to-long-term-job-growth/

40 WordFinder. (2023). *How ChatGPT is catching on in America.* https://wordfinder.yourdictionary.com/blog/how-chatgpt-is-catching-on-in-america/

41 EntryPoint. (2020). *Societal and entrepreneurial trends through the generations: Baby Boomers, Gen X, Millennials, and Gen Z.* https://entrypointmi.com/2020/07/21/societal-and-entrepreneurial-trends-through-the-generations-baby-boomers-gen-x-millennials-and-gen-z/

42 Statista. (2022). *Entrepreneurial spirit index by generation 2021.* www.statista.com/statistics/948469/entrepreneurial-spirit-index-generation/

43 Azoulay, P., Jones, B. F., Kim, J. D., & Miranda, J. (2020). Age and high-growth entrepreneurship. *American Economic Review: Insights, 2*(1), 65–82.

44 MBO Partners. (2019). *The state of independence in America.* https://s29814.pcdn.co/wp-content/uploads/2019/06/MBO-SOI-2019.pdf

45 Upwork. (2022). *Freelance forward 2022.* www.upwork.com/research/freelance-forward-2022

46 Statista. (2023). *Freelance participation in the United States as of 2020, by generation.* www.statista.com/statistics/531012/freelancers-by-age-us/

Mindsets in the Workplace 3

A mindset is a collection of beliefs and attitudes that influence how people see and operate in the world. In her book *Mindset*, psychologist Carol Dweck provides a detailed overview of how mindsets, especially those related to professional pursuits, play a critical role in achieving success.[1] Two common mindsets are fixed and growth. Those with a fixed mindset see abilities and talents as innate and unchangeable, which then pre-determine factors for success. Those with a growth mindset believe talent and intelligence can develop over time, where success is achievable through effort, perseverance, and hard work. Dweck's research also suggests that those with a fixed mindset are more risk-averse and might avoid failure altogether rather than seeing obstacles as an opportunity to learn or improve. Those with a growth mindset, on the other hand, are more likely to experience success due to their ability to confront challenges, take risks, and integrate feedback, even if they first face setbacks.

There's a good reason the topic of mindsets in the workplace has received much attention. Employees can align their efforts with values and aspirations, and employers can design better working environments that align with the mindsets of their workers, leading to greater profitability and productivity, as well as lower levels of employee turnover and absenteeism.[2]

Why People Work

Let's take a look at some of the factors related to mindset. In 1980, famous country singer, Dolly Parton, came out with the song "9 to 5," which

DOI: 10.4324/9781003541035-3

chronicles an experience many can relate to: hopping out of bed to get ready for the workday, but not without pouring a cup of ambition. While some people's morning routine does involve coffee, Dolly's catchy lyrics and tune, even after decades, lead us to wonder more about motivation. What moves people to get up, go to work, and pursue careers? And, are there generational nuances at play?

Universal Motivations to Work

In our Generations in the Workplace study, we asked participants to select the top three reasons they work from a list of 15 options. We found that, across cohorts, the universal reasons include to earn money, feel a sense of purpose, and use their skills.[3]

EARNING INCOME

Earning an income is reasonably one of the biggest reasons individuals work. People have bills to pay and lives to support. And, an income provides the money needed to pursue personal passions, hobbies, and experiences outside of work. However, only roughly one-third of employees in the United States are satisfied with their pay and benefits.[4] And those who are dissatisfied are not necessarily staying. Nearly two-thirds of employees who left their jobs in the last year did so because their salary was too low, and nearly half left because of insufficient benefits, such as health insurance or time off.[5]

Generational Considerations and Strategies
Despite Baby Boomers, Gen Xers, and Millennials having higher rates when it comes to ranking income in their top three priorities, the vast majority of employees, across all generations, are motivated to work to make money.[3]

While the most obvious solution is good pay for everyone, there is also a value in transparency. For example, listing the salary and benefits in the job posting can help prospective applicants make informed decisions before even submitting a resume. Further, during hiring and onboarding, it can be useful to provide clear expectations for how one can earn a merit-based pay raise, as well as how to become eligible for advancement opportunities. Doing so can help lay out the path for working toward achieving future financial and professional milestones. Finally, making sure employees understand the benefits package can provide a fuller picture of the monetary incentives available. This may include holding information sessions or developing video overviews, which can allow for more engagement from younger audiences.

SENSE OF PURPOSE

Along with compensation, our study uncovered another top-cited reason for working shared by all generational cohorts – to have a sense of purpose.[3] Richard J. Leider's book, *The Power of Purpose*, narrows in on how purpose is a deeply energizing aspect of being because it communicates the innate desire to matter and have meaning in life.[6] Through a study of employees and business leaders across various industries, professional services firm, PwC found that having purpose and engaging in meaningful work is essential, even more so than feeling a sense of community and creating an impact.[7]

Generational Considerations and Strategies

Although a greater number of Millennials, followed by Gen Xers, noted "a sense of purpose" as being in the top three reasons for working, all generations expressed this sentiment. Thus, helping employees across all cohorts find purpose in their work is paramount to engaging them in the workplace. This can be achieved through intentional discussions during hiring, onboarding, supervision, and ongoing performance feedback. For example, supervisors should be transparent with their answers to the following questions in order to provide clarity in purpose for the employee:

- Why does this role exist?
- How does this role help the organization achieve its goals?
- How does the current project, initiative, or duties support the larger goals and priorities of the organization?
- What impact does this role have in advancing these goals?

While these discussions might be more targeted and productive in one-on-ones, regularly sharing goals and priorities during organization-wide meetings and communication efforts can help clarify and reinforce purpose.

UTILIZING ONE'S SKILLS

We found that another common reason for working shared among generational cohorts is to utilize one's skills.[3] While skills vary, the desire to be useful and contribute knowledge or expertise makes people feel valued and worthy. A report published by the Organisation for Economic and Co-Operation Development (OECD), an international member organization of democracies focusing on policies for economic growth, noted that leveraging one's skills in the workplace leads to higher levels of well-being and satisfaction.[8] And employers benefit, too, in terms of employee retention, engagement, productivity, and innovation.

Generational Considerations and Strategies

While indicated by members across all generations, the importance of skill utilization is highest for Baby Boomers, decreasing with each subsequent younger generation. This makes sense in that older employees who have been in the workforce longer might have developed strong skill sets over time that they want to make use of.

When working with Baby Boomers then, it is important to point out any impact their skills have had or could have on their assigned tasks and duties. Younger cohorts, on the other hand, are still growing and refining their professional skills and would benefit from opportunities to develop competencies needed for success in their organizational roles now and in the future. Encourage them to take advantage of online courses, certifications, and training programs; job shadowing opportunities to cross-train and learn from others; and mentorship with colleagues who have a skill set they want to develop. Additional ideas are offered in the Learning and Development chapter.

Nuanced Motivations to Work

Despite similarities across generational cohorts, there are some notable differences in why they work. Understanding these motivations can help supervisors and managers as well as coworkers better understand what is important for different constituents of employees.

STRIVING FOR LEGITIMACY

Legitimacy is essential within organizations. Many employees strive to prove their value to their peers, in particular, putting forth the sentiment, "I deserve to be here." But, some, particularly those who are younger or less experienced, have to contend with imposter syndrome, which can be defined as "doubting your abilities and feeling like a fraud at work."[9] This can cause stress, pressure to fake it, and negative self-talk. Thus, a sense of legitimacy could be powerful on both an emotional and practical level for employees to be successful.

Generational Considerations and Strategies
Imposter syndrome, however, is more disproportionately an issue for younger employees. Working as a way to create a sense of legitimacy appears to be more important for Millennials and Gen Zers than Gen Xers and Baby Boomers.[3] This isn't surprising in that older employees are likely to possess more robust skill sets and a longer work history, leading them to feel more apt to leverage that expertise and experience to prove their contributions are worthy and useful. However, this phenomenon may not simply be attributable to age alone. Research from the leadership and management apprenticeship agency, the Executive Development Network, found that rates of having experienced imposter syndrome increases with each younger generational cohort, meaning that far fewer (25 percent) who identify as Baby Boomers have ever had to contend with it compared to Gen Zers (66 percent).[10]

To help younger generations feel a sense of legitimacy in their work, clearly state how their involvement and their role positively benefits the team, organization, or consumers (patients, clients, students, etc.), making sure to reflect with them, after-the-fact, on the impact their contribution made. For Generation Z, it is important to acknowledge what they bring to the table, seek their feedback, and provide opportunities for them to apply the knowledge and skills they have gained thus far during their career. To help Millennials, it's advantageous to allow them to take more control of their work, lead projects or teams, and engage them in decision-making to leverage their skills. For both groups, helping them confront any imposter syndrome messaging they may be harboring can help reinforce that it is possible to be a contributing member of the organization while also still learning.

The Desire to Feel Productive

Feeling productive is a top reason for working shared by Baby Boomers and Gen Xers, but not Millennials and Gen Zers.[3] While these findings serve as a key indicator as to why someone works, they do not reflect actual productivity disparities between generations. For instance, a Bureau of Labor Statistics study found there were no significant differences in the level of time committed to work or being productive when comparing Gen Xers and Millennials when they were the same age.[11] Also, media coverage that frames younger employees as less productive pits generations against each other when it comes to viewpoints on productivity.

Generational Considerations and Strategies
Despite discussions on actual productivity, it is important to recognize that Gen Xers and Baby Boomers like to work in order to feel productive. Thus, recognizing and thanking them for their contributions on an ongoing basis, rather than through periodic formal recognition, can help them feel productive because their efforts are being validated by others. In addition, providing mechanisms for them to track their progress may help them feel accomplished as they complete specific tasks.

Craving Connection and Collegiality

Collegial relationships play an important role in feeling connected, as they prioritize cooperation, collaboration, and positive interactions. They also serve as the impetus for engaging in effective communication, demonstrating respect, and striving toward understanding one another. Having meaningful relationships can boost workplace productivity and satisfaction[12] and decrease the likelihood of leaving.[13] In some cases, collegial connections turn into friendships. And, 57 percent believe having a "friend at work makes their job more enjoyable."[14] The importance of strong collegial relationships hasn't gone unnoticed in the workforce. For instance, Salesforce established a team dedicated to the employee experience to ensure their workers feel connected and engaged with others as well as offers employee resource groups to connect those with similar interests and backgrounds.[15]

Generational Considerations and Strategies
We found Gen Xers and Millennials, more so than Baby Boomers and Gen Zers, are motivated to work because they enjoy connecting with others.[3] These two middle generations also see collegiality as an important factor in the workplace, more so than members of other cohorts.[3]

Knowing the benefits of meaningful collegial relationships, organizations may want to help foster connections between employees, more specifically with Gen Xers and Millennials as they put more weight on its importance. When working with these two generations, it is critical to intentionally craft time for professional relationships to form. While Gen Xers, more so than Millennials, like independence, autonomy, and getting things done quickly,[3] they may be more hesitant to engage in intentional teambuilding activities compared to Millennials. However, by making space for organic connection to manifest, like during lunch breaks, committee meetings, and the like, opportunities could emerge for relationships to forge in their own ways.

Further, to promote an environment of collegiality, recognize and celebrate those who exhibit collegial behaviors such as respect, collaboration, and assisting others. Focused time for connection and celebration of positive behaviors communicates these everyday interactions as pivotal practices in supporting organizational culture.

FILLING TIME

Our society is premised on the notion that people work. That's why one of the first questions we ask when meeting someone is "What do you do?" However, when we don't work, there can be a gap in one's life, eliciting feelings of boredom for some. This is particularly noteworthy with retirees who often struggle with filling their newfound time. While some dive into taking up new hobbies, traveling, or partaking in other interests, some eventually opt to un-retire, re-entering the workforce in their encore careers.[16] Thus, working to combat boredom is significant.

But, filling time by working isn't just specific to those entering retirement. Employees of all ages can partake in side hustles, engaging in work outside of their primary roles. While the main reason for side hustling is to supplement income, a good number also do so to fill their spare time.[17]

Generational Considerations and Strategies
We found in our workplace study that Gen Xers and Gen Zers have higher rates of wanting to work as a means to fill their time.[3] Considering the differences between both cohorts, it's important to understand the circumstances and rationale specific to each generation.

Gen Xers, the industrious and independent generation, are driven by feeling accomplished in the workplace.[3] Without work to fill their time, they may lack other opportunities to gain the sense of achievement they crave. Given the older half of this generation has newly adult children moving out, many Gen Xers experience grief and loss with empty nest syndrome.[18] Thus, to fill their time and distract from feelings of distress, they may take on extra work. This is a generation that seeks flexibility and balance yet feels the pressure to work. Being aware of the mental health reasons they may choose to fill their time working is essential for providing appropriate resources and support for them.

Many Gen Zers, on the other hand, are filling their time by working side gigs, with nearly half having taken on either a part or full-time job alongside their primary one.[19] While their main goals include earning more income and leveraging themselves for career advancement, side hustling also provides an opportunity for them to turn off their minds so they can disconnect from the stress of their primary jobs.[17] The alternative to doing so is having free time to worry about their main roles. In addition, as Gen Zers are the youngest working generation, many don't have partners, spouses, children, or other familial obligations or opportunities that might otherwise fill their time. Thus, when not working their full-time jobs, they may engage in their side hustle or even try to pick up extra shifts at their primary workplace to avoid being alone.

To aid Gen Zers in coping with the worries of their main jobs, organizational leaders may want to provide training, resources, and guidance on reducing and managing stress as well as supervisory check-ins and a supportive culture in which they can share concerns. Further, to combat any loneliness they may be facing, coworkers could invite them to social events so they can fill their time with meaningful interpersonal connections rather than additional work hours.

Workplace Values

Two companies in the same industry can be vastly different because of policies, processes, norms, and expectations. It is the collection of these values that shapes the larger culture of the organization. People want to work for companies with which they share values.[20] On the contrary, some may skip applying for or staying in a job where they don't feel there is a fit. Let's take a look at elements of organizational culture and how they align with generational preferences.

Universal Values

There are three key organizational values that are important regardless of generation. These include trust, communication, and health and safety.

TRUST

Trust is an inherently dyadic relationship, which involves interactions between two parties, entities, or people. In its most basic sense, trust focuses on prioritizing honesty, truth, and reliability. In the workplace, trust looks like creating psychological safety (i.e. feeling able to share thoughts, opinions, and beliefs without negative repercussions), honest interactions, transparency, reliance on one another, and mutual respect.[21] A trusting relationship communicates a sense of certainty and expectation among the involved parties. Trust, or lack of trust, in the workplace can have some profound impacts. Researchers at Great Place to Work, an analytics and consulting firm, studied the role of trust and its effects on companies over three decades and found that high-trust organizations experience greater profits, productivity, employee retention, and innovation.[22] They posited that these environments have credible leaders, prioritize treating people with respect, and are fair.

Generational Considerations and Strategies

Our study found that trust is the most important factor in the workplace for Baby Boomers, Gen Xers, and Gen Zers, with it being the second most for Millennials (of 21 factors).[3] It's clear – all employees want to work in a trusting environment with coworkers and leaders they have faith in. Building trust on an individual level, regardless of generation, includes consistently practicing active listening, following through on tasks, providing timely and open and honest communication, and showing appreciation for others. At an organizational level, leaders can provide transparent updates to team members, solicit and integrate feedback, take responsibility for mistakes, and practice accountability. Managers and supervisors can ensure team members have the information and resources they need to perform and providing consistent and ongoing feedback for employees to help them develop more autonomy in their work. More details on fostering a trusting supervisor-supervisee relationship can be found in the Management and Supervision chapter.

Communication

You've likely had an experience when the message you were trying to convey was not coming across the way you had hoped, eliciting feelings of frustration for both you and the receiver. You are not alone. Half of those surveyed in a Forbes Advisor study indicated having experienced ineffective communication that affected their productivity negatively (i.e. not getting something done, taking longer than necessary, etc.) as well as poor communication that had negative effects on workplace satisfaction.[23] In addition, it created additional stress and led to an erosion of trust.

Generational Considerations and Strategies

Effective communication as an important workplace factor ranked in the top four for all cohorts.[3] However, their expectations, approaches, and preferences may differ. Thus, when working with others, particularly across generations, consider co-creating an agreement that lays out communication guidelines and protocol – around what everyone can agree to in terms of expected response timeframes and platforms to be used. A communications agreement is a formal, but powerful, way to articulate and manage expectations for effective communication while balancing individual and generational preferences.

Another way to prioritize effective communication is by segmenting messaging based on the intended audience. Knowing that different groups will have unique preferences, it's essential to deliver messages through mediums and methods that best align for each group. Details of generational approaches to communication can be found in the Interpersonal Dynamics chapter.

Health and Safety

While generalized safety practices are critical, emotional, and mental well-being has drawn much attention. So much so that it is listed as a priority for the federal government's Department of Health and Human Services priorities.[24] In addition, Gallup asserts it is critical for employee productivity,[25] and the American Psychological Association put forth a guide to help organizations prioritize workplace wellness.[26]

Prioritizing health and safety pays off for companies and employers. For example, organizations experience notable benefits when workers believe their employer cares about their overall well-being.[27] Positive outcomes include a higher likelihood for employees to be engaged in their workplaces, serve as advocates for the organization, and have greater trust in leadership. They also experience lower levels of burnout and are less likely to look for a new job. While many organizations have incorporated well-being into the fabric of their organizational culture, one such program stands out. Microsoft offers the Microsoft Cares program, which serves as an employee assistance program to connect workers with in-person and online therapy and counseling.[28]

Generational Considerations and Strategies
It's no surprise then that health and safety ranks in the top four across all generational cohorts. Therefore, embedding well-being into the organizational culture can benefit everyone, regardless of age. Some initiatives include wellness programs, healthcare benefits, mental health resources, affinity groups, fitness memberships, flexible work options, stress management workshops, and balanced workloads and schedules.

Nuanced Values

While many values cut across all generations when it comes to their importance in the workplace, three stand out as being more aligned with specific generational cohorts – integrity with Baby Boomers, flexibility with Gen Xers, and meaningful work with Millennials and Gen Zers.

INTEGRITY

Integrity is composed of honesty, loyalty, trust, and transparency. Nearly every organization has an explicit value of integrity, whether the word shows up in the mission statement, list of values, or vision and goals.[29] Organizational leaders want their employees to demonstrate integrity, and workers want their employers to do as well.

Generational Considerations and Strategies
Integrity in the workplace is critical for members of all generations.[3] However, we found that Baby Boomers had a slightly higher number who indicated its importance.[3] This cohort's desire for integrity is no surprise, given the weight

they give to ethics in general. For instance, more so than members of other cohorts, Baby Boomers consider the ethical decisions of a company's leaders before making a purchase.[30] This is a generation that wants to shop with and work for organizations they believe demonstrate integrity.

To understand this nuance with Baby Boomers, it's essential to consider the era in which this generation entered the workforce: the 1960s. During this time, pensions were commonplace, gold watches were standard awards for longevity, wages provided ample income to live on, and unions were more abundant. All indicators of organizational loyalty toward employees were still relatively intact. By the 1970s, though, this loyalty started its starker decline.[31] Gen Zers, Millennials, and even Gen Xers, to some extent, began their careers during a time in history in which work had shifted to a transactional exchange between the employer and employees. Salary cuts, downsizing, and increased workloads in the name of record-breaking profits for shareholders were the norm.[31] And while Baby Boomers have spent the majority of their lives in a more transactional workforce, they did get their start when the promises of loyalty and integrity were large and the deliverables were evident.

However, younger employees who entered the workforce never knowing of a time when employer loyalty and integrity were the norm might struggle with giving it in return and even want to buck the system as a way to push back. For instance, research published in the Harvard Business Review describes how monitoring employees at work can lead to more rule-breaking, such as taking unauthorized breaks, stealing, working more slower, damaging property, and not following instructions.[32]

Although a greater share of Baby Boomers place integrity on their list of important workplace attributes, those in younger generations might have their faith restored by working for an organization that demonstrates integrity. Taking responsibility after making mistakes, being transparent about organizational decisions, modeling high standards as leaders, ensuring consistency throughout the organization (where managers aren't able to break rules that employees have to abide by), trusting workers, and limiting the monitoring of employees can go a long way in ensuring a high-functioning workplace with workers who reciprocate ethical behavior.

FLEXIBILITY

Flexibility in the workplace means having more control and ownership of how one's time is used and structured. While flexibility offers the opportunity for employees to create a balance between work and personal life, there are also many other benefits. For example, employees with flexible work options tend to experience fewer burnout symptoms, have a more positive outlook on the organizational culture, see their team as more innovative, and exhibit imposter syndrome at lower levels.[33] And there is no doubt that organizations benefit from this as well, through productivity, retention, and quality of work.

Generational Considerations and Strategies

While flexibility is paramount for workers across all generations, it's Gen Xers who rank it as one of the top three most important factors in the workplace.[3] And one-third of them consider it the best benefit.[34] This makes sense in that members of this cohort are the most likely, by virtue of life stage, to serve as caretakers for children and/or aging parents who need flexibility. Their independent work style calls for management to trust them to decide for themselves how, when, and where to best approach their work.

Recruiting and retaining Gen Xers, in particular, may come down to how flexible the organization is in meeting the needs of this cohort. For instance, job platform, Indeed, utilized data from more than 10 million surveys to rank Fortune 500 companies based on happiness scores, with one scale measuring flexibility.[35] Companies like Intuit, Google, Apple, and Dell rose to the top in this category. It isn't just the tech industry, though. Others, like Nike, Marriott International, American Airlines, and Edward Jones topped the list as well. Using these organizations as examples may help others in designing workplaces where Gen Xers, among all cohorts, feel supported.

In addition, organizational leaders may want to consider offering more flexibility in scheduling (i.e. when people work) and location of work (i.e. where people work). This might look like compressed weeks or allowing employees to determine their preferred schedule, as appropriate. It might also include implementing a hybrid or remote work structure to allow for more location control to be granted to employees. Flexibility can also be reflected through time off and vacation policies, such as generous paid time off, personal leave, and sabbaticals. While these organizational policies and practices are important, so is the interpersonal work environment. Supervisors who verbally and emotionally offer support to their employees, allow time off for those who have to take care of personal issues, adapt worker schedules, and check in about their balanced workloads can create a culture where flexibility is the norm.

MEANINGFUL WORK

Finding meaning in work involves understanding one's purpose, having a sense of accomplishment, and recognizing the impact of one's efforts. Research has found that purpose can be tied to the level of one's organizational role, insomuch that 85 percent of those in upper management say they "are living their purpose at work," whereas that is the case with only 15 percent of frontline managers and workers.[36] Given that older employees are likely to be in higher-level roles, due to their age, meaningful work for them may simply be an expectation, rather than a goal like it might be for younger employees.

Generational Considerations and Strategies

It makes sense then that 89 percent of Millennials in our study reported that meaningful work is important in a workplace, making it their highest-rated attribute for that cohort across all 21.[3] A study of nearly half a million employees by Great Place to Work found that nearly three times as many Millennials who work at "winning" workplaces, or those organizations that score high in other employee-friendly markers, cited feeling a sense of purpose and meaning compared to those that do not.[37] Thus, workplaces that value their employees can cultivate a feeling of purpose.

Finding meaning in work is also of great importance to Gen Zers. We found in our global Generation Z study that nearly 52 percent of open-ended responses about what was most important in a future career reflected the theme of happiness and fulfillment, which was the most prominent theme. Further, 16 percent highlighted making an impact.[38] One Gen Zer responded with, "doing work that I think is meaningful … so I can be best invested in it."

Because meaningful work was also ranked by two-thirds or greater of every generation,[3] fostering a sense of meaningfulness may have impacts beyond just Millennials and Gen Zers. Consider highlighting examples of employees living the purpose of the organization, showing them the results or impacts of their work, giving them time to reflect on their contributions, empowering them to be innovative, listening to their ideas, and embracing social entrepreneurship principles to ensure the organization commits to making a difference. Take, for example, eyeglass company, Warby Parker. Every time a customer buys a pair of glasses, another is donated to those in need of eyewear.[39] Who wouldn't find purpose and meaning in that mission?

Optimism

In the simplest explanation, optimism is an outlook shaped by a positive belief that things will turn out favorably. It is linked to more positive mental and physical health, purpose, and perceived quality of life.[40] And, those who are more optimistic have greater coping abilities to handle challenges and stresses. From a professional perspective, an optimistic mindset helps employees navigate the obstacles and moments of stress they face at work. Optimism can also serve as proactive inspiration and motivation, particularly in that optimistic employees outperform their pessimistic peers in areas related to engagement, productivity, earnings, and promotion.[41]

Generational Considerations and Strategies

In looking at composite scores of five measurements of optimism, Millennials tend to be slightly more optimistic than those in other generations, and Gen Zers slightly less so.[3] This holds true, for the most part, with each distinct measurement as well.

Table 3.1   *Optimism Outlooks*

	Baby Boomers	Gen Xers	Millennials	Gen Zers
I am optimistic about my future.	67%	80%	84%	65%
I believe people are inherently good.	66%	71%	80%	61%
I believe good things will happen for me.	74%	79%	81%	69%
I plan for the worst-case scenario.	56%	64%	69%	62%
I assume others will let me down.	32%	49%	57%	47%

Although Millennials possess some of the highest levels of optimism about their future and believe good things will happen to them, they also have the highest numbers who assume others will let them down. This is also the case with Gen Xers. The inconsistency may manifest as feeling the need to take control of their futures with less reliance on other people in the process. Being aware of these hesitations among the two middle generations is crucial to understanding how they might approach their work – displaying a positive outlook until they have to work with others. Simply knowing this may help alleviate unrealistic expectations in working together. Further, outlining clear and well-articulated responsibilities and assignments as well as modeling dependability might help Gen Xers and Millennials make the mindset shift.

Baby Boomers are the cohort who are least likely to believe that people will let them down. This can be an advantageous mindset because they can role model trust for other cohorts as well as help others learn how to build trust.

Gen Zers possess notably lower levels of optimism compared to other cohorts, specifically in being optimistic about their future, believing that people are inherently good, and that good things will happen to them. Growing up in an era burdened by a global recession, a widespread deadly pandemic, skyrocketing housing prices, limited affordable health care, devastating climate change, social justice regression, and ever-increasing higher education costs, it's no surprise that they lack the optimistic outlook of other cohorts. These lower levels of optimism may show up in the workplace in the form of over-worrying about their performance, distrusting others to follow through on their assigned tasks and duties, not taking risks because the reward isn't guaranteed, and exhibiting a negative or cynical attitude.

There are a few actions that can be taken to bolster the optimistic mindset among Gen Zers, specifically, such as integrating elements of reflection and gratitude into the culture of the organization, unit, or team. This may include leading the employee or team in meaning-making after the completion of a big task through reflective discussion or journaling, modeling, and encouraging appreciation of others, and helping Gen Zers consider the "wins," or good things, about their contributions, rather than focus solely on losses or setbacks.

Entrepreneurial Mindset

Steve Jobs. Oprah Winfrey. Tory Burch. When most people think of entrepreneurship, the idea of creating a huge, revolutionary company comes to mind. But entrepreneurship can take many forms beyond starting the next tech giant, media company, or fashion empire. For some, it might mean opening a restaurant, starting a mobile dog grooming business, or launching a tech start-up. What all of these endeavors have in common is that they include innovative thinking, risk-taking, and proactively going after opportunities.

Research has found that roughly 23 percent of adults in the United States have started a business, and an additional 23 percent are interested in doing so.[42] That's nearly half the population. While not everyone can or will launch their own full-fledged business venture, there are other ways people can deploy an entrepreneurial mindset. These include being a solopreneur (i.e. a sole proprietor), freelancer (i.e. a contract worker), side hustler (i.e. someone with work alongside their primary job), or running a pop-up business (i.e. providing occasional product or service offerings through events).

What is an entrepreneurial mindset? It's a thought process that incorporates innovative thinking, risk-taking, and proactive opportunity-seeking. Let's take a look at elements of this mindset with different generational cohorts. In our workplace study, we used measurements from the Entrepreneurship Mindset Domains Confidence Scale[43] to learn which particular components play more of a role for each cohort.[3] By exploring these nuances, we can better understand any variation in generational perspectives on entrepreneurship that, if appropriately engaged, can positively contribute to the organization.

Table 3.2 *Entrepreneurial Mindset Domains*

	Baby Boomers	Gen Xers	Millennials	Gen Zers
Critical Thinking and Problem-Solving	85%	87%	87%	65%
Flexibility and Adaptability	80%	79%	82%	73%
Communication and Collaboration	63%	73%	81%	63%
Comfort with Risk	71%	74%	83%	70%
Future Orientation	69%	81%	86%	71%
Opportunity Recognition	71%	80%	84%	71%
Creativity and Innovation	67%	80%	85%	67%

Generational Considerations and Strategies
Numbers are relatively high across the board for all elements of an entrepreneurial mindset. However, there are some distinctions worth pointing out.

First, a higher number of Baby Boomers resonate with having skills in critical thinking and problem-solving, along with adaptability, than other entrepreneurial domains. This may be more of a factor of their age and experience than anything. Because of this, most Baby Boomers might be able to jump into critical thinking mode to uncover the root cause of an organizational issue as well as examine and evaluate proposed solutions to identify areas for improvement. And, if circumstances change, many of them should easily adapt.

Gen Xers also have higher numbers indicating their skill sets in critical thinking and problem-solving compared to other entrepreneurial domains. As many in this generation grew up in households in which both parents were working, the level of independence at younger ages provided an opportunity for them to develop and practice problem-solving. It isn't surprising, then, that research conducted by job search platform, LiveCareer, found Gen Xers noted their greatest strength to be problem-solving.[27] Given they also have higher levels of future orientation, they may be able to seamlessly identify opportunities and strategize moving forward. To leverage their strengths when it comes to these mindsets, consider including them in visioning, strategic planning, goal setting, and opportunity identification.

A high number of Millennials identify with all the domains, indicating a strong gravitation toward entrepreneurship across the board. What stands out, though, is the high number who believe new ideas or new ways of doing things are exciting to them. Their attraction to creativity makes sense in that many were at the tail-end of their schooling when the No Child Left Behind Act was implemented, which shifted the focus from creative endeavors to preparation for standardized testing.[44] So, much of their educational experience included art, music, and theater, which could certainly have laid the groundwork for fostering creativity. While not every role or industry is overtly artistic, creative environments can still be cultivated by building a culture that is oriented toward problem-solving, innovation, and productive collaboration. In addition, consider empowering them to take on projects that have a lot of room for creativity, problem-solving, and multiple possible outcomes. And while Millennials may desire outlets for creativity, it could be necessary to coach them through how to work with those who might not. Defining when brainstorming and ideation can take place and when decisions must be made to move forward can prevent others from getting caught in what might feel like an endless creativity loop with no action.

Gen Zers' entrepreneurial mindset is characterized by being flexible and adaptable. Our past research found that they describe themselves as open-minded, which likely contributes to their comfort with flexibility.[45] Many have grown up with nearly limitless ideas at their fingertips, being exposed to a variety of perspectives through the Internet and social media. While it's certainly easy to silo oneself by consuming only information that aligns with one's set thoughts, the sheer amount of it readily available that counters any one viewpoint can make it difficult to acknowledge that other perspectives exist. The open-mindedness and flexibility of Gen Zers make them great ideation partners in generating a multitude of options to pursue. They can also aid in testing new solutions to problems and providing various points of insight to help refine the direction.

Conclusion

Understanding the diverse mindsets about work that exist among cohorts is foundational to effectively engaging employees across generations. The first step is to recognize and leverage the motivation each generation has toward their work, followed by creating working environments that integrate the elements they deem important, and then capitalizing on their optimism and entrepreneurial outlooks. It is with this identification, appreciation, and leveraging of strengths that organizations can thrive.

Notes

1 Dweck, C. S. (2007). *Mindset: The new psychology of success.* Random House Publishing Group.
2 Sorenson, S. (2013). How employee engagement drives growth. *Gallup.* https://news.gallup.com/businessjournal/163130/employee-engagement-drives-growth.aspx
3 Seemiller, C., & Grace, M. (2023). *Generations in the workplace.* Unpublished dataset.
4 Menasce Horowitz, J., & Parker, K. (2023). *How Americans view their jobs.* Pew Research Center. www.pewresearch.org/social-trends/2023/03/30/how-americans-view-their-jobs
5 Parker, K., & Menasce Horowitz, J. (2022). *Majority of workers who quit a job in 2021 cite low pay, no opportunities for advancement, feeling disrespected.* Pew Research Center. www.pewresearch.org/short-reads/2022/03/09/majority-of-workers-who-quit-a-job-in-2021-cite-low-pay-no-opportunities-for-advancement-feeling-disrespected
6 Leider, R. J. (2015). *The power of purpose* (3rd ed.). Berrett-Koehler Publishers.

7 PwC. (2016). *Putting purpose to work: A study of purpose in the workplace.* www.pwc.com/us/en/purpose-workplace-study.html

8 OECD/ILO. (2017). *Better use of skills in the workplace: Why it matters for productivity and local jobs.* OECD Publishing. http://dx.doi.org/10.1787/9789264281394-en

9 Tulshyan, R., & Burey, J. (2021). Stop telling women they have imposter syndrome. *Harvard Business Review.* https://hbr.org/2021/02/stop-telling-women-they-have-imposter-syndrome

10 Moss, R. (2023). *Imposter syndrome: Workplace prevalence by sector, gender and age.* www.personneltoday.com/hr/imposter-syndrome-prevalence-uk-research/#

11 Bureau of Labor Statistics. (2022). *Time use of Millennials and Generation X: Differences across time.* www.bls.gov/opub/mlr/2022/article/time-use-of-millennials-and-generation-x-differences-across-time.htm

12 Mason, K. (2022, July 5). Study: Fully remote workers report 33% fewer friends at work. *JobSage.* www.jobsage.com/blog/coworker-friendships-survey

13 Patel, A., & Plowman, S. (2022). The increasing importance of a best friend at work. *Gallup.* www.gallup.com/workplace/397058/increasing-importance-best-friend-work.aspx

14 Wildgoose. (2021) *The 2021 Workplace Friendship & Happiness Survey.* https://wearewildgoose.com/usa/news/workplace-friendship-and-happiness-survey

15 Hyder, B. (2022). *How salesforce builds meaningful employee experiences – without return-to-office mandates.* www.salesforce.com/news/stories/how-salesforce-builds-meaningful-employee-experiences/

16 Rosenblatt, C. (2013). *Bored with retirement? Then un-retire and go back to work.* www.forbes.com/sites/carolynrosenblatt/2013/12/04/bored-with-retirement-then-un-retire-and-go-back-to-work/?sh=70cfc1a13cc1

17 Davis, M. (2024). *More than half of Gen Zers and Millennials have a side hustle, 80% of whom say they're more reliant on the extra money due to the current economy.* www.lendingtree.com/debt-consolidation/young-side-hustles-survey/

18 WebMD. (2023). *How to manage empty nest syndrome.* www.webmd.com/parenting/how-to-manage-empty-nest-syndrome

19 Deloitte. (2023). *2023 Gen Z and Millennial survey.* www.deloitte.com/global/en/issues/work/content/genzmillennialsurvey.html

20 Glassdoor. (2019). *New survey: Company mission & culture matter more than compensation.* www.glassdoor.com/employers/blog/mission-culture-survey/

21 McKinsey & Company. (2013). *What is psychological safety?* www.mckinsey.com/featured-insights/mckinsey-explainers/what-is-psychological-safety#/

22 Great Place to Work. (2016). *The business case for a high-trust culture.* https://s3.amazonaws.com/media.greatplacetowork.com/pdfs/Business+Case+for+a+High-Trust+Culture_081816.pdf

23 Hoory, L. (2023). *The state of workplace communication in 2023.* www.forbes.com/advisor/business/digital-communication-workplace

24 U.S. Department of Health and Human Services. (2022). *Workplace well-being.* www.hhs.gov/surgeongeneral/priorities/workplace-well-being/index.html

25 Gallup. (2024). *Employee wellbeing is key for workplace productivity.* www.gallup.com/workplace/215924/well-being.aspx

26 Stringer, H. (2023). *Worker well-being is in demand as organizational culture shifts.* www.apa.org/monitor/2023/01/trends-worker-well-being

27 Harter, J. (2023). Leaders: Ignore employee wellbeing at your own risk. *Gallup.* www.gallup.com/workplace/507974/leaders-ignore-employee-wellbeing-own-risk.aspx

28 Microsoft. (2024). *The time is right for work-life integration.* www.microsoft.com/en-us/microsoft-viva/employee-wellbeing

29 Ashkenas, R. (2011). Why integrity is never easy. *Harvard Business Review.* https://hbr.org/2011/02/why-integrity-is-never-easy?

30 Weinberg, N. (2020). *Research findings: Boomers want integrity in work and life.* www.sap.com/insights/viewpoints/boomers-want-value-integrity-substance.html

31 Wharton Staff. (2017). *'The end of loyalty': Shock and awe for many American workers.* Interview with Rick Wartzman. https://knowledge.wharton.upenn.edu/podcast/knowledge-at-wharton-podcast/the-end-of-loyalty-shock-and-awe-for-many-american-workers/

32 Thiel, C., Bonner, J. M., Bush, J., Welsh, D., & Garud, N. (2022). *Monitoring employees makes them more likely to break rules.* https://hbr.org/2022/06/monitoring-employees-makes-them-more-likely-to-break-rules

33 Atlassian. (2022). *The state of teams.* www.atlassian.com/blog/state-of-teams-2022

34 Paczka, N. (2023). Different generations in the workplace – 2023 study. *LiveCareer.* www.livecareer.com/resources/careers/planning/generation-diversity-in-the-workplace

35 Gafner, J. (2023). *Flexibility and wellbeing: The 25 most flexible companies.* www.indeed.com/career-advice/news/most-flexible-jobs

36 Dhingra, N., Samo, A., Schaninger, B., & Schrimpe, M. (2021). *Help your employees find purpose – or watch them leave.* www.mckinsey.com/capabilities/people-and-organizational-performance/our-insights/help-your-employees-find-purpose-or-watch-them-leave

37 Amire, R. (2023). *Fun drives high levels of well-being at the best workplaces for Millennials.* www.greatplacetowork.com/resources/blog/fun-drives-high-levels-of-well-being-at-the-best-workplaces-for-millennials#:~:text=2.,ll%20stay%20at%20their%20company.

38 Seemiller, C., & Grace, M. (2021). *Global Gen Z.* Unpublished dataset.

39 Warby Parker. (n.d.). *The whole story begins with you.* www.warbyparker.com/buy-a-pair-give-a-pair

40 Conversano, C., Rotondo, A., Lensi, E., Della Vista, O., Arpone, F., & Reda, M. A. (2010). Optimism and its impact on mental and physical well-being. *Clinical Practice and Epidemiology in Mental Health, 6,* 25–29.

41 Gielan, M. (2019). The financial upside of being an optimist. *Harvard Business Review.* https://hbr.org/2019/03/the-financial-upside-of-being-an-optimist?registration=success

42 Ipsos. (2022). *Untapped potential: Entrepreneurialism in inflationary times, a 26-country study.* www.ipsos.com/sites/default/files/ct/news/documents/2022-07/Global%20Entrepreneurialism%20Global%20Report%20Final%20July%202022.pdf

43 Network for Teaching Entrepreneurship. (2021). *Entrepreneurial archetypes.* https://nfte.com/archetypes/

44 Sabol, F. R. (2010). *No Child Left Behind: A study of its impact on art education.* https://arteducators-prod.s3.amazonaws.com/documents/452/dccb38a0-8cd8-454a-a997-ccdcc2205dbc.pdf?1452930297

45 Seemiller, C., & Grace, M. (2019). *Generation Z: A century in the making.* Routledge.

Career Planning and Development

4

From the first day on the job to the retirement party, a considerable amount of time and energy is invested in managing one's work life. Some take a methodical approach to planning the various phases of their career, whereas others approach their journey, one step at a time, as they move through their various occupational experiences.

Career development is "the proactive, lifelong process of finding your footing and advancing your career path."[1] There are five phases of this process.[2]

1. Experiment with options
2. Develop skills
3. Pursue opportunities
4. Level up
5. Mastery

Experimentation involves testing one's interests, passions, and fit for a job by volunteering, participating in internships, or simply taking a position in that field. Once a person determines their alignment, the next step is to develop skills through education, apprenticeships, training programs, and on-the-job experiences. This phase is then followed by pursuing actual work opportunities and then leveling up, which is unique for each person, as some may choose to advance within a single company, whereas others do so by engaging in roles outside their organization or starting their own businesses. Mastery occurs when people intuitively address challenges using the wisdom they have amassed over time. While this process is, for the most

DOI: 10.4324/9781003541035-4

part, linear, changing career fields can propel someone back to the start of this process.

Members of all generations go through these phases, albeit perhaps a bit differently based on their outlooks, motivations, and priorities, which is highlighted throughout this book. Throughout the remainder of this book, these variances will be highlighted. However, let's start by looking at what shapes their views on career selection, advancement, and retirement.

Selecting a Career Path

Think back to what propelled you into your field. And, if you are still searching, consider what has impacted your contemplation about the type of work you want to do. Did you know someone who offered to introduce you to a hiring authority? Did you watch a movie like *Jerry Maguire* and decide being a sports agent was in your future? Or did you go through school, preparing for your impending career field by taking courses and engaging in internships? While everyone follows their own path, there are some that align more so with specific generations when it comes to career selection.

Interpersonal Influences

People's values, perspectives, and behaviors are often shaped by their interpersonal interactions and close relationships, particularly those during the early years of their lives. Thus, it is not surprising that these connections play some of the greatest influences on career choices. Let's take a look at a few and to what extent they resonate with members from different generations.

Who You Know

The old phrase "it's not what you know, but who you know" might have some sway when it comes to career exploration and job searching. Perhaps a parent's friend is a pilot and shares stories of flying airplanes or an older sibling just got a job doing marketing at a firm and hosts a tour of her workplace. Those actions may pique one's interest in a field, prompting action to explore further.

In some cases, people may not know what they are interested in but get a job by virtue of a network. Consider a scenario in which a friend offers to make an introduction to the head chef at a restaurant hiring prep cooks. The next thing you know, you are employed in the kitchen, well on your way to becoming a chef yourself. And, this phenomenon isn't just anecdotal. A study by the career networking platform, LinkedIn, reports that the top way job seekers find new opportunities is through referrals, which rely on interpersonal connections.[3] Thus, knowing someone in a field can be incredibly valuable for getting a foot in the door.

Generational Considerations and Strategies

We found in our Generations in the Workplace study that higher numbers of those from the three youngest generations indicated that knowing someone in a particular field had an influence on their career choice.[4] Lower rates among Baby Boomers might be explained by the lesser amount of viral technology available throughout the course of their occupational lifecycles. A study by online talent acquisition suite, Jobvite.com, found that while one in three job seekers look for opportunities through employee referrals or personal networks, over half do so via social media.[5] While in-person connections can be useful, social media allows for a much further reach, as individuals are bombarded with updates on people's careers, links to job postings, and even inspirational photos of work events from their distant acquaintances, who without these online connections, they might not keep up with. With younger generations having been exposed to social media for a larger share of their careers, it makes sense they have had more opportunity to connect with their personal networks online about jobs.

To reach out to prospective employees, particularly in the youngest generations, it's important to have a social media presence beyond general ads and announcements. Instead, consider crafting posts that include "a day in the life" stories of current workers, which can then be shared with their personal networks, as well as asking employees to post or repost compelling stories about the impact of their organizations. This endorsement can go a long way in terms of reaching others in their circles.

ENCOURAGEMENT

"You are so good at explaining things. I think you'd make a great teacher."
"You really should do something with your music. You are so talented."

"Have you ever thought about becoming a physical trainer? You always seem to be reading online about exercise and the human body." People, especially those in our trusted circles, have the ability to see our strengths, interests, skills, and potential from a different angle, and can thus offer unique helpful insight in considering career options. Sometimes, all it takes is for someone to believe in you or simply point you in a specific direction you hadn't thought of. Let's take a look at how often this happens with members of different generations.

Generational Considerations and Strategies

Receiving encouragement from a friend or family member to explore a field or apply for a job is one of the primary influences among Millennials and Gen Xers. Both of these generations were told growing up that "You can be anything you want to be," whereas Baby Boomers were not, and the tides shifted with Gen Zers as it has been suggested to their parents to move away from that phrase.[6] While these two middle generations might have been provided more blanket support, being encouraged to pursue specific career paths has been dependent on time in history when not everyone could access any career. As occupational opportunities have opened up over the years, there is more accessibility to enter into some fields that, regardless of encouragement, simply would have been more difficult to obtain in the past. Even today, though, no matter how much support is given to a woman to be a Navy Seal, engineer, or construction manager, for instance, getting into those roles can be difficult. The same goes for people of color with jobs like veterinarians, lawyers, and farmers[7,8]

Despite the role of encouragement being more prominent among Gen Xers and Millennials, there is still a number of people across all generations who have found that receiving inspiration and support from those they trust has helped them find their career paths. While these individuals are likely family members and friends, don't rule out the impact coworkers and bosses can have in encouraging others to apply for that promotion or seek out a new opportunity.

Family Legacy

Following in the professional footsteps of a parent or family member is a common occurrence. For example, a mom working in a science field might pass on a love for that subject to the child, or a sibling in the field of information technology could inspire a younger one to take a similar path. This makes sense in that those in one's inner circle are some of the first examples of work that young people are exposed to. It's no surprise then that a network analysis conducted by Facebook's parent company, Meta, found that family members do influence career choices to some degree.[9] There are two distinct ways this could happen – children taking over the family business or engaging in the same profession as a parent or family member.

Generational Considerations and Strategies

Let's examine both of these phenomena through a generational cohort lens. While it was more common for Baby Boomers, and even Gen Xers, to be handed the family business when their parents retired, it is less so with Millennials and Gen Zers. Tracey Gillespie, with Wealth & Investment Management at Wells Fargo, notes, "Many parents, especially Baby Boomers, want their kids to become college educated and choose a career path that interests them—and often, the family business doesn't … we're also seeing a shift in societal norms; there's not the same feeling of duty among younger generations to carry on their parents' business legacy. Younger generations want to fulfill their own goals and build their own legacies." Because of this, today, more than half of business owners do not want to pass them on to their children.[10]

Instead of taking the reins of the family operation, if Millennials and Gen Zers do follow in the footsteps of their parents, they are more apt to select a similar career field.[4] Given many younger individuals growing up with two parents have likely had both in the workforce during their childhood, more so than Baby Boomers, for instance.[11] This gives them twice as many opportunities to see what fields resonate most with them.

Considering these nuances, it's important that when working across generations to have an appreciation of what might be drawing each person to their occupational fields. Is it born from a passion? A family obligation? Both?

External Influences

While interpersonal interactions and relationships impact the career paths that individuals explore and pursue, there are external influences that can do the same. These are often experiences, whether intentional or not, that provide new insight into a field, prompting people to investigate options.

Classes

Some kids can remember back as early as grade school excelling in a particular subject, only to pursue a related career field later on in life. For instance, that child who loved writing goes on to publish a book, or the one who was a math whiz becomes a tax accountant. Whether in K-12 or college, school allows individuals to explore strengths, skills, and interests for future careers.

Generational Considerations and Strategies
Of all the potential influences on their career selection, we found Gen Xers, Millennials, and Gen Zers noted taking a class among their top ones.[4] And that may simply be due to exposure. The National Center for Education Statistics reports that the average college enrollment rate of Baby Boomers when they completed high school was 50 percent, while Gen Xers enrolled at an average rate of 60 percent, Millennials at 66 percent, and Gen Zers at 67 percent.[12] The higher rates of younger generations may mean that there are simply greater opportunities for them to take courses that would expose them to career interests and opportunities, at least at the collegiate level. Additionally, programs to help young people explore occupations are prominent in K-12 schools today. For instance, 40 percent of Gen Z high schoolers attend institutions with programs that help them explore potential career paths, and 38 percent have dedicated classes for career exploration.[13]

Given classes have been a prominent force for career planning for many younger generations, it could be beneficial to encourage them to continue this reflection process even in the workplace through participation in professional development opportunities, mentoring, and other career development programs and initiatives.

Media

A study conducted by ZenBusiness, an all-in-one digital platform for small businesses, found that more than half of their survey respondents reported that TV, movies, books, video games, or podcasts had inspired their career choices.[14] It makes sense then that employment trends are correlated with how frequently a profession is portrayed or mentioned in the media, especially for occupations related to office and administrative support, transportation and material moving, building and maintenance, food prep-aration, computer science and mathematics, and production.[15]

So, while it might not be causal, watching a show like The Office could inspire someone to pursue working in a typical 9–5 workplace, or seeing hospitality professions portrayed on The Travel Channel may encourage people to explore the travel industry.

Generational Considerations and Strategies

Although seeing careers portrayed in the media is not one of the main influences for any generation, many Millennials indicate its potency more so than other cohorts.[4] Particularly for Baby Boomers, TV, and movies were far more limited when they were entering the workforce. For some, televi-sion was just becoming accessible to the average household, movies were only seen at theaters, and shows were limited to the few networks available, which is why it's not surprising that so very few believe media consumption is an influencer on their career selection.

While some Gen Xers may have become inspired to be lifeguards after watching *Baywatch*, many of the shows in the era in which they entered adulthood simply didn't highlight potential careers unless you wanted to take up slaying vampires with Buffy.

However, Millennials were thrust into a world marked by highly com-plex shows like *CSI: Crime Scene Investigation* where after watching, it seemed as though everyone wanted to be a forensic scientist and solve cold cases. Some might have been eager to become lawyers as *Boston Legal*, as the show highlighted the fun-filled profession of law. Although inspiring for Millennials, these portrayals were not always accurate – par-ticularly in education and the medical/health care field.[10] However, that didn't stop this generation from wanting to join the medical interns on *Grey's Anatomy*.

Given the sheer amount of content available, why don't Gen Zers see their TV and movie consumption as influential to their career selection? It's likely due to the heavy influx of reality television on channels such as Food Network, HGTV, Discovery, or TLC, to name a few, that, in many cases, more accurately portray occupations than scripted series do. Shows like *Deadliest Catch*, *Dirty Jobs*, and *Dog the Bounty Hunter* reduce the glorifi-cation of particular occupations, potentially deterring young people from entering those fields. So, while media might not have influenced many of them to pursue specific fields, it may very well have, unbeknownst to them, detracted them from others.

HOBBIES

Career inspiration can also come from activities that bring joy. Consider the person who travels frequently, becoming a travel blogger, or someone who enjoys fashion and pursuing a career as a stylist. In some cases, people may go into their full-time careers based on a hobby, whereas others might explore side hustles. Research has found that one in four Americans have already turned a hobby into a side hustle, with another 55 percent wanting to do so.[16]

Generational Considerations and Strategies
Of all generational cohorts, more Millennials and Gen Zers have had a leisure activity or hobby influence their career choices.[4] This phenomenon has grown with access to platforms like Etsy, where creators can monetize their works, and UpWork and Fiverr, where people can freelance. Additionally, individuals are sourcing their talents and hobbies on social media, where they can garner followers and generate an income. While Baby Boomers may have had a greater separation between their hobbies and their professional pursuits on the front-end of their career lifecycles, many are turning these hobbies into their encore, or second careers, during retirement.[17]

PERSONAL ASSESSMENTS

Another form of career exploration can come from taking personality or skills assessments. These tools are designed to provide clarity on interests, strengths, passions, and competencies and help people gain greater insight into careers or industries that might suit them well. They also serve to affirm what individuals already know about themselves and give them the language to best articulate those assets.

Generational Considerations and Strategies
While personality or skills assessments are not at the top for any one generation when it comes to primary influences on career choic es, numbers are far higher for Millennials, Gen Xers, and Gen Zers than for Baby Boomers.[4] The varying levels of influence reported between Baby Boomers and younger cohorts could stem from the timeline in which these types of tools gained popularity. Consider that some of the well-known ones, the Myers-Briggs Type Indicator (MBTI), the Five Factor Model, and

StrengthsFinder, were developed between the 1960s and 1990s.[18] During this timeframe, Baby Boomers, unlike younger generations, may not have had access to these assessments while exploring careers.

However, given their proliferation, it can be useful for schools and even workplaces to utilize them to ensure employees have good alignment with their career choices.

Unplanned Influences

In some situations, an individual doesn't find their career field; instead, it finds the individual. Famous for starring as Han Solo in Star Wars, Harrison Ford was working as a carpenter at Goldwyn Studios when he was asked by casting director, Fred Roos, to help with auditions by reading lines with other actors. After doing so with more than 100 potential cast members, Ford, himself, landed the role that would fully launch his acting career.[19] While he knew he wanted to act and had been cast in one small role prior, being in the right place at the right time helped the stars align for him to land a dream job.

Generational Considerations and Strategies

Falling into a job is the most pronounced with Baby Boomers, Gen Xers, and Gen Zers.[4] Yet, even Millennials have relatively high rates when it comes to the influence of taking advantage of an unplanned opportunity in finding one's career.

Career Advancement

Most employees want to move up as their skills develop and they amass ample experience, particularly because taking one's career to the next level often means increased pay, more responsibility, and possibly more control over one's work. Career advancement might mean being promoted from within an existing organization, leaving a current role for a new opportunity, or leveling up business operations for entrepreneurs. Advancement is critical for most people, so much so that more than half of active job seekers cite it as their top reason for seeking a new role.[5] While the sentiment cuts across employees of various generations, there are several factors related to how each cohort approaches and navigates this process.

Perspectives on Promotions

Many employees expect, at some point, to earn a promotion within their current workplace, which may include a change in title, responsibilities, and/or pay. A study by job search platform, FlexJobs, found that one in three employees indicated that they would leave their organizations if there were a lack of advancement opportunities.[20] And, this is not just an empty promise. Research from the Pew Research Center found that a lack of advancement opportunities was the second most cited reason employees actually left their jobs, after low pay.[21] This presents important implications for organizations in that in order to retain good employees, management will need to ensure possibilities of promotion are accessible and readily available.

Generational Considerations and Strategies

When looking at expectations regarding promotions, there are more similarities than differences across generations. For instance, we found in our study that more than half of employees believe it is reasonable to expect to be promoted sometime between six months and two years, with the average expectation around the one-year mark.[4]

Despite the generalities, there is some nuance between cohorts that is essential to highlight. For one, more Baby Boomers, compared to those in other generations, noted that advancement shouldn't take place until the three-year mark. Gen Xers, too, think a bit longer tenure is required compared to younger generations, with the majority indicating sometime between one and two years.[4] While Millennials might be more apt to seek and then apply for more opportunities in an effort to play career catchup from the Recession,[22] their expectations on internal promotions are not considerably shorter than those of their older counterparts. And, for Gen Zers, their views on when to expect a promotion fluctuate depending on the employment market, hovering around less than a year when jobs are plentiful and up to 18 months when they are less so.[23]

It makes sense that those in older generations may want a little more time to pass before an employee is promoted, given that they have been in the workforce longer and might have had to wait for a promotion. Particularly, equity-minded Gen Xers[4] don't think it's fair to jump the line without having paid some dues.

In addition, each generation has differing views on why someone should be promoted. Baby Boomers believe it should be based on experience, Gen Xers on merit, Millennials on how hard they work, and Gen Zers on time in service.[23]

To manage expectations, organizations should be proactive by communicating performance metrics that will be assessed to determine promotion eligibility. And, being transparent about this during the recruitment process can be critical for helping prospective employees across all generations make important choices about their future.

Upskilling

Dave, a 20-year veteran of his organization, shows up each day, works hard, and gives his best effort. Technology is advancing rapidly, though, and Dave is constantly re-tooling to be able to be successful in his role. If he wants to move into a higher position at some point, though, he will have to upskill beyond what he needs to perform his current duties. Finding adequate opportunities to do this can be challenging. Dave is not alone in grappling with this dilemma. Research has found that 78 percent of employees are concerned that they lack the skills needed to advance in their careers, and 70 percent indicate feeling unprepared for the future of work.[24]

Generational Considerations and Strategies

It's clear that upskilling is necessary for advancement, but let's take a look at each generation's views and approaches around it. While Baby Boomers may be further into their careers, a study conducted by the American Association of Retired Persons (AARP) found that more than half of older employees are willing to learn new workforce skills.[25] However, only one in three Baby Boomers had indicated having participated in a job-related training or education program in the last two years.[25] This presents a gap in interests and reality, but also serves as a call for employers to help better connect Baby Boomers with skill development experiences, perhaps through a personal invitation to participate, work coverage and support while in attendance, and even accessible registration processes.

Gen Xers also see the value in upskilling. Zety, a resume-building platform, found that Gen Xers believe their commitment to professional development and learning is one of their defining characteristics.[26] Further, one in four would consider leaving their current employer if there was a lack of professional development opportunities.[21] So, despite being in the career phase where they are likely leading companies and managing others, Gen Xers are still looking to learn more and gather new skills. If the opportunity to upskill is not readily available, this cohort may be motivated to look elsewhere.

Not having adequate skill development opportunities could be a reason that Millennials decide to pursue new careers as well. Management firm, PwC, reported that training and development programs would make an organization an attractive employer for one in three Millennial employees.[27] On the other hand, a lack of opportunities would motivate 74 percent of them to leave an employer.[18] So, like Gen Xers, a workplace that does not prioritize upskilling risks losing or missing out on engaging Millennial talent.

Skill development is so important to Gen Z that, for some, it is a reason they would remain in a job. In a study conducted by the talent acquisition firm, Lever, Gen Zers are the most likely of any cohort to stay in their current role because of opportunities to reskill or upskill that exist with their employer.[28] Doing so could lead to internal promotions or an enhancement in competencies that could aid Gen Zers in future employment. For example, Darby, a second-year Generation Z employee at a graphic design company, signs up to attend a training session at her work to learn HTML programming for websites, only to then get promoted to a new role where knowing how to build websites is on the list of required criteria.

Changing Jobs

Sometimes advancing to the next level in one's career is achieved by changing jobs or even industries. However, "job hopping" is often viewed as a behavior associated with disloyalty to an employer. There is much more that lies beneath the surface of someone choosing to change occupations. A 2022 Marist Poll found that since the start of the COVID-19 pandemic, nearly four in ten employees have changed jobs.[29] Even beyond the circumstances presented by the pandemic, including layoffs, furloughs, and reduced hours, there are several reasons employees seek new career opportunities – such as wanting to leave a toxic organizational culture, low salary, bad management, and a lack of work–life balance.[14] These reasons are likely universal and would serve as motivation for anyone, regardless of age, to pursue a new opportunity.

Generational Considerations and Strategies
According to the Bureau of Labor Statistics' Current Population Survey, while the median tenure of employees in the United States to stay

with their employer is 4.1 years, that number varies by age group.[30] For those between 55 and 64, it is 9.8 years; 45 and 54 is 6.9 years; 35 and 44 is 4.7 years; 25–34 is 2.8 years. Despite the lower numbers for young employees, research from the Pew Research Center found that job tenure rates for Millennials and Gen Zers today are essentially the same as they were for Baby Boomers and Gen Xers when they were around the same age.[31] Thus, changing jobs during the early years of a career is likely an expected part of one's professional maturation process and less dependent on their generational cohort.

With most Baby Boomers nearing retirement, it is unlikely that many of them will be planning to change jobs or careers before they retire compared to other generations. However, Baby Boomers have the highest reported rates of returning to work for a previous employer because they offer better benefits or have more opportunities for upskilling/reskilling.[25]

Finding and maintaining work–life balance is the most valuable work-place attribute among Gen Xers.[21] It's not surprising then that one in four of them would be prompted to leave their current role if they had to regu-larly work overtime or had poor work–life balance.[21] If a job lacks these characteristics or these erode over time, members of this cohort may be motivated to seek new opportunities.

For Millennials, motivation to advance in one's career can be the reason for changing jobs. In a study of younger professionals, Gallup found that one in three Millennials rated accelerating their career as a very important factor in taking their next job, which is much higher than the rates for older generations.[32] However, Millennials also see opportunities for advance-ment within their current company or place of employment. According to findings from the Lever study, the Millennial cohort is the most likely of any generation to ask their employer for a change of role.[25]

Like those in older generations, Generation Z employees are motivated by salary when considering new career options. Money isn't the sole or pri-mary concern for Gen Zers seeking shifts. More would rather work for an organization where they have a clear sense of purpose than one that would pay them a higher salary,[25] which further reiterates the perspective that they seek out jobs that are fulfilling and provide meaning.

While members of each generation have their criteria for staying in a job, it's clear: people of all ages will leave if their organizations don't provide them with what they need. So, leaders should get to know their employees and help create environments, processes, and opportunities to motivate them to stay and share their talents for years to come.

Retirement

Much of the focus of career planning and development is often designed around exploration and preparation, getting a job, and advancing in one's field. However, an important phase of the career lifecycle that requires intention, thought, and planning is retirement. Most employees do not just wake up one day, stop working, and retire. For many, retirement is a well-thought-out activity based on one's prediction of how long they can sustain financial solvency without working.

Retirement Age

Having a vision for the age at which one retires can serve as a tangible goal for preparation. Some set their sights based on when they will be able to access benefits through Social Security, which is 66 for people born between 1943 and 1954,[33] increasing by a few months each birth year until 1960, at which 67 is the age for full-benefits eligibility. However, those who wish to keep working after these ages can continue doing so, along with others who want to retire earlier before Social Security kicks in. With varying lengths of proximity to retirement ages, each generation has a different set of intentions for when they will retire.

Generational Considerations and Strategies

Of the Baby Boomers still working full time, we found the vast majority plan to retire after the age of 65, with 40 percent planning to retire after the age of 70.[4] These statistics are consistent with findings from the Pew Research Center, which reported employment rates of Americans aged 65+ having doubled in just three decades.[34] Baby Boomers are sticking around because many are healthier than members of their predecessor generations when they were the same age, increasing their longevity; and, some simply still enjoy their jobs and find their work fulfilling.[36] This generation is leaning into "flextirement," where they are slowly decreasing their hours in the workplace to avoid an abrupt transition out.[35] With 54 percent planning to work after they officially retire, many want to ensure they have the finances necessary for full retirement[37] and for later on, when they move into assisted living facilities, which have become nearly unaffordable.[36]

The two middle generations have similar perspectives on when they will retire. More than half of Gen Xers and nearly three-quarters of Millennials believe they will retire before they turn 66.[4] However, as they each get closer to 65, they may find that the feasibility or desire to retire then could have changed over time.

Nearly half of Gen Zers want to retire before they turn 60, with one in five aiming to do so before 55.[4] And, they are already taking retirement seriously. The median age for Gen Zers to start saving is 19, compared to Millennials (25), Gen Xers (30), and Baby Boomers (35).[37] Further, research indicates that for one in three Gen Zers, saving for retirement is one of their financial priorities.[37] While their perspectives might evolve as they age, retiring early aligns with Generation Z's sentiment that work is not the center of one's life purpose, despite wanting to find fulfillment and meaning in it.

One's retirement age is contingent on the financial ability of a person to be able to sustainably support themselves for the duration of their life. Thus, members across all generations are seeking positions with employers who provide substantial retirement benefits that can help them leverage their ability to retire comfortably and when they aim to.

Retirement Preparation

Fidelity Investments' Retirement Savings Assessment provides an analysis of retirement preparedness, which yields a score reflecting a household's ability to cover estimated expenses during retirement. Their average American retirement score is 83, meaning a typical saver is on pace to have 83 percent of the income necessary to manage expenses in retirement by the time they get to that age.[37] The average score of 83 is driven by the 54 percent of households that fall within the good or "on target" category. However, 28 percent are in the category of "needs attention," in which a typical saver would have fewer than 65 percent of anticipated expenses covered.[36] Individuals in this category are more likely to be women, people of color, and those with lower educational levels.[38] One thing is clear: while having adequate resources for retirement feels out of reach for many, most people are making great efforts to prepare themselves in the best way possible.

Generational Considerations and Strategies

In looking at generational cohorts as a whole, is one better prepared than another? The answer is "yes." Fidelity Investments reported Baby Boomers having an average score of 87, followed by Millennials at 82, and Gen Xers at 80. Gen Zers were not included in the analysis. Declining scores make sense in that older individuals would likely have saved and prepared more for retirement than subsequent younger generations, although Millennials' scores are slightly higher than those of Gen Xers, which is no surprise given that 54 percent of them feel they will be financially prepared for retirement.[39] Despite Gen Zers' absence from the analysis, a study by Northwestern Mutual did find that these young employees are the most confident that they will be financially prepared when the time for retirement comes around.[38]

While these scores can provide a snapshot of retirement readiness, it is necessary to dig deeper into the top three financial strategies each generational cohort engages in to prepare for retirement, along with the least used strategy.[4]

Table 4.1   *Retirement Preparation Strategies by Generation*

	Baby Boomers	Gen Xers	Millennials	Gen Zers
1	Contributing to a 401(k) or workplace retirement plan	Contributing to a 401(k) or workplace retirement plan	Contributing to a 401(k) or workplace retirement plan	Contributing to a 401(k) or workplace retirement plan
2	Minimizing debt	Putting money in a savings account	Working with a financial advisor	Putting money in a savings account
3	Putting money in a savings account	Working with a financial advisor*		
Least Used	Contributing to a personal IRA or Roth	Investing* Minimizing debt* Adhering to a budget*	Putting money in a savings account Adhering to a budget	Working with a financial advisor Adhering to a budget

*Indicates equal rating of importance.

401(K)S AND WORKPLACE RETIREMENT PLANS

The 401(k) was established by Congress in 1978 and has a long history in the workforce since then as being a viable retirement strategy for both employers, who use their matching contributions as a recruitment tactic, and employees, who can put away pre-tax money for later. And, its popularity is strong in that 34.6 percent of working-age people have 401(k)s, 403(b)s, or the like, and 18.2 percent have individual retirement accounts (IRAs.)[40]

Generational Considerations and Strategies

The U.S. Census found that age matters. Those in older generations have put more away in their retirement accounts,[39] which isn't surprising as they have been in the workforce longer. However, the interest is there across all cohorts as contributing to a 401(k)s or other plan was cited in our study as the most utilized retirement planning strategy for members of all generations. Despite their younger age, even more than 40 percent of Gen Zers contribute. However, in 2023, 78 percent of Millennials and 80 percent of Gen Zers indicated having scaled back their contributions to deal with inflation and a fear of a recession.[41]

While employer plans are popular across cohorts, Roth and IRAs are not. In particular, we found in our study that far fewer Baby Boomers are investing in these types of plans, likely depending more so on their employer-matched accounts that many started years earlier.

As some organizations shift to 1099 workers or full-time positions without benefits, or reduce or remove retirement account matching or pensions, they may find good employees across all generations pass them up for more lucrative opportunities elsewhere. This isn't speculative. Ninety percent of HR professionals worry that workers will leave if they can't offer a good financial package, and 89 percent of employees agree.[39] Seventy-five percent of workers say they would take a job somewhere else if the benefits they wanted were not provided.[39]

Putting Money in a Savings Account

Having a savings account is a common practice for individuals as a way to tuck away money for a rainy day. Whether as an emergency account to draw from to repair a vehicle or a long-term fund to build up resources for a down payment on a house, Americans are trying to save. According to a 2022 study conducted by the Federal Reserve, the median balance for a savings account across all families was $8,000.[42]

Generational Considerations and Strategies

Members of all generations are socking money away in savings accounts. However, the $13,400 average savings older Baby Boomers have in their accounts is considerably higher than the $8,000 young Baby Boomers, $8,700 Gen Xers, and $5,400 Millennials and Gen Zers have in their savings. These relatively declining amounts, with the exception of young Baby Boomers, make sense given each cohort's age. Numbers, though, vary even within cohorts, where some individuals are more fully prepared for retirement, and others don't even have a savings account. Still, one-third of Baby Boomers believe they do not have enough money saved to retire, and nearly one-half think they will either outlive their savings and investments or have to compensate for the diminishing or disappearing Social Security payments.[37] Gen Xers, like Baby Boomers, have similar concerns as nearly half believe they will outlive what they have saved for retirement.[43] And, Millennials, while having put away a bit less in savings, have more time to make up that ground.

Gen Zers, while amassing an impressive amount of retirement savings for having worked for such a short time, are committed to their financial independence – so much so that Fidelity Investments found that 75 percent of them are saving money as a way to achieve it.[46] On average, Gen Zers put away 14 percent of their income, which is higher than the averages reported by Millennials, Gen Xers, and Baby Boomers.[44] That's because only 45 percent believe they will be able to rely on Social Security benefits as a source of income during retirement.[37]

What can organizations do? Perhaps offer an emergency savings initiative, where employees set a specific amount to be deducted from their paychecks to go into a "savings envelope."[45] By the end of 2022, users of the Wisely prepaid debit card and app which houses some companies' employee savings, reported that workers had saved 1.55 billion dollars.[42] Further, some employers even incentivize participation, like Delta Airlines that contributes $1,000 for employees who complete financial training.[42]

Minimizing Debt

Americans hold an average of $103,358 in consumer debt, with mortgage debt at $241,815 and non-consumer debt at $23,317.[46] With high interest rates, some people can't seem to get out of debt, accumulating so much so that their homes are foreclosed on, and cars repossessed. The implications are steep: bad debt can lead to low credit scores and the inability to rent an apartment or buy a car. Heavy debt can result in simply never being able to get ahead and being wholly unprepared for retirement.

Generational Considerations and Strategies
While paying off debts and remaining debt-free is a primary strategy for preparing for retirement for Baby Boomers,[4] nearly half hold a mortgage balance, as well as credit card balances and an auto loan.[41] Despite the COVID-19 pandemic having presented a great deal of financial uncertainty, many Baby Boomers used this time to pay down an average of 15.5 percent of their overall debt,[47] better situating them as they move toward retirement.

Gen Xers, though, indicated one of their lowest strategies for retirement preparation is paying off their loans, and that is evident in the fact that their debt increased nearly 26 percent from 2021 to 2023.[43] Given that 39 percent of the nation's entire pool of student loan debt is with Generation X, making it the highest of any cohort,[48] this generation will have to confront their debt head on in the near future.

While there may not be much that organizations can do about their employees' personal debt, some workplaces, such as Aetna, Google, Hulu, Penguin Random House, and Staples, are helping to pay off their workers' student loans.[49]

WORKING WITH A FINANCIAL ADVISOR

A financial advisor is an expert who provides guidance to individuals in making decisions regarding money. Whether to help set a budget, plan for long-term goals, or discuss ideas for revenue and spending streams, these professionals can aid in being able to more successfully manage one's finances. According to the Bureau of Labor Statistics, in 2023, there were 272,190 financial advisors in the workforce.[50] That's a lot of people helping others with their finances.

In addition to professionals in the field, finance and money management apps are available for those who might want a low-cost or free resource at their fingertips. In 2021 alone, there were 573.1 million downloads of these types of apps, up from 481.9 million just one year earlier.[51] Thus, people are seeking information about how to manage their finances.

Generational Considerations and Strategies
We found in our study that the three youngest generations seek financial advising as a way to plan for their retirement. However, these are the three cohorts that note their least used strategy is actually sticking to a budget,

which may be a bit counterintuitive, given that would likely be a fundamental recommendation of any financial advisor or money management app.

However, Gen Xers do get other guidance from their advisors – in particular, strategies for achieving long-term financial goals.[43] And Millennials seek advising in order to better navigate uncertainty. They see meeting with an advisor as an essential way to achieve financial success.[52] Gen Zers, on the other hand, more often get their advice online.[53]

Whether through workshops, one-on-one coaching, or links to money management apps, younger employees want, and even expect resources on financial planning as a work benefit. And, while nearly nine out of ten HR professionals reported that their organizations offered financial wellness programs, one out of ten do not.[39] And, that may be a dealbreaker for young employees.

INVESTMENTING

Sixty-one percent of Americans invest in the stock market, whether that is through day trading, active investing, or simply hosting their retirement funds in a 401(k) and letting the market do the work. When it surges, profits soar. When it dips, assets take a loss. Despite the volatility, many see investing as a way to create a retirement nest egg.[54]

Generational Considerations and Strategies
While we found just over a third of the three oldest generations have put money in investment accounts, Gen Xers are the only generation that indicated this as being a primary strategy for retirement preparation. As Gen Zers age, more of them may turn to investing – both because they will likely have more discretionary income and more time to develop their confidence in this practice, especially since 71 percent of them don't feel confident in self-managing investments.[54]

Like financial advising, organizations that offer investment advising may find it to be a valuable workplace benefit. This may help build the confidence of the youngest employees while providing what could otherwise be an expensive or inaccessible service for all workers.

Conclusion

While some aspects of career development are consistent across generational cohorts, there are some slight nuances. Whether the differences in perceptions and approaches to career trajectories may be due to each cohort's place in the career lifecycle or actual defining generational characteristics, the result is the same: different age groups in the workforce have unique wants and needs around career planning and development.

Notes

1 Upwork. (2023). *What is career development? Types, steps, and career tips.* www.upwork.com/resources/what-is-career-development

2 Munro, I. (2022). *A roadmap for career development: How to set your course.* www.betterup.com/blog/career-development

3 LinkedIn Talent Solutions. (n.d.). *The ultimate list of hiring statistics.* https://business.linkedin.com/content/dam/business/talentsolutions/global/en_us/c/pdfs/Ultimate-List-of-Hiring-Stats-v02.04.pdf

4 Seemiller, C., & Grace, M. (2023). *Generations in the workplace.* Unpublished dataset.

5 Jobvite.com. (2023). *Examining employer and job seeker realities in the current job market: How employers can respond to candidate preferences, perceptions, and personas.* https://web.jobvite.com/rs/328-BQS-080/images/2023-03-EmployQuarterlyInsightsReportQ12023.pdf

6 Reischer, E. (2016). *No, honey, you can't be anything you want to be. And, that's okay.* www.washingtonpost.com/news/parenting/wp/2016/02/18/no-honey-you-cant-be-anything-you-want-to-be-and-thats-okay/

7 Luckwaldt, J. H. (2013). *The 10 whitest jobs in America.* www.payscale.com/career-advice/the-10-whitest-jobs-in-america/

8 Weber, L. (2024). *40% of lawyers are women. 7% are Black. America's workforce in charts.* www.wsj.com/economy/jobs/workers-america-jobs-demographics-charts-94a5ff6c

9 Adamic, L., & Filiz, I.O. (2016). *Do jobs run in families?* https://research.facebook.com/blog/2016/3/do-jobs-run-in-families/

10 Gonzales, N. (2024). *What to consider doing with the family business when you're ready to retire.* https://conversations.wf.com/family-business-transition/

11 Livingston, G., & Parker, K. (2019). *8 facts about American dads.* www.pewresearch.org/short-reads/2019/06/12/fathers-day-facts/

12 National Center for Education Statistics. (2022). *Table 302.10: Recent high school completers and their enrollment in college, by sex and level of institution: 1960 through 2021.* https://nces.ed.gov/programs/digest/d22/tables/dt22_302.10.asp?current=yes

13 ECMC Group. (2023). *Question the quo June 2023: Gen Z teens have changed their priorities for education and work.* www.questionthequo.org/news/buzz/report-gen-z-teens-have-changed-their-priorities-for-education-and-work

14 ZenBusiness. (2020). *Influence of media on careers.* www.zenbusiness.com/blog/influence-of-media-on-careers/

15 Baruah, S., Somandepalli, K., & Narayanan, S. (2022). Representation of professions in entertainment media: Insights into frequency and sentiment trends through computational text analysis. *PLoS ONE, 17*(5), 1–37. https://doi.org/10.1371/journal.pone.0267812

16 Hughes, A. (2021). *55 percent of adults want to turn a hobby into a lucrative side hustle.* https://swnsdigital.com/us/2019/07/55-percent-of-adults-want-to-turn-a-hobby-into-a-lucrative-side-hustle/

17 Brooks, R. (2016). *They turned their hobbies into encore careers.* www.washingtonpost.com/business/get-there/they-turned-their-hobbies-into-encore-careers/2016/10/27/e9df96b4-9013-11e6-a6a3-d50061aa9fae_story.html

18 Harrell, E. (2017). A brief history of personality tests: Three assessments that shaped the industry. *Harvard Business Review.* https://hbr.org/2017/03/a-brief-history-of-personality-tests?ab=seriesnav-spotlight

19 Newsweek Special Edition. (2016). Carpenter to Han Solo – Star Wars' impact on Harrison Ford's career. *Newsweek.* www.newsweek.com/how-star-wars-advanced-harrison-ford-acting-career-527310

20 Pelta, R. (2022). Great resignation: Survey finds 1 in 3 are considering quitting their jobs. *FlexJobs.* www.flexjobs.com/blog/post/survey-resignation-workers-considering-quitting-jobs/

21 Parker, K., & Menasce Horowitz, J. (2022). *Majority of workers who quit a job in 2021 cite low pay, no opportunities for advancement, feeling disrespected.* Pew Research Center. www.pewresearch.org/short-reads/2022/03/09/majority-of-workers-who-quit-a-job-in-2021-cite-low-pay-no-opportunities-for-advancement-feeling-disrespected/

22 Rinz, K. (2019). *Did timing matter? Life cycle differences in effects of exposure to the Great Recession.* U.S. Census Bureau. https://kevinrinz.github.io/recession.pdf

23 Fredman, J. (2023). *How fast does Gen Z expect to be promoted?* https://ripplematch.com/insights/how-fast-does-gen-z-expect-to-be-promoted/

24 Workplace Intelligence. (2022). *Upskilling study.* http://workplaceintelligence.com/upskilling-study/

25 Choi-Allum, L. (2022). Job reskilling and upskilling among the 50+. *AARP Research.* www.aarp.org/research/topics/economics/info-2022/reskilling-workforce-trends-older-adults.html

26 Buffet, J. (2023). Generation X in the workplace: 2022 study. *Zety.com.* https://zety.com/blog/generation-x-in-the-workplace#2

27 PwC. (2011). *Millennials at work: Reshaping the workplace.* www.pwc.com/co/es/publicaciones/assets/millennials-at-work.pdf

28 Lever. (2022). *2022 Great Resignation: The state of internal mobility and employee retention report.* www.lever.co/wp-content/uploads/2022/02/Lever_Great-Resignation-Report_2022.pdf

29 Marist Poll. (2022). *The U.S. labor force, Sep 2022*. https://maristpoll.marist.edu/polls/the-u-s-labor-force-sep-2022/

30 U.S. Bureau of Labor Statistics. (2022). *Employee tenure summary*. www.bls.gov/news.release/tenure.nr0.htm

31 Fry, R. (2022). *For today's young workers in the U.S., job tenure is similar to that of young workers in the past*. Pew Research Center. www.pewresearch.org/shortreads/2022/12/02/for-todays-young-workers-in-the-u-s-job-tenure-is-similar-to-that-of-young-workers-in-the-past/

32 Pendell, R., & Vander Helm, S. (2022). Generation disconnected: Data on Gen Z in the workplace. *Gallup*. www.gallup.com/workplace/404693/generation-disconnected-data-gen-workplace.aspx

33 Social Security Administration. (2023). *Retirement benefits*. www.ssa.gov/pubs/EN-05-10035.pdf

34 Fry, R., & Braga, D. (2023). *Older workers are growing in number and earning higher wages*. Pew Research Center. www.pewresearch.org/social-trends/2023/12/14/older-workers-are-growing-in-number-and-earning-higher-wages/

35 Barnes, J. (2024). *I'm a CEO and 12 of my employees are in 'flextirement.' With boomers opting not to retire, the arrangement will become more common*. https://finance.yahoo.com/news/m-ceo-12-employees-flextirement-130227033.html?guccounter=1

36 Rowland, C. (2023). *Senior care is crushingly expensive. Baby Boomers aren't ready*. www.washingtonpost.com/business/2023/03/18/senior-care-costs-too-high/

37 Fidelity Investments. (2020). *Retirement savings assessment 2020: Executive summary*. www.fidelity.com/bin-public/060_www_fidelity_com/documents/about-fidelity/2020-rsa-executive-summary.pdf

38 Picchi, A. (2024). *Baby boomers are hitting "peak 65." Two-thirds don't have nearly enough saved for retirement*. www.cbsnews.com/news/retirement-baby-boomers-peak-65-financial-crisis/#

39 Northwestern Mutual. (2023). *Planning and progress study 2023*. https://news.northwesternmutual.com/planning-and-progress-study-2023

40 Hoffman, M. G., Klee, M. A., & Sullivan, B. (2022). New data reveal inequality in retirement account ownership. *U.S. Census*. www.census.gov/library/stories/2022/08/who-has-retirement-accounts.html

41 Morgan Stanley at Work. (2023). *State of the workplace III*. www.morganstanley.com/content/dam/msdotcom/atwork/state-of-workplace-financial-benefits-study-2023/state-of-workplace-study.pdf

42 Merritt, J. (2024). *The average savings account balance*. www.usnews.com/banking/articles/the-average-savings-account-balance#:~:text=The%20median%20savings%20account%20balance,living%20expenses%20as%20a%20goal.

43 Northwestern Mutual. (2023). *Planning and progress study 2023*. https://news.northwesternmutual.com/planning-and-progress-study-2023

44 BlackRock, Inc. (2023). *See the moment: 2023 BlackRock read on retirement.* www. blackrock.com/us/individual/literature/presentation/2023-read-on-retirem ent-report.pdf

45 Weston, L. (2023). How your employer can help you save for emergencies. *NerdWallet.* www.nerdwallet.com/article/finance/employer-provided-emerge ncy-savings-accounts

46 Satov, T. (2024). *What is the average American debt by age?* www.synchronybank. com/blog/average-american-debt-by-age/

47 Davis, M. (2023). Baby Boomers and Gen Xers wound down their nonmortgage debt over the past 2 years, while Gen Zers and Millennials increased their burdens. *Lending Tree.* www.lendingtree.com/debt-consolidation/generatio nal-debt-study/#:~:text=Gen%20Xers%20are%20the%20most,most%20lik ely%2C%20at%2045.0%25.

48 Bareham, H. (2023). Which generation has the most student loan debt? *Bankrate.* www.bankrate.com/loans/student-loans/student-loan-debt-by-generation/

49 Argento, M. (2021). *20 companies that help employees pay off their student loans.* www.lendingtree.com/student/companies-that-pay-off-student-loans/

50 Bureau of Labor Statistics. (2023). *Occupational and employment wages.* www.bls. gov/oes/current/oes132052.htm

51 Lebow, S. (2022). *Finance apps flew past 500 million mark in US downloads.* www. emarketer.com/content/finance-apps-downloads

52 Business Wire. (2023). *Fidelity research spotlights significant growth opportunity for advisors with young investors.* www.businesswire.com/news/home/20230124005 076/en/Fidelity%C2%AE-Research-Spotlights-Significant-Growth-Opportun ity-for-Advisors-With-Young-Investors

53 Rose, K. (2023). *Gen Z's social media dependency is a bridge, not barrier, for advisors.* www.forbes.com/sites/forbesfinancecouncil/2023/09/28/gen-zs-social-media-dependency-is-a-bridge-not-barrier-for-advisors/

54 Gallup. (2023). *What percentage of Americans own stock?* https://news.gallup. com/poll/266807/percentage-americans-owns-stock.aspx#:~:text=U.S.%20St ock%20Ownership%2C%20Annual%20Trends&text=Sixty%2Done%20perc ent%20of%20U.S.,52%25%20in%202013%20and%202016

Thriving at Work   5

Across all industries and roles, one thing is certain: employees desire an environment where they can thrive, allowing them to "achieve their full potential in their work, home, and community."[1] While Gallup found that slightly more than half of employees in the United States report being in a state of thriving, while the rest do not.[2] And those who don't report a higher likelihood of burnout, daily worrying, ongoing stress, and sadness or anger.[2]

The concept of thriving has a potential impact that extends beyond the workplace context. If someone is happy and healthy at work, they are more likely to be happy and healthy in their personal lives, within their communities, and as citizens of a larger society. Conversely, those who are unhappy or operate in unhealthy conditions at work can easily carry those feelings into other aspects of their lives. Thus, thriving has even bigger implications than just in the workplace.

Work Environment

Because working conditions contribute to thriving at work,[1] it's important to look at the structure of the work environment, including where people work, their hours, and the control they have over their scheduling.

As the workplace has evolved, so have the preferences of employees in how they structure their work. With advances in technology, innovation, and the impact of the COVID-19 pandemic, recessions, and other significant societal events, many employees, particularly those in older

DOI: 10.4324/9781003541035-5

generations, have experienced different structures over the course of their career lifecycles. Therefore, it is not surprising that each generational cohort has their own set of preferences and practices related to their work environments.

Work Settings

Prior to the COVID-19 pandemic in 2020, working on-site was the predominant practice for many employees. According to the U.S. Census Bureau, 84 percent of adults in the United States worked in an on-site or in-person capacity, and only 12 percent worked remotely in 2019.[3] In 2021, the number of adults in the United States working from home doubled to roughly 21 percent.[3] However, the Pew Research Center estimates that nearly two-thirds of jobs in the United States are not feasibly conducted remotely.[4] Thus, the growth in remote work may be more pronounced if one simply looks at office workers.

REMOTE WORK

Many workers, though, have since been called back to the office once the pandemic began to wane. Yet, not all have been eager to return,[5] especially given the benefits they would have to give up. These include fewer distractions, more flexibility, reduction of or elimination of a commute, better work–life balance, greater opportunity for creativity, higher levels of motivation,[6] being able to create a sense of balance between work and personal life, as well as managing projects and deadlines more effectively.[4]

Generational Considerations and Strategies

So, in looking by generation, is the desire for remote work concentrated within one or two cohorts, or is it more generalized? To examine this question closely, we asked employees in our Generations in the Workplace study. Given all the benefits, unsurprisingly, we found that members across all generations prefer remote over on-site work.[7] However, Baby Boomers seem to be the most pro-remote,[8,9] essentially because they feel more productive when working from home,[9] and without a commute, they enjoy being able to spend more time with loved ones.[8] Gen Xers and Millennials also enjoy remote work, mainly to save time and money,[8] but also for family and childcare reasons.[9] And, Gen Zers like the technological aspects of remote work, as many are comfortable with virtual collaboration,[10] so much so that 17 percent are more likely to apply for remote jobs compared to those in other generations.[10]

Hybrid Setups

Research has found that 86 percent of employees would prefer to work at least one day a week from home and then come to the office when needed for collaboration sessions, idea generation retreats, networking, or talks and events.[8] And, in some cases, accessing resources from the office may be necessary – like wanting to use the copier or printer, get supplies, or utilize meeting rooms.[8]

Generational Considerations and Strategies

In our study, hybrid work emerged as a preferred setup, more so with younger generations.[6] Both Millennials and Gen Zers like the face-to-face time they can get with those in executive roles.[7] In addition, those who work fully remotely cite it as hurting their opportunities to be mentored in the workplace and to feel connected with their coworkers.[4] With both younger cohorts having a greater desire for mentorship and believe it will help with their development,[7] lacking in-person opportunities may impede their career goals.

Gen Zers, in particular, want hybrid setups because they like the benefits of remote work but enjoy the perks they get from coming to the office, such as lunches and snacks,[9] free coffee, and having a focused place to work.[8] While our research found that many Millennials actually work in a hybrid capacity, more of them would like to be fully remote.[6]

Working On-Site

Before the proliferation of technology, working remotely was more of a rarity. Nearly every office worker got up every day, commuted to a building across town, and worked the 9 to 5 shift. With the advent of digital communication, video-based platforms, productivity apps, and document-sharing resources, it became easier and easier to work from anywhere. Yet, many CEOs have called people back to the office in the name of collaboration and camaraderie, making on-site work still more common than might be expected. However, one of the reasons employees cite for not wanting to come back to the office is that their coworkers are dispersed,[11] and when they show up on-site, they simply spend their day in video meetings.

Generational Considerations and Strategies
More employees, across all generations, work on-site than would prefer to.[6] After having had the advantage of engaging in remote work during the pandemic scaled back with a callback, this changeup can be jarring for some. And, for those who have never worked remotely, the explicit benefits they have witnessed others receive might be alluring for them. It makes sense then, that in our study, we found on-site work to be the least preferred setup for members of all cohorts when compared to remote and hybrid work.[7]

Leaders should be mindful to construct workplace setups that do not solely align with their personal preferences but effectively engage their employees of all ages. Organizations that require fully in-person work may struggle to recruit and retain younger generations who would prefer to work remotely. Conversely, organizations that only offer remote work may have difficulty attracting those who prefer a hybrid setup. All in all, having a flexible working arrangement is a primary motivator across all generations when it comes to looking for a new job.[12] Thus, despite any generational differences, organizational leaders will want to keep in mind the importance of flexibility and autonomy when hiring.

Scheduling Preferences and Control

Another important factor related to thriving is the level of control employees have over their schedule. The Work and Well-Being Initiative, a joint research-for-action project between Harvard University and the Massachusetts Institute of Technology, found that employees who have more control over their schedules reported feeling less stressed and were less likely to quit due to the benefits of better balance in personal lives, more family time, and increases in physical health and sleep.[13]

Generational Considerations and Strategies
In looking at both actual and preferred scheduling practices, our study uncovered some slight differences by generation.

Table 5.1   *Preferred Scheduling Control*

	Baby Boomers	Gen Xers	Millennials	Gen Zers
Preferred	Full Control	Some Control	Full Control	Full Control* Set Schedule*
Actual	Set Schedule	Set Schedule	Full Control	Set Schedule

*Indicates equal rating of importance

Across all generations, employees like to have some say in their scheduling, with Baby Boomers, Millennials, and Gen Zers wanting full control.[7] These align with findings from another study that highlight the significant role autonomy plays for employees and their desire to be the primary decision-makers of their work schedules.[14]

While members from all cohorts want at least partial, if not full, control, other than Millennials, most adhere to a schedule set for them.[7]

Table 5.2   *Level of Preferred and Actual Scheduling Control*

	Baby Boomers	Gen Xers	Millennials	Gen Zers
Full control	Equally preferred and actual	Equally preferred and actual	More preferred than actual	Equally preferred and actual
Some control	Equally preferred and actual	More preferred than actual	More preferred than actual	Equally preferred and actual
Set schedule	Less preferred than actual	Less preferred than actual	Less preferred than actual	More preferred than actual

It's clear that those in older generations would prefer more control and less set scheduling than they actually have. It may be less likely these employees are handed a shift schedule, although that can be the case. More so, their set schedules are reflective of needing to attend standing meetings or events due to their more senior roles.

Many Gen Zers, though, prefer to have a set schedule. This could be related to their need for defined hours, so they know exactly when they have time to engage in a side gig[15] or work their second job.[8]

It's important that organizations keep in mind that scheduling preferences are unique to generational cohorts and even individuals. Thus, a customized approach might be best. For instance, information technology firm Alley has no set hours. Instead, employees work when they choose to.[16] The company has found that there is a heightened sense of accountability in that workers do not want to let each other down.[11]

However, in any situation where employees have a say in scheduling, there must be equitable and clear guidelines[9] to demonstrate fairness and consistency. Further, being transparent about schedules is critical. For example, if Baby Boomer Tanya, who reluctantly works a set schedule, never interacts with A.J., a Gen Xer, because he determines his own hours, resentment could brew between the two.

Well-being

Structure is just one factor that contributes to thriving at work. Organizational culture, which consists of the "shared values, attitudes, behaviors, and standards that make up a work environment,"[17] may positively or negatively impact the well-being of employees and ultimately, their ability to thrive. So much so, that 96 percent of employees only look at companies with a "clear emphasis on employee wellbeing" as they seek out their next jobs.[18] Further, 87 percent would leave their current company if it lacked a focus on well-being.

The level of commitment that organizations have toward the well-being of their employees can have a profound impact on the success of the organization and the individuals who work within it. In a longitudinal study conducted by Gallup, researchers found that the perception that organizations are committed to employee well-being peaked among U.S. employees in the spring of 2020 at 49 percent but dropped to 24 percent post-pandemic.[19] This is lower than pre-pandemic perspectives in 2019 at 29 percent. In a separate 2023 study, Gallup reported that when employees agree that their employer cares about their overall well-being, they are less likely to job search and experience burnout, more likely to thrive in their lives, be engaged, advocate for the organization as a good place to work, and be more trusting of their leaders.[20] Simply put, when organizations are committed to the well-being of their employees, employees are committed in return.

Margaret Swarbrick's model highlights multiple dimensions of well-being.[21] These include physical, financial, intellectual, emotional, social, spiritual, environmental, and occupational. Each of these plays an important role in an employee's experience.

Generational Considerations and Strategies

So, which dimensions do members of each generation rate as their highest in terms of what they possess? Lowest? Which ones do they believe organizations should focus on?

Table 5.3 *Dimensions of Well-being*

	Baby Boomers	Gen Xers	Millennials	Gen Zers
Highest	Intellectual Spiritual Occupational	Intellectual Emotional Occupational	Intellectual Occupational Physical	Intellectual Occupational Spiritual
Lowest	Financial	Financial	Social	Social
Highest Priority for Organizations	Occupational Emotional Intellectual	Financial Occupational Intellectual	Occupational Social Physical	Financial Occupational Social

Intellectual Well-being

Imagine working in a job where your assigned task was so repetitive and mundane that you became bored and disengaged. You want to share ideas, solve problems, be creative, and innovate. But, there is no option to do so, as you are consistently thrust back into the day-to-day grind. While some employees like that kind of work, a lot would rather have opportunities to be intellectually stimulated, engaging in tasks that allow them to utilize their creativity and critical thinking skills. Doing so can reinforce a sense of legitimacy in their contribution and validate that their skill sets are being adequately leveraged. The benefits also extend beyond employees. When workers are intellectually stimulated, organizations often see increases in quality and productivity.[22]

Generational Considerations and Strategies

Although members across all age groups believe their intellectual well-being is high,[7] it is those in the two oldest generations that are more prone to think that it should be a top priority for organizations. Perhaps, as employees progress through their career lifecycle, they develop a greater desire for creative and intellectual stimulation in their work, or the tasks they have become accustomed to are more complex, creating a higher standard for the type of work they are willing to do at this point in their careers.

Despite the high rates across the board, organizations can continue to offer support by encouraging continued learning and skill development, engaging employees in critical thinking and problem-solving scenarios, and incentivizing brain health activities outside of work, such as reading, journaling, games, and engaging with the arts. Having employees with strong critical thinking skills, the ability to solve problems, and the capacity to approach situations with creativity can lead to stronger teams, greater productivity, and better outcomes.

Occupational Well-being

Even if work does not play a central role in one's personal identity, people often commit a significant portion of their lives to their jobs – approximately 2,100 hours per year or roughly 24 percent of their time annually.[23] With nearly a quarter of an adult's life being spent working, its reasonable that individuals would desire to have some level of occupational well-being, which involves "feeling good about what you do," including passionate, fulfilled, balanced, and inspired.[24] When one feels positive about their work life, that often carries over into their home life. However, research has found that 27 percent of employees believe their job is actually getting in the way of their well-being rather than contributing to it.[20] Thus, occupational well-being has the potential for greater holistic impact on a person's life and is critical for thriving in and out of the workplace.

Generational Considerations and Strategies
To what extent do employees feel like they are "well" in this dimension? In our study, we found that members across all generations report their occupational well-being as higher than most other wellness dimensions.[7] The two youngest cohorts rank second, whereas Gen Xers and Baby Boomers put this in the third slot.[7] While there is some nuance in that, the main theme is that the factors related to occupational wellness are critical for everyone. This may be due to greater opportunities for flexible work arrangements since the COVID-19 pandemic, more employees prioritizing well-being over salary, and increases in usage of employer wellness benefits.[19]

When asked to prioritize wellness dimensions that employers should support, occupational well-being ranked in the top two across all generations,[7] which is not surprising in that this dimension is most aligned with what is in the purview of organizations to control.

Despite most employees noting high levels of occupational well-being, organizations will want to continue efforts to support this area. For instance, supervisors should ensure balanced workloads for their employees, offer opportunities for them to upskill and engage in professional development, create open channels of communication, and find ways to connect employees to projects and tasks that are meaningful to them.[25]

Spiritual Well-being

Spiritual well-being involves the search for meaning in life. At its core, it is associated with feeling connected to oneself and a greater purpose. For some, it involves religion or engaging in a faith community. Others opt to practice spirituality through activities like yoga, mindfulness, meditation, volunteering, reflection, or spending time in nature.

In some cases, people find their sense of purpose through their work or link their career to their purpose or passion. We often see this in fields such as education, health, public administration, and the nonprofit sector. With 86 percent of employees noting that they find meaning in their work,[19] it's easy to see that most employees feel a personal alignment between their jobs and their values.

Despite meaning-making that occurs on the job, many also seek spiritual fulfillment outside of work. In those instances, employers are more hesitant to offer support. For example, only 25 percent of employees say their employers give them time off to engage in their religious practices, and 36 percent believe their organizations either rarely or never provide time off to participate in volunteer work.[19]

Generational Considerations and Strategies

So, which generations believe their spiritual well-being is high? Baby Boomers and Gen Zers. Let's take a deeper look, though. For Baby Boomers, spiritual well-being is second just to their intellectual well-being.[7] And, this is no surprise in that compared to other cohorts, more Baby Boomers identify with a formalized religion,[23] and a greater number use religion as a source of guidance around determining what is right and wrong.[26]

While more Baby Boomers align with the religious element of spiritual well-being, Gen Zers tend to execute their spirituality differently. For one, this cohort is less likely to be involved in formal religion or faith-based practices.[27] This may be because those in Generation Z draw inspiration from multiple faiths and regularly participate in other activities, such as prayer or being in nature.[28] Further, many seek purpose in activities that aren't explicitly aligned with spirituality, like engaging in meaningful work,[7] advocating for causes they believe in, and making a difference for others.[29]

Regardless of whether one has spiritual well-being and wants to continue investing in it or is seeking it altogether, like some Gen Xers and Millennials might be, organizational leaders may want to pay attention to the role meaning-making has in the lives of their employees. To do this, supervisors can have intentional conversations with their direct reports about the purpose of their work as well as provide support for them to participate in practices that enhance their spirituality, even if they are on the clock. Further, it is helpful to understand that individuals have different definitions of spiritual fulfillment, and that to work best across generational lines, honoring their personal commitment, however they define it, is essential.

Emotional Well-being

Emotional well-being involves having an awareness of and an ability to manage one's feelings and emotions, particularly in responding and coping to challenges and adversity.

In an international study of more than 5,000, employees noted emotional wellness as the dimension most likely to impact their productivity, with stress being one of the main causes.[21] With 95 percent being stressed out in their jobs,[19] it's clear that a lack of emotional well-being can have both a personal and organizational effect.

Generational Considerations and Strategies

Gen Xers are the only cohort we found that ranks their level of emotional well-being in the top three, although Millennials did report high scores on this dimension.[7] What's more telling, though, is Gen Zers' poor levels of emotional well-being.[7] And, it's not just a lifecycle effect – young people struggling more than their older counterparts. A study conducted by the Walton Family Foundation and Gallup discovered that Gen Zers have had more difficulty with emotional well-being than those in other generations did when they were the same age.[30] Let's explore why.

For one, Gen Zers have lower levels of resilience,[7] which means it might take more time or effort to recover from a setback. It's hard to bounce back when there is an ongoing barrage of issues they have to face – whether political headlines that pop up on their phones, statistics about the planet dying being shared on social media, or doom and gloom messages about the economy embedded in the many videos they watch for entertainment. Add to that, their higher levels of stress, anxiety, loneliness, and sadness.[30] This stems from their concerns over gun violence in school, lack of financial security,[30] along with social media and worries over the climate crisis.[31] Further, some lack competence and confidence in interpersonal communication,[41] which has led to having fewer close relationships they can lean on during challenging times.

To help Gen Zers develop emotional well-being in the workplace, coworkers might want to offer support, modeling, and guidance so these young employees can learn effective coping strategies. In addition, the National Institutes of Health offers the Emotional Wellness Toolkit, which includes various resources for building resilience, stress reduction, and mindfulness.[32] Human Resources departments may find these tools useful for aiding Generation Z employees in developing their emotional well-being.

While Baby Boomers didn't rate their Emotional well-being the lowest, many still believe it should be a priority for employers to support.[7] This may come as somewhat of a surprise given that this generation grew up when stigmas of mental and emotional health issues were pervasive, preventing many from seeking the care they needed. In addition to the day-to-day issues they faced that could have benefited from therapy, consider that 40 percent of male Baby Boomers served in the military prior to post-traumatic stress disorder (PTSD) becoming a diagnosis.[33] Soldiers came home from Vietnam, for example, and just carried on with life. Now that they are older, emotional health is even more paramount for them, especially since depression increases with age.[33]

In addition to access to therapy, organizations may also want to consider structural changes like limiting work after hours, instituting a four-day workweek, and offering mental health days,[34] to aid Baby Boomers, along with members across all generations, in preserving positive emotional well-being.

Physical Well-being

Physical well-being refers to one's state of personal health and wellness. Many factors contribute to this, including nutrition, exercise, and health management. Employees rate physical well-being as the second most important wellness dimension for its impact on productivity,[19] meaning that one's health can affect their performance on the job. On the other hand, the job can also impact physical well-being. For example, 63 percent say that their job gets in the way of working out, and 58 percent note that it prevents them from eating healthy.[19]

Generational Considerations and Strategies

Millennials were the only cohort to indicate their level of physical well-being falls within the top three of all eight dimensions.[7] Many in this generation are taking steps to be proactive in maintaining good physical health so as to promote life longevity.[35] McKinsey & Company found that Millennials prioritize nutrition, sleep, and fitness more so than the average consumer.[36]

We discovered that the lowest rate of physical well-being across generations is with Generation Z.[7] Some of this is related to sedentary lifestyles,[37] consumption of fast food,[33] and not getting enough sleep, which is a serious enough issue that some Gen Zers have taken to TikTok to share their suggestions for prioritizing rest and sleep through extensive rest periods called "bed rotting."[38] In addition, given their high rates of stress and anxiety,[30] it's not surprising that these can take a toll on their bodies – in the form of fatigue, illness, gastrointestinal issues, and the like.

Despite rating themselves high in this area, Millennials would like to see organizations prioritize physical well-being. This is the generation who championed nap pods, fitness rooms, free food, and, even "fur-ternity" leave to allow for time off after adopting a pet.[39] They want to see this continue as they age.

It's clear that when organizations offer wellness programs, they work. For instance, 78 percent of HR leaders indicated that these types of programs in their organizations contributed to reduced spending on healthcare benefits for employees, and 85 percent highlighted that sick day use decreased.[19] However, for the youngest two generations, it might also help to provide fitness memberships, massages, stress reduction apps, wearable fitness technology, and discounts for healthy food purchases, given their salaries are likely among the lowest in the organization.

Financial Well-being

While money can't buy happiness, it sure can impact one's ability to live comfortably and thrive, like being able to afford groceries and gas, pay down credit card debt, or save for a big purchase. The Consumer Financial Protection Bureau defines financial well-being as "how much your financial situation and money choices provide you with security and freedom of choice."[40]

But, with more than 66 percent of Americans living paycheck to paycheck[41] and only 34 percent living comfortably,[42] it makes sense that personal finances are the number one source of stress among employees.[43] This worry can cause distraction, which has been found to take up nearly a quarter of an employee's workweek, as well as result in lower retention and engagement and poor physical and mental health.[44]

When employees feel in control of their financial well-being and on track to meet their goals, they are more likely to be satisfied with their job, remain in their role, and report feeling happy, engaged, and productive at work.[15]

Generational Considerations and Strategies

One thing is for sure – people across all cohorts are worried about money, with an even more pronounced focus on those in the two oldest generations as they rank this as their lowest dimension of well-being.[7] This makes sense in that many Baby Boomers are coming up short in their retirement funds,[45] and Gen Xers have the highest rates of student loan debt.[46]

For members of both generations, though, the main issue seems to center around a shortage of financial resources. While educational initiatives can be helpful, more monetary ones, like tuition assistance programs for Gen Xers' college-bound children or higher matching programs for the company 401(k) could go a lot further.

While Baby Boomers may rate themselves low in this area, many believe employers should instead be prioritizing other dimensions of wellness, particularly ones around their ability to mentally and emotionally thrive on the job. However, it is the highest ranked wellness dimension for Gen Xers and Gen Zers in terms of what they think employers should focus on. This is likely because Gen Xers report having low financial well-being, and many Gen Zers tend to have the lowest salaries in the organization, given their tenure.

Only 40 percent of organizations offer financial wellness programs,[47] it might be time to invest in one. According to Great Place to Work, some ideas include offering salary increases, interest-free loans, financial planning and education programs, tuition awards, and employee discounts.[48] Financial firm, KPMG, offers assistance with college advising, and hotel chain, Hyatt, provides hardship grants to employees suffering setbacks from unexpected events. These resources could prove to be helpful, particularly to those in the youngest cohort, who may be struggling financially and not have experience managing their salaries or benefits.

Social Well-being

Imagine going to work every day, yet not having any social connections there. Coworkers gather during breaks to chat, yet you have no one to talk to. Or, maybe you work remotely, and while you interact through your messaging app with colleagues around work topics, there is not anyone asking how your day is or interested in hearing about your weekend. While not everyone wants to make friends in their workplace, having no social connection can take a toll. According to Gallup, 20 percent of workers say they felt lonely "a lot" the previous day.[49] High levels of loneliness can lead to greater mortality rates.[47] In addition, with 17 percent of engaged employees feel lonely compared to 31 percent of disengaged employees, it's clear that there is a relationship between employee engagement and social well-being, which is rooted in connection and belonging.

Generational Considerations and Strategies
The two younger generations rate their social well-being lowest.[7] This could be linked to the decreasing levels of social connectedness among Americans in the last two decades when both of these cohorts were growing up and coming into adulthood.[50] Now, we see the norm of neighbors who have never met, lack of participation in community organizations, and general social disengagement. Thus, it's no surprise that Baby Boomers and Gen Xers spend more time on leisure activities, including socializing with others.[51] They grew up going to the neighborhood block parties and hanging out with their friends at the mall.

While Millennials and Gen Zers have low levels of social well-being, they are also turning to their workplaces to provide it. In more formal ways, organizations can offer employee resource groups, teambuilding activities, intentional time for relationship building, and mentoring. And, given these two cohorts are more likely to want to hang out with their coworkers outside of work than members of the two older generations,[7] informal connections might be a viable path to enhancing their social well-being.

Environmental Well-being

Think of a circumstance in which your organization offered something for your workspace that helped you thrive – maybe it was an office with a window, a comfortable chair, or an ergonomic keyboard. Or, virtually, perhaps it was a simple online communications platform that made working across geographic areas easier. Regardless, our surroundings can have a serious effect on our ability to do our jobs.

Environmental well-being involves feeling physically safe and healthy within our micro-environments (the places we live, learn, work, etc.) and macro-environments (our communities, country, and whole planet).[52] For one, studies have shown that more time in nature during the workday can reduce stress and ailments.[53] In addition, everything from good lighting to better air quality can lead to increased health for employees, along with reduced absenteeism and greater productivity.[54]

Generational Considerations and Strategies
More than 80 percent of employees across all cohorts reported positive environmental well-being, which explains why far fewer think that organizations should prioritize this dimension.[7] However, in looking more closely, the story becomes clearer. On a macro level, Millennials and Gen Zers want their workplaces to embrace sustainability, with 20 percent reporting that they have changed jobs to something that better aligns with their environmental values.[15] Older generations, on the other hand, are focused more on internal elements of environmental well-being. For instance, Baby Boomers want quiet and private workspaces as well as high-quality meeting rooms,[55] and Gen Xers want private offices, either on-site or in their home, to engage in independent work.[7] And, while Millennials and Gen Zers are focused on macro-environmental impact, they like their internal workspaces to be comfortable and feel like home, as well as have good lighting, plants, and patio workspaces.[56]

Employee Engagement

The level of engagement that employees commit to their job also serves as a prominent contributing factor to thriving. Employee engagement is "the personal commitment an employee has to their organization's goals and overall success. It's the amount of passion they have for their work and their willingness to put forth effort."[57] With countless benefits, including productivity, well-being, quality, and customer loyalty,[58] it makes sense that companies like Gallup have invested inordinate amounts of resources into helping organizations increase their employee engagement.[22]

Generational Considerations and Strategies

In looking at generational perspectives, there are both similarities and differences that cut across the various types of engagement. These types include intrinsic (excitement, values alignment, and commitment), support (connection, value, and recognition), leadership (invested in, utilized, and listened to by organizational leaders), and structural (challenging work, opportunities for growth, and adequate training).[7]

Table 5.4 *Engagement Perspectives by Generational Cohort*

	Baby Boomers	Gen Xers	Millennials	Gen Zers
Intrinsic	74%	78%	87%	69%
Support	66%	77%	86%	68%
Leadership	65%	74%	85%	65%
Structural	72%	81%	89%	73%

We found quite a bit of consistency across cohorts – as the majority of members from all generations feel engaged at work.[7] In looking closer, though, we can see some unique indicators that might help organizational leaders, supervisors, and coworkers more effectively foster employee engagement.

For example, the three youngest generations are more engaged through structural means than any other type of engagement. However, in narrowing in more closely, they have much higher rates in terms of feeling adequately prepared through training than feeling they have ample growth opportunities, which is particularly low for Gen Zers.[7] Not only does this cohort believe they can advance in their organizations, upwards of 60 percent do not even think they will land a good job in the next year.[59] What this means for organizations is to continue to focus on offering training and development, but pay more attention to also ensuring that opportunities for growth and advancement are offered and that employees know about and are encouraged to pursue them.

Baby Boomers feel more intrinsically engaged, more so by being committed to doing their best work every day rather than feeling excited about coming to work.[7] This may be explained by the fact that they have a high level of integrity[7] and would likely not be satisfied with doing marginal work. However, excitement is a different story. Research conducted by 360 Learning found that far more Baby Boomers believe their job is just okay, necessary but unenjoyable, or they hate it, compared to those in younger age groups. One of the primary reasons is because many think their work is not valued,[60] which is consistent with findings from our study.[7] Addressing this, however, will take more than just words to convince Baby Boomers their contribution is important. Consider writing thank-you notes, providing flexibility and trust, engaging in daily check ins, and offering stretch opportunities to capitalize on their talents.[61]

Members across all groups rated leadership engagement the lowest.[7] However, the nuances lie in the details, as Baby Boomers feel utilized but not heard, and Gen Xers, Millennials, and Gen Zers feel heard but not utilized.

The greater number of Baby Boomers feeling unheard could be explained by their more extensive experience in the workforce, warranting a desire to provide more thoughts more frequently than they are afforded. This cohort has expressed a need to be intellectually stimulated within the workplace. So, it is reasonable that they would also want to share their thoughtful opinions and perspectives to help improve the organization.

In working across generations, understanding what creates engagement for each employee is paramount. For instance, a Baby Boomer boss who works tirelessly to make sure her Gen Z employees are heard, when they already feel their opinions are considered, could benefit more so from finding ways to better utilize the talents of these young workers. That may involve attempting to notice any instances of boredom, lack of motivation, or procrastination and then talking to them about better leveraging their skills.[62] Overall, however, being able to cue into the needs of each worker, regardless of generation, is the key to employee engagement.

Diversity, Equity, and Inclusion

Thriving also means feeling a sense of belonging – both from how one is treated in the workplace by others and from the policies and practices embedded into the organizational culture. It makes sense, then, that the Pew Research Center found that 56 percent of employees, in general, believe that increasing diversity, equity, and inclusion (DEI) in their workplaces is positive.[63]

Generational Considerations and Strategies

The concepts and practices related to diversity, equity, and inclusion have evolved over the years, impacting the way each cohort sees DEI. For instance, a slightly higher number of Baby Boomers, Gen Xers, and Millennials place importance on integrating DEI policies over conducting educational initiatives, like training, discussions, and meetings.[7] This aligns with findings from the Pew Research Center in that 72 percent of survey respondents noted that having policies that ensure equity in hiring and pay has had a positive impact on them, compared to 57 percent who indicated the same with DEI meetings and trainings.[49]

The largest disparity we uncovered is with Baby Boomers, where there was more than a 20-point difference between support for DEI policies and support for DEI training.[7] This is not surprising in that fewer than half of Boomer respondents indicated finding this type of training in the workplace important or very important.[7] Further, this generation sees diversity more related to representation and equality, which align more with policies, rather than developmental, which ties more to education.[64]

Millennials and Gen Zers, on the other hand, had the smallest difference between the two measures,[7] meaning that employees in these cohorts see both DEI policies and education as being critical for organizations to embrace.

Why might this be? For one, more Gen Zers and Millennials believe efforts focused on DEI are "a good thing."[49] Second, despite their desire for policies, a majority of Millennials also find diversity trainings to be important, higher than the rates for any other cohort.[7] This is likely due to their perspectives on diversity being about respecting identities,[64] which lends itself to developmental initiatives like enhanced exposure and educational trainings that can expand people's worldviews.

For Gen Zers, DEI training goes beyond simply providing an opportunity for them to grow and develop. It can also help them feel reassured that their older coworkers and supervisors are being trained on DEI, resulting in a more open, supportive, and welcoming organizations. One Gen Zer in our Global Gen Z study noted, "I think many see diversity as a bad thing, but uniqueness is amazing."[65] And, young people want others to view diversity as an asset to the organization.

Understanding the nuances in how cohorts view DEI practices can be helpful in better forging authentic relationships with them. Baby Boomers, in particular, may have a commitment to DEI, but execute it in more of a tactical way with measurable policies. Younger employees, though, might advocate for more developmental opportunities to foster a welcoming culture.

Perspectives on Diversity

Diversity "refers to the representation or composition of various social identity groups in a work group, organization, or community."[66] It is well-documented that high levels of diversity have benefits for companies, such as increased business performance, greater employee retention, improved decision-making, and elevated innovation.[67]

Generational Considerations and Strategies

Data from the Pew Research Center found that a majority of workers believe that having people of different races, ethnicities, ages, and genders at work is important.[50] We uncovered the same in our study – an array of diverse voices is essential in the workplace.[7] When you look closer at our research, though, the numbers were slightly higher for Millennials and Gen Xers.[7] Let's explore this further.

Many Baby Boomers came of age during Civil Rights when diversity was positioned as a personal and political issue to be dealt with outside of work.[55] Companies and organizations were not only staying out of the fray during that time; many were continuing discriminatory practices and were subject to lawsuits.[68] Thus, diversity and workplaces did not mix. Gen Xers, though, grew up post-Civil Rights, having experienced more inclusion efforts in school and greater exposure to a diverse array of people,[55] making diversity more of a norm as they aged into adulthood.

The perspectives on diversity held by Millennials and Gen Zers differ considerably from their older counterparts. They are more prone to recognize cognitive diversity, which includes variations in opinions, experiences, worldviews, and identities, than demographic representation.[69,70] Cognitive diversity plays an influential role with Millennials. With their desire for teamwork,[7] this is a cohort that wants to create diverse teams that bring together people with differing ideas and perspectives to make the collaborative process richer.

On the other hand, many Gen Zers believe that diversity is simply a reality and that organizations should focus should more on equity and inclusion than trying to enhance representation, demographic or cognitive, that already exists.[55]

Perhaps a key to better engagement between cohorts is to first begin by discussing what diversity means to them. Could some be talking about demographic representation, whereas others are referring to cognitive differences? Further, honoring different definitions could also have an impact on inclusion. For instance, if a Millennial feels supported in that their view of diversity includes personality type or communication preference, the notion of having that view validated could be inclusive in its own right.

While it is important to embrace cognitive diversity, as the younger cohorts want, as well as acknowledge existing diversity, as Gen Zers want, so is ensuring diverse representation, as it is still lacking in many industries and organizations. Some companies, though, are investing in efforts to enhance diversity. Consider the pharmaceutical company Johnson & Johnson that has 43 percent of their management positions filled by women and has a virtual museum, highlighting the contributions of women since the company's founding in 1886.[71] As this company has ranked in the top 50 most admired places to work for 21 years,[72] it's clear that their commitment to diversity is paying off.

Perspectives on Equity

Where diversity looks at the composition of the identities, demographics, and worldviews present in any given group or organization, equity narrows in on how people are treated in terms of fairness. Research has found that employees who believe that they will be treated fairly are 9.8 more times likely to want to go to work and 5.4 times more likely to stay at their company.[73] Equity can include many factors, including pay transparency, disability accommodations, access to promotions, time off for religious holidays, non-discrimination policies and practices, and parental leave.

However, research has found that very few employees are seeing efforts toward organizational equity realized. For instance, only 30 percent believe they are treated fairly, and just 33 percent think they have the same opportunities for promotion or advancement.[74]

Generational Considerations and Strategies
In terms of all factors related to DEI, it is equity that stands out as most important.[7] While the vast majority of members across cohorts believe that organizations should treat employees fairly and equitably, we noticed a divergence in other measures that helps explain a lot about

generational perceptions. Millennials and Gen Zers lean more toward external equity – wanting their organizations to advocate for equitable laws and policies, whereas Baby Boomers and Gen Xers preference internal equity – having their workplaces free from bias.[7]

Younger generations' desire to work for companies that advocate for policies on a larger scale is tied to their more prominent concerns around climate change[75] and social inequality.[15] Many believe corporations, in particular, have a moral obligation to address these issues, given both their responsibility in exacerbating them and the power and resources they have to create change.[15] This desire for corporate responsibility is so great with younger cohorts that 75 percent look to an organization's engagement in the community and propensity to make a positive social impact when considering where to work.[15]

Baby Boomers and Gen Xers, though, place more importance on anti-discrimination policies, likely tied to their view of diversity as more demographic. However, it's important to look a bit deeper. For instance, a greater number of Millennials and Gen Zers believe that workplaces should have policies that prohibit workplace discrimination around gender identity.[76] So, while Baby Boomers and Gen Xers support policies in general, there may be varying levels of support depending on the actual policy.

In order for organizations to effectively address equity issues, it is necessary to implement processes that will ensure equity is achieved. For instance, pay transparency has become more widespread in recent years, particularly due to legislation requiring companies to advertise salaries.[77] This is one shift that companies can do to ensure applicants experience a fair hiring process.

While there are some nuances in terms of what different generational cohorts believe is important regarding equity, one thing is clear – they all want to work in places that treat them fairly.

Perspectives on Inclusion

Inclusion builds upon both diversity and equity by aiming to make people feel welcome in being their authentic selves in the workplace. By definition, an inclusive environment is one that "offers affirmation, celebration, and appreciation of different approaches, styles, perspectives, and experiences."[50] McKinsey & Company, for instance, discovered that among people who left their jobs, over half did so because they felt like they didn't belong.[78] Other research has found that inclusive practices result in better recruitment, retention, and engagement of employees as well as create gains in innovation, resilience, and market growth for organizations.[79]

Generational Considerations and Strategies

So, what is most important to each cohort when it comes to inclusive practices? We found that across all generations, being encouraged to express oneself freely and openly was a priority, followed by using one's preferred pronouns and being able to wear what makes one comfortable.[7] However, these last two practices scored considerably lower for Baby Boomers than other measures for that cohort and compared to other generations.

Let's look at why this might be. Baby Boomers entered the workforce during a time in which women wore pantyhose and men wore ties to work. Today, a necktie is a rarity, and it's actually difficult to figure out where one would even buy pantyhose. And, given gender fluidity, who would wear what these days? This shift, though, has not been embraced equally by all. For instance, Gen Zers tend to dress more informally than most, eliciting concerns from older HR managers that they lack professionalism due to what they deem as inappropriate attire for a work setting.[80]

While some older folks may be less concerned about being inclusive around pronouns and dress, younger employees are. And, integrating practices that support people's identities and expression can go a long way. For instance, using gender-inclusive pronouns in organizations promotes positive organizational attitudes and identity safety.[81] Essentially, when supervisors, in particular, engage in an overt example of inclusive behavior such as this, doing so has the effect of signaling to even cisgender people that leaders in the organization care about inclusion and belonging. Efforts toward inclusive behaviors rarely cost organizations money but can be profound in their ability to make employees feel like they belong.

Conclusion

Regardless of industry, role, or generation, people want to thrive and feel successful in their work. Certainly, individuals stand to benefit, but organizations also do, particularly as a thriving culture can lead to enhanced productivity and retention, fewer errors, and heightened morale. Thus, it is imperative that organizational leaders find ways to support individuals, as best as possible, by creating healthy, supportive, inclusive, engaging, and flexible work environments that meet both generational and individual needs.

Notes

1 Peters, S. E., Sorensen, G., Katz, J. N., Gundersen, D. A., & Wagner, G. R. (2021). Thriving from work: Conceptualization and measurement. *International Journal of Environmental Research and Public Health, 18*(13), 7196. https://doi.org/10.3390/ijerph18137196

2 Gallup. (2023). *Employee wellbeing.* www.gallup.com/394424/indicator-employee-well-being.aspx

3 United States Census Bureau. (2023). *Home-based workers: 2019–2021.* www.census.gov/library/publications/2023/demo/p70br-184.html

4 Pew Research Center. (2023). *About a third of U.S. workers who can work from home now do so all the time.* www.pewresearch.org/short-reads/2023/03/30/about-a-third-of-us-workers-who-can-work-from-home-do-so-all-the-time/

5 Thompson, P. (2024). *Almost half of Dell's full-time US workforce has rejected the company's return-to-office push.* www.businessinsider.com/us-dell-workers-reject-return-to-office-hybrid-work-2024-6

6 Kowalski G., & Ślebarska K. (2022). Remote working and work effectiveness: A leader perspective. *International Journal of Environmental Research and Public Health, 19*(22):15326. https://doi.org/10.3390/ijerph192215326. PMID: 36430045; PMCID: PMC9690707.

7 Seemiller, C., & Grace, M. (2023). *Generations in the workplace.* Unpublished dataset.

8 Watkins, H. (2023). *Gen Z and Millennials are much more pro-office than Gen X and Baby Boomers.* https://hubblehq.com/blog/future-of-work-different-age-groups

9 Kantar. (2023). *New ways of working from Gen-Z to Boomers.* www.kantar.com/north-america/inspiration/research-services/new-ways-of-working-from-gen-z-to-boomers-pf#:~:text=Generally%2C%20younger%20generations%2C%20who%20are,to%20only%208%25%20of%20Boomers

10 Reid, K., & Lewis, G. (2021). *LinkedIn data shows women and Gen Z are more likely to apply to remote jobs.* www.linkedin.com/business/talent/blog/talent-strategy/women-gen-z-more-likely-to-apply-to-remote-jobs

11 Sorensen, K. (2023). *5 reasons for employees not wanting to return to the office (and how to address them).* www.officespacesoftware.com/blog/5-reasons-for-employees-not-wanting-to-return-to-the-office-and-how-to-address-them/#:~:text=In%20a%20recent%20poll%2C%2065,of%20the%20traditional%20office%20model

12 McKinsey & Company. (2022). *Americans are embracing flexible work-and they want more of it.* www.mckinsey.com/industries/real-estate/our-insights/americans-are-embracing-flexible-work-and-they-want-more-of-it

13 Harvard University and MIT Work and Well-being Initiative. (2023). *Work design for health: A promising approach to worker well-being.* https://workwellbeinginitiative.org/module-2-enhancing-employee-control-work#:~:text=Enhanced%20schedule%20control%20enabled%20employees,%2C%20heart%20disease%2C%20or%20stroke

14 Reisinger, H., & Fetterer, D. (2021). *Forget flexibility. Your employees want autonomy.* https://hbr.org/2021/10/forget-flexibility-your-employees-want-autonomy

15 Deloitte. (2023). *2023 Gen Z and Millennial survey.* www.deloitte.com/global/en/issues/work/content/genzmillennialsurvey.html

16 Fox, M. (2022). *Flexible hours allow employees at this company to fit work around their lives.* www.cnbc.com/2022/03/18/flexible-hours-let-this-companys-workers-fit-work-around-their-lives.html

17 Debara, D. (2022). *What is company culture and how do you develop it?* www.betterup.com/blog/what-is-company-culture

18 Carrington, M. (2024). *The state of work-life wellness.* https://assets-cdn.gympass.com/docs/Lead-Magnets/US/WLW24/WLW_Report_EN_US_1011_B_db7fc6d705.pdf?ajs_aid=02378fcb-61a0-4d86-8b0d-a117c399f16e&__hstc=238227295.6fb20c9261ddef429609d3857d818545.1719597928608.1719597928608.1719597928608.1&__hssc=238227295.2.1719597928608&__hsfp=2021361107&_gl=1*ho1n2w*_gcl_au*MTE0NDI2NTY5NS4xNzE5NTk3OTI3

19 Harter, J. (2022). *Percent who feel employer cares about their wellbeing plummets.* www.gallup.com/workplace/390776/percent-feel-employer-cares-wellbeing-plummets.aspx

20 Harter, J. (2023). *Leaders: Ignore employee wellbeing at your own risk.* www.gallup.com/workplace/507974/leaders-ignore-employee-wellbeing-own-risk.aspx

21 Swarbrick, M. (2006). A wellness approach. *Psychiatric Rehabilitation Journal, 29*(4), 311–314. https://doi.org/10.2975/29.2006.311.314. PMID: 16689042.

22 Gallup. (2023). *The benefits of employee engagement.* www.gallup.com/workplace/236927/employee-engagement-drives-growth.aspx

23 Bureau of Labor Statistics. (2022). *American time use survey – 2022 results.* www.bls.gov/news.release/archives/atus_06222023.pdf

24 Mansveld, C. (2024). *Occupational wellbeing*. www.wellbeingtherapyspace.com. au/occupational-wellbeing/

25 Rotman, S. (2022). *8 ways to improve occupational wellness*. https://embodiedwel lnesscenter.com/8-ways-to-improve-occupational-wellness/

26 Pew Research Center. (2014). *Religious landscape study: Baby Boomers*. www.pewr esearch.org/religion/religious-landscape-study/generational-cohort/baby-boomer/

27 Cox, D. A. (2022). *Generation Z and the future of faith in America*. www.americans urveycenter.org/research/generation-z-future-of-faith/

28 Springtide Research Institute. (2022). *An inside look at Gen Z's spiritual practices*. https://springtideresearch.org/post/religion-and-spirituality/an-inside-look-at-gen-zs-spiritual-practices#:~:text=They%20are%20explorers%20by%20nat ure,as%20ways%20to%20connect%20spiritually

29 Holcombe, M. (2024). *Gen Z is less happy than the rest of us. Here is what would make a difference*. www.cnn.com/2024/04/09/health/gen-z-happiness-gallup-wellness/index.html

30 Walton Family Foundation and Gallup. (2023). *Voices of Gen Z: Perspectives on U.S. education, wellbeing and the future*. https://8ce82b94a8c4fdc3ea6d-b1d23 3e3bc3cb10858bea65ff05e18f2.ssl.cf2.rackcdn.com/bb/55/146dc5d6447cb4686 de1054bfe49/walton-gallup-voices-of-gen-z.pdf

31 Kreimer, S. (2023). *Gen Z perceives more dangers than previous generations, study shows*. www.upi.com/Health_News/2023/12/13/gen-z-study/465170 2478618/

32 National Institutes of Health. (2022). *Emotional wellness toolkit*. www.nih.gov/ health-information/emotional-wellness-toolkit

33 Bogenberger, R. (2024). *Baby Boomers and mental health*. https://therapist.com/ generations/baby-boomers/

34 McGlauflin, P., & Abrams, J. (2023). *3 initiatives employees say have the greatest impact on their wellbeing*. https://fortune.com/2023/11/14/well-being-emplo yee-benefits-impact-mental-health/

35 Lifesum. (2024). *2024 state of healthy eating and wellbeing report*. https://drive.goo gle.com/file/d/1FU_p4ZAi8S23Pg6lb2rcdiv9sVNGdOyD/view

36 McKinsey & Company. (2022). *Still feeling good: The US wellness market continues to boom*. www.mckinsey.com/industries/consumer-packaged-goods/our-insig hts/still-feeling-good-the-us-wellness-market-continues-to-boom

37 Tilley, C. (2024). *Why are Gen Zers aging faster than Millennials? Experts blame stress, fast food, sedentary lifestyles and not having a purpose*. www.dailymail.co.uk/ wellness-us/body/article-12996699/gen-z-aging-millennials-fast-food-stress-lifestyle.html

38 Hui, A. (2024). *What is 'bed rotting'? Gen Z's newest self-care trend, explained.* www. health.com/what-is-bed-rotting-trend-7561395

39 Lansat, M., & Aydin, R. (2019). *20 of the best job perks and benefits millennials have that their parents didn't.* www.businessinsider.com/best-job-perks-benefits-for-millennials-2018-8

40 Consumer Financial Protection Bureau. (n.d.). *Why financial well-being?* www. consumerfinance.gov/consumer-tools/financial-well-being/about/#:~:text= Financial%20well%2Dbeing%20means%20how,of%20your%20financial%20w ell%2Dbeing

41 Henderson, R. (2024). *Paycheck to paycheck statistics: 66.2% of Americans report struggling between paydays.* www.marketwatch.com/guides/banking/paych eck-to-paycheck-statistics/#:~:text=Our%20survey%20revealed%20that%20o ver,the%20first%20quarter%20of%202024

42 Board of Governors of the Federal Reserve System. (2023). *Economic well-being of U.S. households in 2022.* www.federalreserve.gov/publications/2023-economic-well-being-of-us-households-in-2022-overall-financial-well-being.htm#:~:text= Current%20Financial%20Situation,by%22%20(8%20percent)

43 MetLife. (2023). *Financial wellness programs foster a thriving workforce.* www. metlife.com/content/dam/metlifecom/us/ebts/pdf/MetLife_Financial_ Wellness_Programs_Foster_a_Thriving_Workforce.pdf

44 Herron, A. (2023). *Financial stress in the workplace: How to help employees cope.* www.webmdhealthservices.com/blog/financial-stress-in-the-workplace-how-to-help-employees-cope/

45 Fidelity Investments. (2020). *Retirement savings assessment 2020: Executive summary.* www.fidelity.com/bin-public/060_www_fidelity_com/documents/ about-fidelity/2020-rsa-executive-summary.pdf

46 Bareham, H. (2023). Which generation has the most student loan debt? *Bankrate.* www.bankrate.com/loans/student-loans/student-loan-debt-by-generation/

47 Bank of America. (2023). *BofA survey finds many American workers optimistic about their financial future, though feeling the strain of inflation.* https://newsroom. bankofamerica.com/content/newsroom/press-releases/2023/09/bofa-survey-finds-many-american-workers-optimistic-about-their-f.html

48 Kitterman, T. (2023). *How great companies prioritize financial wellness for employees.* www.greatplacetowork.com/resources/blog/how-great-companies-prioritize-financial-wellness-for-employees

49 Pendell, R. (2024). *1 in 5 employees worldwide feel lonely.* www.gallup.com/workpl ace/645566/employees-worldwide-feel-lonely.aspx

50 Kannan, V. D., & Veazie, P. J. (2022). US trends in social isolation, social engagement, and companionship — nationally and by age, sex, race/ethnicity, family income, and work hours, 2003–2020. *SSM – Population Health, 21,* 101331. https://doi.org/10.1016/j.ssmph.2022.101331

51 Bureau of Labor Statistics. (2022). *American time use survey – 2022 results*. www.bls.gov/news.release/archives/atus_06222023.pdf

52 Swarbrick, M., & Yudof, J. (2017). *Wellness in 8 dimensions*. https://cspnj.org/wp-content/uploads/2021/09/Wellness-8-Dimensions.pdf

53 Largo-Wight, E., Chen, W. W., Dodd, V., & Weiler, R. (2011). Healthy workplaces: The effects of nature contact at work on employee stress and health. *Public Health Reports, 126*(1), 124–130.

54 Timm, S., Gray, W. A., & Sung Eun Hung, S. (2018). Designing for health: How the physical environment plays a role in workplace wellness. *American Journal of Health Promotion, 32*(6), 1468–1473.

55 Baba, R. (2024). *Boomers & Millennials in the workplace*. www.mccoyrockford.com/blog/boomers-and-millennials-generational-transition/#:~:text=When%20it%20comes%20to%20Baby,and%20high%20quality%20meeting%20rooms.

56 Hushoffice. (2022). *What does each generation want from the office?* https://hushoffice.com/en-us/what-does-each-generation-want-from-the-office/

57 Quiambao, L. (2021). Generations engagement survey. *Wrike*. www.wrike.com/blog/generations-engagement-survey/

58 Gallup. (2023). *The benefits of employee engagement*. www.gallup.com/workplace/236927/employee-engagement-drives-growth.aspx

59 Ripplematch. (2023). *Gen Z in losing confidence in the job search in 2023*. https://ripplematch.com/insights/gen-z-is-losing-confidence-in-the-job-search-in-2023

60 Nichols, R. (2024). *American Baby Boomers don't love their jobs*. https://360learning.com/guide/great-resignation-us/baby-boomers-quit-us/

61 Gibson, K. R., O'Leary, K., & Weintraub, J. R. (2020). *The little things that make employees feel appreciated*. https://hbr.org/2020/01/the-little-things-that-make-employees-feel-appreciated

62 Indeed. (2022). *How to tell if your skills are underutilized at work*. www.indeed.com/career-advice/career-development/underutilized-at-work

63 Minkin, R. (2023). *Diversity, equity and inclusion in the workplace*. www.pewresearch.org/social-trends/2023/05/17/diversity-equity-and-inclusion-in-the-workplace/

64 Smith, C. (2020). *The radical transformation of diversity and inclusion: The Millennial influence*. www2.deloitte.com/content/dam/Deloitte/us/Documents/about-deloitte/us-inclus-millennial-influence-120215.pdf

65 Seemiller, C., & Grace, M. (2021). *Global Gen Z*. Unpublished dataset.

66 American Psychological Association. (n.d.). *Equity, diversity, and inclusion*. www.apa.org/topics/equity-diversity-inclusion

67 McKinsey & Company (2022). *What is diversity, equity, and inclusion*. www.mckinsey.com/featured-insights/mckinsey-explainers/what-is-diversity-equity-and-inclusion

68 Hauser, S. (2012). *The dream, the reality: Civil Rights in the '60s and today*. https://workforce.com/news/the-dream-the-reality-civil-rights-in-the-60s-and-today

69 Monster.com. (2024). *What workforce diversity means for Gen Z*. https://hiring.monster.com/resources/workforce-management/diversity-in-the-workplace/workforce-diversity-for-millennials/

70 Kratz, J. (2023). *How to stop generational differences from derailing DEI initiatives*. www.linkedin.com/pulse/how-stop-generational-differences-from-derailing-dei-julie-kratz/

71 Johnson & Johnson. (2024). *Our commitment to women*. www.jnj.com/discover-j-j/our-commitment-to-women

72 Johnson & Johnson. (2023). *Johnson & Johnson named a 2023 Fortune world's most admired company and ranked #1 on the pharmaceutical industry list*. www.jnj.com/latest-news/johnson-johnson-named-a-2023-fortune-worlds-most-admired-company

73 Bush, M. (2023). *Why is diversity and inclusion in the workplace important?* www.greatplacetowork.com/resources/blog/why-is-diversity-inclusion-in-the-workplace-important

74 Brecheisen, J. (2023). *Research: Where employees think companies' DEIB efforts are failing*. https://hbr.org/2023/03/research-where-employees-think-companies-deib-efforts-are-failing

75 Tyson, A., Kennedy, B., & Funk, C. (2021). *Climate change activism, social media engagement with issue*. www.pewresearch.org/science/2021/05/26/gen-z-millennials-stand-out-for-climate-change-activism-social-media-engagement-with-issue/

76 AP-NORC Center for Public Affairs Research. (2021). *MTV/AP-NORC poll: Younger generations stand out on identity, acceptance, and progressive policies*. https://apnorc.org/projects/younger-generations-stand-out-on-identity-acceptance-and-progressive-policies/

77 Lewis, C. (2023). *Pay transparency is spreading. Here's what you need to know*. https://apnews.com/article/business-new-york-city-california-washington-0e4b2754b08d4e1ab4ffd2708cd759f7

78 McKinsey & Company. (2021). *'Great Attrition' or 'Great Attraction'? The choice is yours*. www.mckinsey.com/capabilities/people-and-organizational-performance/our-insights/great-attrition-or-great-attraction-the-choice-is-yours#/

79 Frei, F. X., & Morriss, A. (2023). *10 reasons why inclusion is a competitive advantage*. https://hbr.org/2023/10/10-reasons-why-inclusion-is-a-competitive-advantage

80 Intelligent.com. (2023). *Nearly 4 in 10 employers avoid hiring recent college grads in favor of older workers.* www.intelligent.com/nearly-4-in-10-employers-avoid-hiring-recent-college-grads-in-favor-of-older-workers/

81 Johnson, I. R., Pietri, E. S., Buck, D. M., & Daas, R. (2021). What's in a pronoun: Exploring gender pronouns as an organizational identity-safety cue among sexual and gender minorities. *Journal of Experimental Social Psychology, 91*, 104194.

Learning and Development

6

If it weren't for employees acquiring new knowledge and skills, workplaces would be stagnant, operating in the status quo. Being in this state can make it challenging for organizations to innovate, as novel viewpoints, subject matter mastery, and enhanced competence are necessary for moving forward. Thus, opportunities, and even expectations, for learning and development are often built into the fabric of organizational culture.

Equipped with new information and skills, employees are better able to do their jobs, have more opportunities for advancement, and are happier, which can lead to enhanced performance.[1] It's no surprise, then, that 92 percent of workers believe professional development is important.[2] Further, those who engage in it have a 34 percent higher job retention rate than those who do not and are more likely to move into future leadership roles in the organization.[2]

Organizations also benefit from learning and development opportunities because employees who expand their knowledge or enhance skill sets can better engage in activities that expedite work processes. This may include technical skills, such as learning a new online platform that speeds up a protocol, or interpersonal skills, like conflict resolution strategies. In addition, companies that over-invest in learning and development have a higher rate of innovation,[3] and employees are more likely to stay at their place of work if they participate in these activities.[1] Retention has important financial implications, as it can cost upwards of 33 percent of an employee's annual salary to find a replacement.[4]

DOI: 10.4324/9781003541035-6

Given these benefits, understanding how employees prefer to learn and develop can be the key to leveraging their potential for both organizational success and their own well-being.

Learning

Have you ever been in an in-person training where you thought, "Why am I here? I could just watch a video about this." Or, maybe you had to complete an online module and thought, "This would be so much easier if we could meet in person for an hour and go over this information." Neither modality is more correct than the other since both offer value. Sometimes, the variation is based on the context of what one sets out to learn. But in other cases, it comes down to what people prefer. Let's take a look at six different learning modalities: demonstrated, experiential, video-based, interpersonal, intrapersonal, and social to better understand variance in preference, particularly across generational cohorts.

Demonstrated learning involves watching others successfully perform a task, similar to witnessing a high school teacher conduct a science lab. Learning may take place in a live setting or through an instructional video that can be replayed and paused at points for the learner to acquire the necessary knowledge or skills. Experiential learning happens through hands-on application of instructional material. This may involve, for example, someone mastering a computer program by practicing what was already taught or clicking around until figuring out how to use it on one's own. Video-based learning involves viewing an instructional video, either live or pre-recorded, that includes information, often in the form of a presentation or tutorial covering specific content or showcasing a skill or process. Interpersonal learning occurs when two or more individuals learn with and from each other to develop a more comprehensive understanding of the subject matter. This modality can involve group discussions, pair-shares, and team projects. Intrapersonal learning is a self-directed process where people are given specific assignments to do on their own, without interaction with others, like a research paper or individual project, or independently seeking out information, like through an Internet search or reading a book on a topic of interest. Social learning takes place individually as well, but in the presence of others, for instance, new employees gathered in a training room to complete online onboarding modules on their own or people studying next to, but not with, each other. The purpose is to be around others for accountability and motivation, not for interaction.

If organizational leaders understand learning modality preferences of generational cohorts, they can be more strategic in offering experiences that meet their employees' needs, fostering greater interest, engagement, and knowledge acquisition.

In our workplace study, we asked employees which modalities they enjoyed. Those with the highest percentage by generation varied between all four cohorts, while the lowest was the same.[5]

Table 6.1   *Enjoyment of Learning Modalities*

	Baby Boomers	Gen Xers	Millennials	Gen Zers
Highest	Intrapersonal	Video-Based	Demonstrated	Experiential
Lowest	Social	Social	Social	Social

Generational Considerations and Strategies

While Baby Boomers might not engage in intrapersonal learning as much by taking a deep dive on Google or watching a YouTube video, they do like to collect printed materials on topics of interest to refer to later. Consider it a permanent repository of information they can consult when they need to. It's recommended then to provide hard-copy instructional handouts for Baby Boomers, making self-learning accessible without technology.[6]

Gen Xers like video-based learning, which is often done independently, resonating with their preference for workplace autonomy.[5] And, they can watch from anywhere, tapping into their desire for flexible workspaces.[5] This cohort likes interactive components, which may work well with videos that can be paused for them to complete self-assessments, quizzes, games, and reflections.[6]

Millennials enjoy demonstrated learning, particularly given their need to make sure they are on the right track. If they watch a demonstration, they can feel more confident in executing the task on their own. Further, they may be less likely to ask clarification questions, which can be beneficial for Generation X supervisors, who embrace autonomy[5] and want to empower their employees to be self-sufficient. It might be helpful to begin with in-person instruction with this cohort, followed by the use of apps, videos, and websites.[6] The face-to-face time could be spent on demonstrating, while the digital space could be conducive for reiteration, as well as practice.

Gen Zers like rolling up their sleeves and applying the content through experiential learning. They are a Do-It-Yourself (DIY) generation, ready to jump in and start "doing." And many like engaging online,[6] which may mean they could benefit from case studies, simulations, and games.

While there is diversity among the generational cohorts in what is considered enjoyable, social learning ranked lowest for all generations. So, if there is a training in which all individuals need to be present, it is critical that there is a clearly defined and communicated purpose for bringing people together in person to interact rather than to listen to a presentation or complete individual work in the presence of others.

Given the differences across generational cohorts, there are two approaches to setting up learning experiences. One involves integrating various modalities into the same program so that all learners experience each type of learning. For example, offering a live demonstration accompanied by an associated handout, followed by a practice session using an online module. Another approach could include allowing individuals to select the same training from among different modalities, aligning best with their preferences.

Professional Development

Professional development is the term for any learning opportunity that helps individuals develop their knowledge or skills to be more effective in their job roles or advance within their career fields. While employees benefit from professional development, so do organizations – so much so that they are paying a hefty price. Research has found that workplaces in 2021 spent an average of $1,280 per employee on learning and development.[7] And, in looking at the aggregate, those numbers are staggering. In 2021–2022, training expenditures in the United States rose to over 100 billion dollars for the year.[8]

Despite its universal proliferation, how and why people engage in professional development can vary, particularly at the generational cohort level. For instance, many Baby Boomers want to re-skill and re-certify to get that one last promotion or raise before retiring, and both Gen Xers and Millennials want management and leadership training.[9] However, Gen Xers' desire focuses more on developing skills to effectively lead others, whereas Millennials may seek out training as a way to set themselves apart from their peers for career advancement.[5] And, given Gen Zers' participation in the freelance economy,[10] they may want to find ways to hone their knowledge and skills to ultimately work for themselves.

Types of Professional Development

There are four main types of professional development: cultural, technical, competency, and diversity, equity, and inclusion (DEI). Cultural development is about orienting employees to the culture of the organization, which may include meetings with colleagues and an overview of organizational protocol, as well as socializing them to the norms and expectations of the profession as a whole. These types of programs are common in workplaces and can be as simple as a one-day new employee orientation or as comprehensive as an ongoing program. Streaming platform, Netflix, offers an onboarding experience for new employees that includes a handbook of the organizational values, a quarter-long orientation stage, and mentorship – all designed to help workers transition into the Netflix culture.[11]

Technical development involves training on technical skills required to do one's job, for example, an advanced HTML class for a web programmer or a payroll system workshop for the Human Resources team. This type of development is focused on ensuring professionals can successfully navigate and leverage platforms, software, tools, systems, and services to be effective in their work.

Competency development involves sessions on topics such as communication, supervision, leadership, or critical thinking, to name a few, with the goal of enhancing skills essential for the workplace. This type of training is commonplace and found in a variety of industries. And, it makes sense why – organizations benefit when employees have high skill sets, particularly in those that make them more collaborative, innovative, and productive. Training ranges from one-time topical workshops to longer-term developmental experiences. For instance, CliftonStrengths is a comprehensive program that includes activities, discussions, and reflections to aid in understanding and appreciating each person's top five talent themes, such as "Achiever," "Relator," and "Learner." According to Gallup, this program has been used by more than 90 percent of Fortune 500 companies.[12]

Professional development around DEI is also often embedded into organizations. While DEI was already a focus for many, during the summer of 2020, in response to the deaths of George Floyd, Breonna Taylor, and others, businesses shifted their prioritization. They adopted DEI statements, created executive-level diversity and inclusion positions, pledged vast amounts of money to DEI efforts, and instituted policies and training to assist in creating fair, flourishing, and welcoming environments. In the 1 year following, 29 percent of companies had put into place educational programs on racism and bias, 28 percent set up racism training, and 25 percent offered training on how to be an inclusive leader.[13] For example, global consulting firm Accenture instituted mandatory sessions on antiracism and unconscious bias.[14]

Generational Considerations and Strategies

All types of professional development are important. However, each generation may require something different. For instance, Baby Boomers may need less cultural and competency development if they have worked in a particular organization for any substantial length of time and developed strong skill sets. But, with the proliferation of technology and the ever-changing diverse workforce, technical and DEI development may be most useful. The latter more so in that only 47 percent believe DEI training is important compared to 70 percent of Gen Xers, 80 percent of Millennials, and 73 percent of Gen Zers.[5] Part of that training could be to help shed light on the value of DEI training to begin with.

Gen Xers may resonate with any type of development, so long as it is delivered in a way that supports their need for autonomy and independence and allows them to develop critical leadership skills.

Millennials may benefit greatly from competency and cultural development as most are mid-career and want to build their skills and political savvy to advance in their organization or profession. They likely don't need as much DEI training, as many identify as open-minded and value DEI to begin with.[5] They also may need less technical training, given the majority have great comfort in the digital world.

Because Gen Zers often engage in their own self-learning online, they may find they can get technical and competency development on their own. But, they crave DEI opportunities, not only for expanding their own knowledge but also for validation of their organization's commitment to DEI. And, most are in need of cultural development to learn the ropes of the organization and industry.

Professional Development Modalities

When looking at professional development opportunities, there are a variety of modalities within which they can be offered. They could be in-person or online, in-house or off-site, or informal or formal. Let's take a look at all of these options and how they align with generational preferences.

In-Person

In-person professional development entails people coming together face-to-face to listen to a presenter, participate in activities, or do both. Gathering in person can provide opportunities for employees to take a break from the day-to-day grind and focus entirely on the experience by being away from their homes, workspaces, and technology. They can offer a chance to work with others, allowing for certain exercises to take place that couldn't otherwise be done the same online, for example, having a group try to untangle a rope as a way to highlight strategies for communication and collaboration.

In-person learning does have some drawbacks. One is the temptation for the facilitators to cover a great deal of content in a short period.[15] This "fire-hose" method is typically overwhelming for the learner and ineffective in terms of retaining information. Other drawbacks include the commute, having to get work coverage, and being offline from other job tasks for an extended period of time.

Generational Considerations and Strategies

We asked employees across all generations about their participation in various professional development experiences over the previous year. Our findings show Baby Boomers have the highest rates of attendance at in-person events, with numbers declining with each younger generation.[5] This aligns with other research that highlights Baby Boomers' desire for learning in a physical classroom.[16] With having spent the majority of their careers participating in in-person classes, networking events, conferences, training, and the like, it makes sense this modality is comfortable for them.

Gen Zers, on the other hand, had the lowest rates of attendance, perhaps due in part to their preference for consuming bite-size pieces of content, typically from online sources. They may not have as much experience with in-person professional development as many started or were in the early phases of their careers during the COVID pandemic, which made gathering less feasible.

It's important to keep in mind that some people, particularly Baby Boomers, prefer in-person opportunities more than others. If a Baby Boomer is in charge of a training session and only offers it face-to-face, those in other cohorts may be reluctant to participate. Thus, event planners of all generations should consider which modalities are most conducive to the specific outcomes and intended audience.

ONLINE

Before the Internet became mainstream and accessible, professional development sessions almost always took place in person. But, as the ability to live stream speakers, watch recorded webinars, complete online modules, and attend virtual events has become more commonplace, the notion of professional development has expanded entirely. And there are many benefits.

For one, online opportunities are often less expensive, eliciting lower registration fees and no cost for travel, which makes it more affordable for people to attend or possible for organizations to sponsor more participants. Those who can't take significant time off work or be away from home may find these options useful, especially those that are asynchronous.

There are some drawbacks, though. Asynchronous online opportunities, in particular, require a lot of self-accountability along with the technological infrastructure and support to participate in them.[14] And, they might not be as interpersonally engaging, which may make them less appealing to those who want to learn from and with other participants. Plus, employees can be easily distracted, as it has become typical to log into a training and simultaneously work on other projects, respond to messages, or even change out laundry.

Considering these benefits and drawbacks, certain online modalities stand out. For instance, webinars, which are broadcasted virtual educational seminars, are the preferred format for online learning among employees of all ages.[17] According to communications platform, Zoom, 45 billion webinar minutes were recorded in the last quarter of 2021 on their site alone. This doesn't even include the 3.3 trillion minutes for meetings![18] Research has found that the majority of viewers watch live versus on-demand and that the number of webinars using breakout rooms doubled between 2021 and 2022, indicating a shift to interactive sessions.[19]

Generational Considerations and Strategies

While we found Gen Xers having slightly higher rates of webinar participation, the nuances were negligible, reflecting consistency across generations.[5] It's clear that members from all cohorts participate in webinars. However, there are ways to make them more aligned with their preferences. For example, Baby Boomers like interaction and relationship-building. So, using breakout rooms and instituting interactive components in the main session are a must. In addition, posting links to hard copy resources in the chat might resonate with their desire for a professional development paper trail.

Gen Xers want to get to business – moving straight into the substance. So, it's important to dive into the content of the webinar as quickly as possible. Hold true to the start and end times, and make the session worth their while by outlining the purpose, intended outcomes, and plans for follow-up.

On the other hand, Millennials see webinars more as experiences. They want exciting visuals that will keep them engaged. Instead of packing the slides full of small text, include images, symbols, and short flash points. Further, given they like accolades,[5] consider awarding a certificate or digital badge at the completion of the webinar. Don't forget that Millennials also love to advertise their participation. Research shows a whopping 61 percent indicated having attended an event just to post it on their social media.[20] So, make it worthy of being posted, perhaps even beforehand, as a marketing tool.

As for Gen Zers, they want to be engaged. Consider using the webinar platform's audience participation tools, like chats, polls, quizzes, and hand raising. Have them use the markup on the screen, give them breaks to do an activity and then come back to the main room, and integrate short-form videos. The key is to toggle between a variety of modalities to keep them connected. Also, given this is generation is purpose-driven, they will want to know right from the start what the intended outcomes of the session are.

IN-HOUSE

Professional development opportunities are typically situated either inside or outside of the organization. In-house training might include a presentation delivered by a coworker (i.e., a colleague sharing information about how to enhance communication in the office), a training run by human resources (i.e., an emerging leaders program for mid-level managers), a session that overviews a protocol or process (i.e., someone from IT presenting how to use the new payroll system), or an event where an external speaker is brought into the organization specifically to share their expertise (i.e., an expert on emotional intelligence). Regardless of the purpose, the under-lying fundamentals are the same: professional development comes to the employee and not the other way around.

Generational Considerations and Strategies

In looking at who goes to in-house trainings, it's mostly Baby Boomers, who also, along with Gen Xers, find the most value in those experiences.[5] Consider this scenario: An email is sent out to everyone in the organization about a local speaker coming to talk about understanding personality styles. While this topic seems to be of interest across the board, the responses from employees vary by generation. Patty, a Baby Boomer, is happy to take a detour from her regular schedule and go to an event that is only a short stroll from her workspace to the conference room. Travis, a Gen Xer, while interested, is trying to figure out how to move his schedule around to fit it in, knowing he has to hurry from an earlier meeting to get to the confer-ence room on time. Priyanka, who is a Millennial, is excited about coming together as a group but isn't necessarily excited that the program falls on one of her remote work days. And, Gen Zer, Mia, after watching a YouTube video of the presenter she finds online, realizes the session is going to be exactly the same as what she saw on the recording. Both she and Priyanka would rather stay home and stream videos of prominent experts on the topic and skip the onsite event altogether.

While in-house programs can reach a wider audience for a lesser cost, getting employees motivated and excited about them takes more than just good advertising or an organizational mandate. Consider focusing on an event structure that has more universal appeal. For instance, participants could watch a TED Talk or other video given by a prominent expert, followed by a processing discussion with someone from HR. And, those who are onsite could make their way to the conference room to gather in person for the session while others participate virtually.

CONFERENCES

Conferences are typically full-day or multi-day experiences focused on a specific topic or audience. While virtual conferences are much more com-monplace, face-to-face ones still make up the vast majority, often necessi-tating more coordination, for example, registering for the event, submitting budget paperwork, and setting up travel. But, getting off-site, avoiding distractions, and being offline from everyday matters can do wonders for employee learning and development.

Generational Considerations and Strategies
While it seems the benefits are clear, our study found that a higher number of Millennials who attended a conference in the past year noted that it was somewhat or very valuable compared to other generational cohorts, particularly Generation Z.[5] This isn't surprising given many Millennials love to travel and are drawn to events that are held in places they are interested in exploring.[21]

As for Baby Boomers and Gen Xers, conferences have been the way of the world for much of their careers. Thus, it is important to be mindful that some may want to continue attending them to reskill and connect with professional colleagues, whereas others could opt to just stay home.

Although Gen Zers might not find as much value in conferences and fewer of them attend,[5] the draw to a new and exciting destination could be compelling enough for them to register.[22] If they are able to add a day or two to their trip after the conference to enjoy the area, it could be worth going. And attending with a coworker could make it even better.

Reading

One of the lowest cost and most informal forms of professional development is reading, as it can usually be done anytime and from anywhere – pick up a book on your train commute, surf a news aggregator on your phone, or search the web for a journal article specific to a topic you are interested in. And, unlike having to sit through an entire program or session, reading is customizable. For instance, Google only what you want to learn about or skip to the chapter in the book that covers the content you are looking for.

Generational Considerations and Strategies
Despite how easy it is to engage in reading for professional development, universally, rates are low. Only 17 percent of Gen Zers, along with 23 percent of Millennials and 24 percent of Gen Xers and Baby Boomers, had read an article, book, or publication related to their field sometime during the past year.[5] Given the exceptionally low-cost option, it can be useful for organizations to make reading more accessible and encouraged among workers, for example, by hosting a resource library or online repository.

Another idea to enhance reading includes offering a book club. For one, employees can learn new insight about a topic related to the workplace that might help increase job effectiveness. Second, gathering workers to connect over a common read can aid in developing relationships, leading to better collaboration, communication, and appreciation.

However, different generations have their preferences in what they like to read. Baby Boomers read more about home and garden, Gen Xers about crafts and hobbies, Millennials about business, wellness, and sociology, and Gen Zers about self-help and psychology.[23] Thus, Baby Boomers may prefer bonding with their coworkers by discussing a home remodeling book unrelated to work, whereas Gen Xers may want to discuss a book about pickleball and then go play together to form connections. Millennials may opt to read a biography of a CEO to get inspired about work, while Gen Zers may want to process with through a self-help paperback on a topic such as enhancing communication skills.

Given this diversity, if offering a book club, consider selecting a unique genre to target a specific audience. This could create cohesion among members of a cohort seeking to discuss topics of interest. However, some employees might be drawn in because the selected book is spot-on but then stay for future offerings because they feel like part of the community. In this case, being able to rotate genres could elicit sustained participation from members across all generations.

COURSES AND CERTIFICATIONS

Although training courses and certifications can be offered in person, the proliferation of online options over the past decade has been monumental. Consider that platforms such as Udemy offer more than 100,000 online courses, Skillshare more than 30,000, EdX nearly 3,000, including more than 100 professional certificate programs, and Coursera nearly 1,000.[24] That's a lot of courses, and those are just four of the more well-known course platforms!

What's different about courses and certifications, though, is that they typically extend beyond a single training session and offer a deeper and more formal dive into content through an expert-designed pathway. Upon completion, participants usually earn a certificate to showcase their achievements.

These types of programs, however, can be expensive and time-intensive, making them less accessible to employees. Further, sometimes, a participant will already know a lot of information about a subject but enroll in the course simply to get the credential.

Generational Considerations and Strategies
Regardless of the downsides, people are engaging in online courses and certifications – some generations more than others, with the vast majority who have participated finding them valuable.

Table 6.2   *Participation and Importance of Online Courses and Certifications*

	Baby Boomers	Gen Xers	Millennials	Gen Zers
Participation in online courses	28%	32%	43%	43%
Courses were valuable	81%	81%	97%	82%
Participation in certifications	24%	30%	35%	27%
Certifications were valuable	89%	88%	98%	82%

It's clear that online courses and certifications are crucial professional development experiences across all cohorts. Thus, encouraging participation and providing funding to all employees may enhance engagement for everyone.

Learning from Others

Interpersonal connection offers a great way to foster learning and development.[25] Employees are able to gain new perspectives, gather resources and tools, and solve problems that may benefit from an outside viewpoint. Let's take a look at some of the ways in which employees learn through their connections with others and how various generations approach each of those.

PROFESSIONAL ASSOCIATIONS

Professional associations are organizations typically tied to a specific industry that have the goal of advancing the profession and developing its members. These groups may offer webinars, conferences, and publications, as well as opportunities to take on leadership roles in the organization and learn from colleagues within the field. Associations vary in size but usually range from the hundreds to the low thousands. However, some are considerably larger, like the Academy of Management with more than 18,000 members worldwide,[26] and the American Psychological Association with 146,000.[27]

Generational Considerations and Strategies

While associations are booming with membership, Gen Zers' engagement is considerably lower than other generations.[5] Perhaps, it will pick up as they move through their careers and establish themselves within specific industries. But, associations could address some of the fundamental issues that may be getting in the way of their present participation. Given Gen Zers want meaning and purpose in their chosen occupations, they need a clear understanding of how the association can directly benefit them – what is the value proposition? Further, because they enjoy customizable and personalized experiences, hordes of irrelevant emails and paper magazines on subjects not of interest to them can be a turnoff. Instead, utilize digital subscriptions and limited text-only message options. Also, consider bringing technology up to date with platforms and processes that are easy to use rather than hosting content and resources on archaic, clunky sites. Finally, many who are new to the workforce are likely earning far lower wages than their older counterparts. Perhaps waiving the membership fees for one year for new members could draw in this young cohort.

NETWORKING

Networking involves interacting with others, particularly in a professional setting, to exchange ideas and create collaborations, which can lead to general career success along with increased satisfaction, innovation, collaboration, retention, and pay.[28] While networking can happen anywhere, standalone events have become commonplace; attendees are able to mingle with other professionals, often among a spread of food and beverages. In other cases, it is interwoven into the structure of a conference, perhaps as a meet and greet.

The virtual world also offers the ability to network. For instance, social media sites, like LinkedIn and Facebook, provide spaces for professionals to connect individually. People can message each other directly, share and read posts, and engage in group chats. Virtual meeting spaces have also opened up new ways to connect with others.

Generational Considerations and Strategies

However, engagement is not equal. Gen Xers and Millennials more often attend networking events than those in other generations.[5] They also tend to rate their experiences as "very valuable" at higher levels than their older counterparts. Given Gen Zers are just entering the workforce and may have amassed fewer professional connections, and Baby Boomers already have contacts in their fields, this makes sense. But, there are also generational nuances that might affect how each cohort approaches networking.

For example, Gary, a Baby Boomer, who enjoys in-person training, would likely prefer face-to-face events where he can connect with people he already knows. His circle of colleagues might all share stories of the past and catch up on the latest in each other's lives. But, if Gary has to go to an event where he doesn't know anyone, he may not see as much value.

Jennifer, a Gen Xer, might show up to a networking event with a specific goal in mind – for example, to introduce herself to someone she highly regards in her field. She will want to avoid superfluous small talk that appears to lack purpose, given her generation is marked by being independent and autonomous, direct, and fast-paced.[5] Instead, she wants to get down to business. So, she beelines for the person she's seeking out and chats her up. After finishing, she may end up leaving altogether, unless she runs into some old friends to chat with.

Aiden is a Millennial who likes collaboration and prefers attending networking events with others he knows. He came with Susannah, DaShawn, and Riley from his workplace, and the four of them stick together the entire time, socializing only with each other.

Lucy, a Gen Zer, comes from a generation where many lack interpersonal skills.[29] She would likely skip in-person networking, which isn't surprising, given that 59 percent of Gen Zers will avoid an event if they don't know anyone.[30] Or, if she does go solo, she might feel more comfortable off to the side, messaging with a friend on her phone rather than introducing herself to new contacts.

Because each cohort has different reasons for and, perhaps hesitations with, attending networking events, it is critical to gain an appreciation of where each is coming from. If a Millennial or Gen Zer is nervous about going to an event alone, encourage them to group up and attend together. But, to avoid insularity, have them think of something they want to accomplish, like meeting one new person, introducing themselves to an influential professional in the field, or getting resources for an upcoming project. Further, those in older generations may want to take younger colleagues under their wings and introduce them to people rather than letting them fend for themselves.

MENTORING

A mentor, as defined by the American Psychological Association, is "a coach who provides advice to enhance the mentee's professional performance and development." A mentee, on the other hand, is an "individual who may be in the role of 'learner' in [a] mentoring relationship."[31]

But, who receives mentoring varies by generation. Baby Boomers are more often the mentor than the mentee, likely given their tenure in the workforce. Thus, it's no surprise that only 23 percent had received mentoring in the last three years compared to 74 percent of Millennials, 56 percent of Gen Zers, and 55 percent of Gen Xers.[5] In looking at Gen Zers, in particular, research from the Adobe Future Workplace study found nearly the same rates as we did in terms of who had indicated having a mentor – 52 percent.[32] However, 83 percent believed a mentor is crucial to career success.

While traditional mentoring is useful, let's look at other types that can capitalize on the knowledge of all generations – flash, reverse, peer, and intergenerational mentoring. Flash mentoring occurs when one person teaches or guides another in learning a specific skill or topic.[33] It often involves a short-term relationship, spanning only the time it takes to address the identified reason for coming together, and it can occur between people in any generation. For instance, Sam, who is a Millennial, asks her Gen X coworker, Peter, to lunch to ask for advice on best practices for dealing with a conflict between two team members. Peter offers guidance from his experience but provides no formal follow-up or continued work with Sam on the issue.

Reverse mentoring occurs when younger generations mentor those who are older to aid in their skill development.[34] Doing so can create an empowering culture in an organization in that everyone, regardless of age, is a mentor to others. Research has found that reverse mentoring can aid in promoting diversity, retaining talented young workers, and saving time and money by instituting cost-effective and sustainable ways to capitalize on knowledge transfer from within the organization.[34] Sachse Construction in Detroit uses reverse mentoring, where Millennials offer Baby Boomers assistance with technology.[35]

Intergenerational mentoring is an ongoing collaborative relationship where "Everyone leads, Everyone learns."[36] Unlike traditional, flash, or reverse mentoring that occurs in a unidirectional manner, intergenerational mentoring relies on both parties to be mentor and mentee simultaneously. And, it doesn't always have to take place in dyads, but instead can be triads. Three-person teams of employees, primarily from a mix of age groups, come together to forge relationships, work in collaboration on projects, and share wisdom with each other. Research from the National Institute on Ageing reported that intergenerational triads increase employee productivity and engagement, help new connections form, decrease age bias, and allow each member to give and receive mentoring.[37]

For instance, consider a triad like Sarah from Generation X, who is great at setting up deadlines and independent workflow processes; Navi, who is a Gen Zer and skilled at using several digital apps, and Millennial, Rosie, who excels at collaboration. They can all mentor to their strengths. Rosie may get slowed down by the interpersonal dynamics surrounding a group project but could benefit from Sarah's advice to help her set up more formal processes to move the project along. Sarah might find utility in connecting with Navi to learn how to use an app to institute a better plan for workflow. And Navi might tap Rosie to help him with an interpersonal issue on one of his teams.

Peer mentoring involves the pairing of two employees of the same level from different units to provide each other with professional and personal support. This connection offers an opportunity to connect with someone who understands the organizational context but who isn't a supervisor or day-to-day peer. Each person in the relationship may then be able to be more transparent about concerns or questions that they wouldn't want to discuss with those in their immediate work circle.

Several companies have formal mentoring programs, whether traditional or peer, reverse or flash, or intergenerational. Consider New York Life, where two members of the same employee resource group are paired together, or Caterpillar's reverse, peer, and traditional mentoring programs to support employees from new hires to senior leadership.[38] Given their success, other organizations could use these as models.

Generational Considerations and Strategies

Regardless of the type of mentoring, members of each generation often have differing needs based on the characteristics, motivations, and preferences aligned with their cohorts. For example, Baby Boomers identify as practical, and motivated by accomplishment, caring about the project or task, and wanting to do well because they committed.[5] They also, unless new to the organization, aren't necessarily looking for advisement on navigating organizational culture. Instead, many might want mentors who will help them set specific goals and measurable milestones around their careers, in general, or provide guidance or skill development to aid with a project they are working on.

Gen Xers are the latch-key kids all grown up and who have figured out life on their own. They identify as authentic and sensible and are motivated by caring about the project or task, accomplishment, opportunity for advancement, and advocating for something they believe in.[5] They might seek fewer ideas about tactical steps and more about how to take their passions and turn them into actionable accomplishments.

Being confident and realistic, Millennials are driven by resume-building, rewards, accomplishment, learning, and the opportunity for advancement – all motivators that have to do with achievement.[5] Many Millennials would prefer mentoring that focuses on gaining skills, ideas, and networks that will assist them in moving up in their organizations and professional fields.

Gen Zers are determined and motivated by advocating for something they believe in, accomplishment, meaning and fulfillment, and resume-building.[5] They may best be served by mentors who can help them connect with, build experience, and achieve goals around their passions. Doing so might lead this young generation to find a good career fit and feel assured they are making a difference.

Despite the varied ways in which each generation may view mentoring, the vast majority believe it is valuable.[5] So, for organizations without formal mentoring programs, particularly for young professionals, it's time to start one up. This may involve employees being matched with a more seasoned professional in the organization or even individuals selecting a mentor they want to work with based on the mentee's goals and the strengths of the mentor. Regardless of the structure, the purpose behind the mentoring program would be to provide support and guidance to employees who may need it.

Conclusion

Learning and development initiatives are fundamental to both employees and organizations. However, there is no one size fits all. Some people are eager to gather in the company's conference room to learn about the newest tech platform, whereas others would rather watch an instructional video from their desk. Being aware of these differences, and customizing or offering varied options when possible, can go a long way in ensuring high levels of participation, satisfaction, and learning transfer across all generations.

Notes

1 Gallup. (2017). *State of the American workplace.* www.gallup.com/workplace/238085/state-american-workplace-report-2017.aspx

2 University of Pennsylvania's Wharton School of Business. (2021). *5 reasons to offer employees learning & development opportunities.* https://online.wharton.upenn.edu/blog/5-reasons-to-offer-employees-learning-development-opportunities/

3 Deloitte. (2021). *Becoming irresistible: A new model for employee engagement.* www2.deloitte.com/us/en/insights/deloitte-review/issue-16/employee-engagement-strategies.html

4 Indeed. (n.d.). *Estimating the cost of high employee turnover.* www.indeed.com/hire/c/info/estimating-cost-of-higher-turnover

5 Seemiller, C., & Grace, M. (2023). *Generations in the workplace.* Unpublished dataset.

6 Moore, G., Parker, S., & Baksh, L. (2021). Generational learning preferences. *American Nurse Journal, 16*(12), *33–36.*

7 Statista. (2023). *Average spend on workplace training per employee worldwide from 2008–2021.* www.statista.com/statistics/738519/workplace-training-spending-per-employee/

8 Freifield, L. (2022). *2022 training industry report.* Training Magazine: The Industry Report. https://trainingmag.com/2022-training-industry-report/

9 Payscale. (2019). *Professional development: What employees want.* www.payscale.com/research-and-insights/professional-development-employees-want/

10 Statista. (2023). *Freelance participation in the United States as of 2020, by generation.* www.statista.com/statistics/531012/freelancers-by-age-us/

11 Onboarding FAQ. (2022). *Insight into Netflix onboarding process.* https://onboardingfaq.com/netflix-onboarding-process/

12 Gallup. (2019). *The CliftonStrengths movement continues to accelerate.* www.gallup.com/cliftonstrengths/en/253754/history-cliftonstrengths.aspx#:~:text=More%20than%2090%25%20of%20Fortune,development%20to%20their%20workplace%20culture

13 Seramount. (2021). *From pledge to progress.* https://seramount.com/wp-cont ent/uploads/2021/08/From-Pledge-to-Progress-Corporate-America-One-Year-After-George-Floyds-Death.pdf

14 Accenture. (n.d.). *Racial and ethnic equality.* www.accenture.com/us-en/about/inclusion-diversity/ethnic-diversity

15 LinkedIn Employee Training. (n.d.). *What are the pros and cons of online vs. in-person training for employee development?* www.linkedin.com/advice/1/what-pros-cons-online-vs-in-person-training-employee

16 Wiley. (2022). *Meeting different generational needs for a strong adult learner experience.* https://universityservices.wiley.com/meeting-different-generational-needs-for-a-strong-adult-learner-experience/

17 Statista. (2020). *Preferred digital tools among event visitors in the exhibition industry worldwide as of December 2020.* www.statista.com/statistics/1260172/favorite-digital-tools-exhibition-industry-visitors-worldwide/

18 Woodward, M. (2023). *Zoom user statistics.* www.searchlogistics.com/learn/sta tistics/zoom-user-statistics/#:~:text=Annual%20Webinar%20Minutes&text=You%20can%20share%20your%20screen,quarter%20which%20was%2042%20billion.&text=3%20billion%20webinar%20minutes%20registered%20in%20Q4%20of%202020.

19 On24. (2023). *Digital engagement benchmarks.* www.on24.com/resources/asset/state-of-digital-engagement/

20 Grate, R. (2017). New data on Millennials reveals what draws them to events. *Eventbrite.* www.eventbrite.com/blog/millennials-event-trends-ds00/

21 Mission Bay Conference Center. (2019). *Millennials expect more from their conference experience.* www.bizjournals.com/sanfrancisco/news/2019/02/01/mill ennials-expect-more-from-their-conference.html

22 Smith, T. (2023). *The Z: Planning for the Gen Z attendee.* www.meetingstoday. com/articles/143757/z-planning-gen-z-attendee

23 Rea, A. (2020). Reading through the ages: Generational reading survey. www. libraryjournal.com/story/Reading-Through-the-Ages-Generational-Reading-Survey

24 Learning. Where? (2024). *4 online learning platforms: EdX, Udemy, Coursera, Skillshare (How do they compare?).* https://learningwhere.com/online-courses-platforms/

25 West, K. (2023). 5 surprising benefits of professional networking that you need to know about. *Entrepreneur.* www.entrepreneur.com/leadership/5-surprising-benefits-of-professional-networking/448862

26 Academy of Management. (2024). *Membership.* https://aom.org/membership

27 American Psychological Association. (2024). *About APA.* www.apa.org/about#:~:text=APA%20is%20the%20leading%20scientific,and%20students%20as%20its%20members.

28 Wolff, H. G., & Moser, K. (2009). Effects of networking on career success: A longitudinal study. *Journal of Applied Psychology, 94*(1), 196–206.

29 Seemiller, C., & Grace, M. (2017). *Generation Z goes to college.* Jossey-Bass.

30 Gervis, Z. (2021). *Research reveals how the average American defines a party.* Eventbrite. https://swnsdigital.com/us/2019/08/research-reveals-how-the-average-american-defines-a-party/

31 American Psychological Association. (2012). *Introduction to mentoring: A guide for mentors and mentees.* www.apa.org/education-career/grad/mentoring

32 Adobe Communications Team. (2023). *Adobe Future Workforce Study: What U.S. employers need to know about Gen Z in the workplace.* https://blog.adobe.com/en/publish/2023/09/27/adobe-future-workforce-study-what-us-employers-need-know-about-gen-z-workplace

33 Rahmani, S. (2023). Age diversity in the workplace. *AARP.* https://trainingmag.com/age-diversity-in-the-workplace/

34 Madhavanprabhakaran, G., Francis, F., & Labrague, L. J. (2022). Reverse mentoring and intergenerational learning in nursing. *Sultan Qaboos University Medical Journal, 22*(4), 472–478.

35 SACHSE Press. (2019). *Knowledge is best shared.* https://sachseconstruction.com/knowledge-is-best-shared/

36 Satterly, B. A., Cullen, J., & Dyson, D. A. (2018). The intergenerational mentoring model: An alternative to traditional and reverse models of mentoring. *Mentoring & Tutoring: Partnership in Learning, 26*(4), 441–454.

37 National Institute on Ageing. (2022). *Why foster intergenerational triads?* www.niageing.ca/commentary-posts/2022/11/15/whyfosterintergenerationaltriads

38 Reeves, M. (2022). 10+ examples of successful mentoring programs. *Together.* www.togetherplatform.com/blog/examples-of-successful-mentoring-programs

Getting Things Done   7

Organizations thrive because work gets done. And, both quantity and quality matters – since no business wants to provide goods or services that aren't top-notch. So, what is important to employers then mainly comes down to productivity, which is the rate of efficiency of their workers. While productive organizations can accomplish a great deal, a lack of productivity can result in a loss of revenue, reduced employee retention, and in some cases, closing its doors.

There are several phenomena that impact productivity, one of which is organizational drag – those processes and structures that waste time, such as over-collaboration, endless digital communication, unnecessary meetings, and a culture that supports interruption from others, like having to work with an open office door. Many organizations diligently attempt to combat this drag and create workplaces that foster more, and not less, productivity. For example, the commerce platform, Shopify, instituted policies that eliminated all meetings on Wednesdays and cut other recurring ones, resulting in the elimination of 320,000 hours of meeting time in one year. With 11,600 employees, that's nearly 28 hours per year of productivity gained back per person.[1]

Productivity isn't just impacted by the amount of time a worker has – it's also about the effect of its utilization. Adobe's "The Future of Time" study found that an "always on" mentality and overworking can cause burnout, mental health issues, and inability to have work–life balance.[2] To test the structural effects impacting productivity, educational technology company, Curriculum Associates, conducted an experiment in which 300 of their 2,000

DOI: 10.4324/9781003541035-7

employees agreed to say "no" to meeting requests.[3] Those who participated noted reallocating the saved 8000 hours of meetings toward more creative thinking and task completion. Further, the participants reported greater levels of workplace happiness. Thus, saying no, if empowered to do so, has its benefits.

Beyond larger strategies to reduce organizational drag and help avoid overworking employees, individuals may approach productivity differently. Allowing people to work from their strengths can ultimately lead to optimal outcomes for a task because they are working in ways that are best for them. The effectiveness of using strengths is supported by Gallup's study of more than 1 million workers across 45 countries, which found that leveraging people's strengths led to increased sales, profit, and engagement, as well as lower turnover.[4] Appreciating the strengths each employee brings to approach their work can foster understanding and trust across generations. For instance, believing a subordinate or a coworker is going to get something done, even if in their own unique way, allows for everyone to thrive without restriction or judgment.

Generational Considerations and Strategies

Strengths can differ from generational cohort to cohort. For example, Carlos, who is a Gen Zer, works better late at night when he has a burst of energy and fewer interruptions. Celina, however, is a Millennial who thrives in a collaborative environment in the middle of a busy workday. Instead of their company requiring one specific way of working, using an outcomes-based standard might work best here. It allows both employees to be evaluated on their output regardless of when, where, and how they generated it – and it leads to greater employee engagement. And, as discussed in the Mindsets chapter, the Bureau of Labor Statistics found no significant difference between in productivity levels when comparing generations at the same age.[5] So, the variance in approaches likely doesn't yield significant disparities in output.

To help reduce organizational drag for members of all generations, consider instituting "dark hours" when employees and supervisors are asked to refrain from messaging. Or, adopt a "no meeting Fridays." Doing so allows people to concentrate on projects that need focused and sustained attention without interruption.

In addition, capitalizing on the strengths of an intergenerational team can lead to higher levels of productivity across all employees.[6] This is particularly true when it comes to complex decision-making, where different approaches and perspectives can complement each other. In action, this may resemble a Millennial focusing on team dynamics, while a Gen Xer urges the group to set aggressive deadlines. Together, both can lead to a better overall outcome.

Finding the Right Motivation

Motivation is a reason someone acts in a specific way. For instance, one person may be motivated to seek out a new job to earn a higher salary, whereas another person might be seeking working hours more aligned with their preferences. On a day-to-day level, motivation is critical for striving for goals and following through on tasks. If someone lacks the drive to get something done, that task will likely be left unfinished or take longer to achieve. Uncovering the unique motivations of different generational cohorts is instrumental for energizing employees to do their best work in a productive manner.

Motivators

Motivation can be categorized into three types: intrinsic (I), extrinsic (E), and relational (R). Intrinsic motivation develops from within oneself and is derived from the feeling of satisfaction or contribution (e.g., taking on a project because you enjoy the work or organizing your desk because you like tidy spaces). Extrinsic motivation is an influence outside oneself and is often an impetus to engage in behavior to avoid punishment or gain some type of reward (e.g., showing up to work on time to prevent getting written up or taking on additional tasks so your boss considers you for a promotion). Relational motivation develops from interpersonal connections and is marked by doing something out of a desire to positively impact others (e.g., helping someone move because you know that it would be difficult if they had to do the task on their own, or attending a meeting in someone's place because an emergency arose for them).

Generational Considerations and Strategies

Let's look at what motivates each generation in the workplace through the lens of two different studies. In the first, our workplace study, we created a master list for each generation using the three highest-ranking general motivators.[7] We compared this list with the top career-specific motivators from a study conducted by the global management consulting firm McKinsey & Company.[8] The combination of results is displayed in the following table, where an X means that the motivator appeared in at least one of the two studies.

Table 7.1   *Motivators in the Workplace by Generation*

Motivators	Baby Boomers	Gen Xers	Millennials	Gen Zers
Accomplishment (I)	X	X	X	X
Compensation (E)	X	X	X	X
Caring about the task (I)	X	X	X	
Advancement potential (E)		X	X	X
Meaningful work (I)	X	X		X
Workplace flexibility (E)	X	X	X	
Advocating for something (I)		X		X
Experience for resume (E)			X	X
Made a commitment (I)	X			
Learning and development (I, E)			X	
Tangible rewards (E)			X	
Fulfillment and purpose (I)				X
Diversity, equity, and inclusion (E)				X

Note: Each motivator is marked with an I for intrinsic and E for extrinsic. No Relational (R) motivators emerged in the findings from either study.

One can conclude that of all the extrinsic factors, employees across all generations are motivated by compensation. Other extrinsic factors, like advancement potential and workplace flexibility, also play a role in motivating three of four cohorts.

In terms of intrinsic, all cohorts are motivated by accomplishment, and three of the four are motivated by caring about the task. Researchers have found that intrinsic motivation has more positive benefits than does extrinsic.[9] Employees who are intrinsically motivated have less burnout, higher rates of satisfaction, better performance, and greater levels of commitment. Ways to leverage intrinsic motivation include gamifying experiences so employees can see their accomplishments on an app or tracking platform and helping them understand the value and impact of a task so they can find meaning in it for themselves.

Despite the similarities across generational cohorts, the nuances are also instructive. For one, Baby Boomers as a cohort want to work in an organization that honors their worth through compensation and allows them the ability to make decisions about their schedules and where they work. They are also motivated by a sense of accomplishment, caring deeply about the task and following through on it, and prefer work that has meaning and is contributory to the larger picture. Critical for them is trust and flexibility to drive their own work. They are motivated by intrinsic rationale, so much so that in having a connection to the duties and roles in their jobs, they will likely supervise themselves. When working with Baby Boomers, supervisors and colleagues will find it helpful to set up initial goals and timelines with them at the beginning of a project, checking in only periodically to ask if they need help, and thanking them for their contributions.

Like Baby Boomers, Gen Xers also desire meaningful work embedded in a culture of trust where they can dictate their own workflow. They need space to determine their own goals and processes for going about tasks and do not fare well-being micromanaged. For many Gen Xers, this is an un-motivator, meaning that hovering too closely over the details of their work may lead them to be disengaged. When working with a Gen Xer, give them autonomy, independence, and trust. And like Baby Boomers, they will manage themselves.

While Millennials tend to be motivated by some intrinsic factors, more of their motivators are extrinsic, such as compensation, tangible rewards, career advancement, flexibility, and gaining experience for their resumes. Because of this, when working with a Millennial, it is helpful to lay out a clear reward structure at the beginning of an assignment. Supervisors might say, "Working on this project will help you stand apart from your peers and draw accolades from upper management," "Finishing this project early means you get an extra day off," and "The more sales you close, the bigger bonus you will earn for the year." Peers are also in a position to motivate Millennial colleagues by reminding them of other incentives, such as formal recognition from organizational leadership or pride in a job well done.

Uniquely, Gen Zers, while motivated by some extrinsic factors, tend to be driven by engaging in meaningful work that gives them purpose and fulfillment. They enjoy advocating for something they believe in and then feeling accomplished when they make a difference. Using a tracking process, project management app, or even a shared to-do list can allow them to view their micro-achievements in progress. In addition, incorporating a looped supervisory model can be useful, in which the employee would learn about the purpose of the task or duty, complete it, and then receive an after-action update about its impact.

Productivity Skills

The essence of productivity is getting things done, which requires the deployment of a variety of skills. For example, the ability to stay focused can influence the amount of time it takes to finish a project and how much intentional effort is put into it. The capacity to organize one's space can eliminate the need to waste time sifting through extraneous information. Further, exacting determination can affect one's persistence to complete a challenging task. Let's take a look at how each generation leverages these productivity skills as well as strategies for enhancing any that may be challenges for that cohort.

Maintaining Focus

People are confronted with a variety of distractions every day, whether external, such as coworkers stopping by one's workspace to chat, or internal, such as daydreaming and mind-wandering. Focus is the ability to have the willpower to enact sustained concentration on a task without interruption, and involves being able to ignore, redirect, and avoid the temptation of possible distractions. Lacking focus can result in errors, being inefficient, as well as feeling overwhelmed and drained, none of which are helpful to an organization or its employees.

Generational Considerations and Strategies
The ability to focus can vary among generations. Gen Xers and Millennials tend to be perceived by members of other generational cohorts as better able to focus than Baby Boomers and Gen Zers.[7] Perception, however, may not fully represent truth, allowing assumptions to get in the way of productive functioning between cohorts. It's important to talk with members of different generations to find out what focus looks like for them and where they may shine as well as struggle.

However, perceptions can be based on reality. Let's consider the lower numbers across the board who say that Baby Boomers demonstrate focus.[7] If that is true, what might help explain this? It likely has to do with the proliferation of technology. Over the course of their careers, many processes have gone from analog to digital and paper to technical, requiring them to retool and relearn over and over just to complete simple tasks in their jobs. While some may have jumped on board and embraced this shift, this is a generation that overall has lower levels of tech adoption than younger generations.[10] They may be distracted trying to learn new technology while having to simultaneously deploy it for a task. Given this, consider providing adequate tech training and support so they feel comfortable with any new processes. In addition, providing options that are more analog during the interim of the transition might provide ease for any Baby Boomers feeling the pressure to quickly learn and transition.

Generation Z's focus may be attributed to entirely different causes. For instance, with the bombardment of news, entertainment, communication, and day-to-day tasks that can be done with a click or swipe, Generation Z has been embedded in a digitally distracting world since their birth, pulling their focus in several competing directions. What might help with this generation would be reduced device activity. Rather than creating an extrinsic "no phone at work" policy, unless warranted by job duties, instead provide Gen Zers with stimulating and creative work, which helps them connect their passions to their jobs and fall more seamlessly into the flow, mitigating the temptation to jump on their phones. And, in the event the work just isn't exciting, leaning on Gen Zers to come up with their own unique ways to engage in a project could at least make the process more engaging for them.

ATTENTION SPANS

An attention span is the amount of time a person stays focused on a particular goal or task without diverting their focus to something else. In 2004, attention spans were 2.5 minutes; by 2012, they were 1 minute and 15 seconds; and since 2018, they have been measured at 47 seconds.[11] However, people more often lose focus because of self-created interruptions rather than interruptions from external factors.[11] In particular, the desire to be on devices pulls them away from conversations with people, tasks, and even other online activities, such as drafting an important email. And, it takes people, on average, 25 minutes to reset after an interruption, wasting precious time for concentrated work.[11]

Generational Considerations and Strategies

While there are claims in popular news that assert that those in younger generations, particularly Generation Z, have shorter attention spans than their older counterparts today, actual research that supports this is scant.[12]

Members across all cohorts face this. So, to help everyone, videos need to be shorter, instruction manuals more concise, and tasks need to be broken down into more bite-sized steps.

Attention spans might be similar today across generations. However, in comparing generational cohorts when they were the same age, the numbers do differ. For instance, in 2018, the attention span of an 18-year-old Gen Zer would have been 47 seconds compared to an 18-year-old Millennial in 2004 at two and a half minutes. Thus, training sessions, supervisory meetings, and entry-level tasks given to Gen Zers must be done knowing that their attention spans are likely shorter than those of older supervisors when they were the same age. Until there is a way to lengthen everyone's attention spans, being aware and retrofitting processes is the best approach for those across all generations.

MULTITASKING

Multitasking is the ability to transition between tasks, in real time, either moving rapidly back and forth between unique tasks or taking on more than one task simultaneously. In some cases, this can save time. For instance, there might be a one-minute delay in downloading a document, during which the time could be used to send a short response to a colleague's message; or, waiting for a customer to bring signed forms back to the registration counter might create just enough time to scan three documents.

However, multitasking doesn't always equate to higher levels of productivity as it can be difficult to fully comprehend more than one piece of information at a time, especially across differing contexts, as well as direct one's full attention to multiple places simultaneously.[13] Thus, the notion of multitasking being a desired skill in a workplace may actually lead to reduced, not increased, productivity.

With the pervasiveness of digital communication, organizational structures are inherently set up to encourage multitasking. For example, Emma is trying to finish a big project but keeps getting "pinged" through instant messaging by her coworkers and supervisor with what are supposedly quick questions. It isn't an option for Emma to delay a response, which might be more acceptable through email. So, she responds, then returns to her project, only to be interrupted again. And, if it takes significant time to concentrate after being interrupted, Emma is bound to get behind and feel overwhelmed.

Generational Considerations and Strategies

While multitasking pressures affect everyone, younger generations engage in the practice more often, simply because of their earlier lifetime exposure to technology.[14] With the ability to toggle between texting, social media, Internet searches, and entertainment all on one device, these teens and young adults don't know a world without the ease of technological multitasking.

There are a few ways supervisors can mitigate multitasking in the workplace, such as proactively managing schedules and workloads to avoid employees being overburdened with too many tasks as well as limiting interruptions. Further, it can be helpful to integrate platforms and apps that assist with managing multiple simultaneous projects, ensuring that backup support and resourcing are available during busy periods with competing deadlines.

Organizing

Also critical to productivity is organization, which entails having systems in place to easily keep track of items and tasks. Whether using online apps, following routine processes, utilizing filing systems, creating a standardized method of saving documents, or just getting a drawer organizer, people who are organized save themselves and their organizations time. For example, Jim has worked as an insurance adjuster for several years, situating himself at the same cubicle during his entire tenure with the company. Although Jim continually demonstrates stellar work ethic and great follow-through, he is described by his colleagues as scattered. Often, he misplaces paperwork and has trouble tracking down digital files on his computer because they are not labeled with obvious naming conventions. On average, Jim spends 10 minutes per workday looking for important items. That equates to 50 minutes per week, and nearly 42 hours per year. At $25/hour, that is $1,050 in lost wages per year for his company!

Disorganization can also affect customer relationships, as some tasks or correspondence may be delayed or even missed. This has a reputational cost that can hardly be measured.

Generational Considerations and Strategies

As people are typically organized in their personal and professional lives alike, it makes sense that the state of one's personal closet could be telling in terms of general organization skills exacted in the workplace.

A study by ClosetMaid, a closet organization company, uncovered how different generations manage clutter. Baby Boomers are more likely to keep unwanted items, those they can't or won't yet part with.[15] Taking up room in their closets, they have no intention of disposing, donating, or selling these. Consider a Baby Boomer's workplace then. Their workspace may have several books, documents, and other items accumulated from a lifetime of working, along with family photos and personal décor. They may store a "paper copy" of a digital file for backup, resulting in having stacks of paperwork or overfilled filing cabinets. While this could be reflective of their reluctance to save important information in the digital space, often these paper copies result in countless duplicate files that make their workspaces more cluttered.

Gen Xers generally are quite organized,[15] and were even perceived by other generations in our study as being the most organized cohort.[7] This perception makes sense in that it's hard to imagine an independent, entrepreneurial, fast-moving Generation X employee trying to navigate their autonomous workloads while lacking systems and misplacing important items.

Compared to other generations, ClosetMaid found that Millennials are the most organized at home.[15] They often utilize storage systems and containers, and can easily part with items they don't need, particularly by selling them. If Millennials approach their workspaces in the same way, one might expect them to have highly organized bookshelves and files, as well as rid themselves of things they find no immediate use for. This would apply to employee lockers, work trucks, and the like – wherever employees can accumulate items.

While many Gen Zers also have sparse workspaces free from physical clutter, they are more likely using digital organization systems than physical ones. For example, members of this generation use distraction-blocking software, virtual to-do lists, calendars, note-taking systems, time-tracking, and mind mapping apps more than those in other generations.[16] These tools are so important that 70 percent of Gen Zers said they would change jobs to have better access to these types of apps, a number considerably higher than the 37 percent of Baby Boomers who would.[17]

While Baby Boomers, by virtue of their generational characteristics and longevity in the workforce, have more items accumulated in their workspaces, some in this generation fail to declutter. It's not because they don't want to, but because they are overwhelmed and don't know where to start.[18] Instead of decluttering, they often re-arrange, just moving their things around. Downsizing designer Rita Wilkins suggests helping Baby Boomers develop a clear goal, and then have them either declutter in 15-minute blocks, which she calls the "burst" method, or sorting items only related to one particular category at a time (e.g. files).[18] In addition, providing high-speed scanning services could offer a way for Baby Boomers to keep their paper copies, albeit in a digital format.

Those in other generational cohorts who are familiar with technology can also aid any tech-novice Baby Boomers in becoming more organized in the digital space. This may include helping them create folders with naming conventions, save items in those folders rather than on their desktops, assemble contact groups for calendaring and messaging, and use online apps and tools to sort, store, and communicate important information. And, while this could be an employee-to-employee mentoring situation, organizations might find it useful to integrate digital organizing trainings for workers to learn strategies.

In working together, each generational cohort may find that not only are their organization levels different, but they are spurned by unique rationale. Gen Zers crave productivity apps, Millennials quickly purge anything they deem unnecessary as well as refrain from over-personalizing their workspaces, Gen Xers create systems for efficient and autonomous work, and Baby Boomers keep record of nearly everything. But, all can learn from each other about strategies for better organization, perhaps through sharing best practices and discussing underlying motivations and habits that lead to these behaviors.

Determination

Determination involves not giving up on a task or goal, even when it becomes difficult. Consider the 2004 U.S. Olympic men's basketball team, assembled with an impressive roster of players slated to win Gold that year. After coming home with the Bronze medal instead, the players trained tirelessly for four years to usher in a comeback Gold medal win in 2008. The documentary *The Redeem Team* chronicles their determination.[19] Most jobs, though, don't come with trophies and gold medals. But, staying the course might mean the difference between landing or losing a big contract, inventing or walking away from an idea, or persisting through all odds to get a product to market after testing it for years. And, determination can offer hope, opportunities to push beyond one's limits, and motivation.

Determination is driven by intrinsic, rather than extrinsic, motivating factors, meaning the internal desire to complete a task would trump tangible rewards for doing so. Research on this phenomenon dates back decades with Richard Ryan and Edward Deci's self-determination theory, and helps us uncover what drives people to persist.[20]

Generational Considerations and Strategies

Given Gen Xers' propensity for independence and Millennials' desire for learning and development, it's not surprising that a greater number of employees across all generations perceive both of those cohorts to be determined.[7] For instance, a Gen Xer tasked with an individual project may aim to see it through because its success rests solely on them. And, with Millennials, the drive for constant improvement could help them see that while the outcome of the task is important, what they learn and the skills they develop during that process would set them apart from others. While their motives might be different, their behaviors likely look the same – not giving up easily.

On the other hand, fewer members across all generations view Baby Boomers and Gen Zers as determined. And, when asked to rate their own levels of determination, these two cohorts had lower numbers than Gen Xers and Millennials.[7] Although this could be attributed to unique motivating factors facing each generation, there is likely a lifecycle rationale that is more explanatory – Baby Boomers have already worked through the prime of their careers and may be winding down their efforts, whereas Gen Zers are just starting up and are exploring their passions before diving in head first with relentless persistence.

In working across generations, it's critical to understand the link between determination and motivating factors, as knowing what drives a cohort also explains why and to what extent they may stay the course. It is then that we can best tap into the strengths of each generation to help set them up for success.

GRIT

An important component of determination is grit, which is the "perseverance and passion for long-term goals."[21] Grit is critical to productivity as it involves sticking with a project through completion, despite any challenges one might face.

What makes a person gritty, though? For one, having a growth mindset, which is the belief that with learning, hard work, and practice, people can develop their skills and abilities. Further, obstacles and setbacks are just bumps in the road rather than signals of dire conclusions that one is not talented enough to be successful.[21] A fixed mindset, on the other hand, is linked to lower levels of grit, emphasizing innate talent and supporting the belief that there is no need to work harder since failure is inevitable.

Generational Considerations and Strategies

A study conducted by Shane Sanders and associates, in observing generations over time, found that grit levels don't increase with age. While interventional efforts like identifying and pursuing passions, selecting a skill to develop and then engaging in deliberate practice, and finding meaning in each task, can increase individual levels, essentially without concerted effort, a person's grit score now will likely remain unchanged in the years to come.

The researchers also found a significant variance between grit scores by generation, making it a more telling indicator than age. They ascribe this to individuals within the same cohort developing similar responses to social forces, and thus, affecting their grit levels.[22] In essence, this assertion is reflective of generational theory.[23] Gen Xers had the highest level of grit, followed by Baby Boomers, Millennials, and then Gen Zers.

Differing levels of grit, though, can be a point of contention between employees across generational cohorts. For instance, a hardy Gen Xer not accepting failure after multiple attempts may become frustrated at the Gen Zer who wants to cease efforts after fewer tries. Or, that very Gen Zer may grow tired of what might be perceived as a waste of time trying to salvage an unsuccessful idea championed by a Gen Xer. So, while developing the grit of a Gen Zer can go a long way in helping them stay the course on a challenging project, so too can opening lines of communication between generations to ensure everyone is on the same page in deciding whether to persist with an idea or project.

RESILIENCE

Another component vital to determination is resilience, which is the ability to recover when things don't go as expected. Resilience is positively correlated with productivity, meaning that the more resilient a person is, the higher their productivity levels are. This is mainly due to managing stress and burnout more easily.[24]

Generational Considerations and Strategies

A study by Lya Cartwright-Stroupe and Jean Shinners looked at the resilience levels of Gen Xers, Millennials, and Gen Zers (Baby Boomers were not included in their study). They used the Psychological Capital Questionnaire, which measures self-efficacy (confidence), optimism, hope, and resilience. They found in both their 2019 and 2020 data collections that Gen Zers had lower resilience scores compared to the two older generations.[25] We found the same in our study when participants were asked to report the extent they described themselves as resilient – Gen Zers lagged behind their older counterparts.[7]

However, there is also the perception of resilience, which can be helpful in understanding generational nuances. For example, Baby Boomers and Gen Xers believe Gen Zers have the lowest resilience levels.[7] This perception by older generations may also be perpetuated by the notion that young workers give up when things get hard.[26] However, some young employees would rather walk away from a toxic organization or detrimental situation than stay. For them, it's not about lacking resilience; but instead about seeking something better. It's no surprise then that millions of Gen Zers have taken to the social media app, TikTok, to share their workplace frustrations upon leaving their jobs, using the hashtag, Quittok,[27] and further, earning them the name "Generation Quit."[28] However, their propensity to leave for other opportunities may elicit judgment from members of other cohorts, which can foster contention. It's important, though, to understand why younger employees are quitting, beyond attributing it entirely to a lack of resilience. Factors, like low wages, stagnant career progression, and inability to have a voice are also at play.

On the other hand, some Gen Zers do need a boost in their resilience levels. And, this is where members of older generations can help. Modeling failure, processing one's own shortcomings, teaching them to anticipate barriers and derive workarounds, and providing them opportunities to develop their confidence are some useful strategies. This may come in the form of mentorship, dialogue, or even formalized programs where more seasoned employees offer their "lessons learned" and advice to this cohort.

Fulfilling Employee Needs

Let's consider this scenario. A week beforehand, a memo comes out informing employees that the office will be closed the day after Thanksgiving so everyone can spend time with their families. However, this mandatory vacation day must be deducted from each worker's annual two weeks of paid time off. In the past, most people elected to take the day off. However, others did not and often relied on this time to be able to engage in uninterrupted and highly productive work when the majority of their colleagues were out. While the company has good intentions in supporting work–life balance, this policy misses an opportunity to capitalize on each employees' motivations and drive, particularly in allowing them to work during a time they feel most productive.

It's not surprising then that what people need in order to be productive varies. For instance, one person may want validation and reassurance to start a project, whereas another might require an uninterrupted block of time, like employees in this case. While these preferences can be individual, some can be attributed to generational differences.

Generational Considerations and Strategies

Wrike, a project management software company, conducted a global study of employees across various sectors and identified each generation's three most important productivity needs.[29]

Table 7.2   *Productivity Needs by Generational Cohort*

	Baby Boomers	Gen Xers	Millennials	Gen Zers
1	Workload balance	Flexible work arrangements	Flexible work arrangements	Connecting work to company's larger goals
2	Cross-team collaboration	Workload balance	Automation	Flexible work arrangements
3	Flexible work arrangements	Cross-team collaboration	Workload balance	Clearly defined accountability

Let's take a deeper look at each of these needs and how they play out with various generational cohorts.

Workload Balance

Workload balance involves the selection and prioritization of work to ensure that an appropriate amount of time is allocated to successfully complete each task. Having too much to accomplish can lead to lower quality output, incompletion of tasks, overwhelm of the employee, and a situation where the individual doesn't know where to begin and simply freezes. A balanced workload, however, can allow for time for creative thought, thorough and thoughtful decision-making, fewer errors, and higher employee morale.

Generational Considerations and Strategies

An unbalanced workload is a concern for most employees, particularly those in the three oldest generations.[29] Baby Boomers need to feel valued and appreciated,[7] so, for them, an overbearing workload might feel as though their well-being isn't a priority and they are not being valued by the leadership in the organization. Gen Xers equate a heavy workload with a lack of work–life balance, which is critically important to them. And Millennials may feel the pressure to take on more as a way to gain experience and good favor from organizational leaders they believe they need to advance through their careers.

While the reasons why the need for workload balance differs among generations, the solutions are similar. Supervisors will want to check in regularly with their employees to evaluate their workloads, help them prioritize tasks, and adjust deadlines as needed. Further, it's important to remove or replace duties in their workloads to ensure they can be successful, engaging in the most critical tasks at hand. It can be challenging to do this when units are already short-staffed or there is a project that could benefit from the involvement of an already busy employee with a strong track record. Realigning work rather than piling on more is imperative if employees are to be productive and believe they are set up for success. Baby Boomers can feel more valued, Gen Xers more balanced, and Millennials more supported in their career advancement.

Cross-Team Collaboration

Cross-team collaboration involves employees from different functional units working together to achieve a common goal. For example, to increase sales of a new fitness app, a group might be convened with members from the marketing, sales, and product design teams. All bring in differing ideas, which may result in greater innovation and streamlined processes, faster goal completion, and distributed workloads. It's no surprise then that 55 percent of early stage companies, 71 percent of developing companies, and 83 percent of maturing companies use cross-functional teams.[30]

Generational Considerations and Strategies

Being a part of a collaborative team ranks higher in importance with the two oldest generations.[7] Although Baby Boomers enjoy face-to-face communication, especially that which builds trust and connection, many Gen Xers see it as unnecessary and time-consuming, preferring instead to maintain a project's pace at a clip.[7] This may make Baby Boomers feel disconnected and rushed. So, it's important to agree to a process that works for everyone.

Although Millennials and Gen Zers didn't prioritize cross-team collaboration in regard to aiding in productivity levels, they do thrive in cases where they work with others. Millennials desire a great deal of feedback as they work through a project, which can slow the process and momentum for fast-paced Gen Xers. Gen Zers are often reluctant to speak up in meetings, given their lack of experience and challenges with some interpersonal skills (such as making conversation, sharing ideas and opinions face-to-face, and introducing themselves to new people).[31] Feeling confident in their experience, you might see Baby Boomers doing most of the talking in cross-team meetings, Gen Xers pushing the process forward, Millennials asking a lot of questions to ensure they have a complete understanding of the project, and Gen Zers waiting to be invited to share their ideas. Once we can better understand the variance in these perspectives and behaviors can we then best leverage involvement across all generations.

Flexible Work Arrangements

During the COVID pandemic, many office employees who shifted to remote work became accustomed to having some flexibility in their work lives. Once the height of the pandemic subsided, organizational leaders began calling workers back to the office. The rationale was presented as a way to enhance collaboration and effectively navigate organizational culture. However, executives are four times more likely than their general employees to have no constraints on their schedules.[32] Thus, those calling staff back for onsite work are, in many cases, senior leaders who have far more flexibility in their own schedules and work locations.

While some companies have held firm about return-to-work policies, others have embraced more innovative approaches. For example, retail giant, Target, launched an "On Demand" program so that employees who aren't on a regular schedule can add shifts when they want.[33] And their mobile scheduling app has made the process easier and more seamless. Further, other companies haven't leaned into the notion that onsite means better collaboration. For instance, in 2020, Pinterest canceled its office lease and integrated remote work through their program PinFlex.[34] Their website says, "With PinFlex, we believe work location is situational and we let the work guide the collaboration style." The program is based on the notion that employees' best work happens when they are most inspired, wherever that is.

Generational Considerations and Strategies
Flexibility with location matters for members of all generations, but so do work hours – at least in terms of when employees feel most productive. Research has shown that the majority across all cohorts are productive during the typical 9 a.m.–6 p.m. workday.[17] This isn't surprising as this time block is essentially the customary business workday. However, Gen Zers and Millennials, in particular, "feel pressure to appear working during office hours, even when [they] know [they] won't be productive." They do so to signal to their older coworkers and supervisors that they are present in ways that follow the norm of what work looks like.[2]

Other time blocks throughout the day can also lead to feelings of productivity, with early morning appealing more to older generations and late-night to those in Generation Z.[2]

Table 7.3 *Productivity Preferences Across Generations*

	Baby Boomers	Gen Xers	Millennials	Gen Zers
3 a.m.–9 a.m.	39%	36%	32%	27%
9 a.m.–6 p.m.	74%	76%	74%	62%
6 p.m.–3 a.m.	6%	13%	18%	26%

Note: Percentages exceed 100 percent as participants could select all that apply.

As important as it is to foster generational understanding when it comes to honoring what each generation needs in terms of workplace flexibility, the reality is that this issue is mostly reflective of organizational policies and supervisory practices. Over time, employees who prioritize flexibility will end up leaving their jobs for ones that are a better match, ultimately forcing the hands of executives to reconsider their expectations and workplace culture.

Automation

Automation is the use of systems and online platforms to perform tasks without human intervention. These are often repetitive or rote tasks, such as automatic email sorting, calendar scheduling, and digital invoicing. Freeing up employees from these types of duties allows for them to engage in more complex and creative endeavors as well as more time to learn new skills. A study conducted by Salesforce found that 92 percent of their users cited being more satisfied with their productivity since using automation.[35]

Generational Considerations and Strategies

The desire for automation seems to follow a positive age trajectory, with younger employees being more optimistic about it compared to older employees.[36] Interestingly, Millennials reported the highest rates of wanting more automation. This aligns with findings from Wrike's study in which Millennials were the only cohort to note automation as a top three need in order to be more productive. Thus, integrating it into one's organization can be a critical productivity tool, especially for younger employees.

Baby Boomers, on the other hand, are most reserved about the idea of automation due to the fear of AI taking over their jobs,[37] the high learning curve to acquire new technology skills,[10] and a hesitance to change how they approach work. For example, Baby Boomer, Derek, may be reluctant to use his online calendar to autogenerate a meeting invitation when he is used to reaching out individually to all invitees. As Baby Boomers invest deeply in relationships with those they work with, employees like Derek may not want to automate interpersonal tasks. Thus, his shift to online calendaring may be more than just a technological change; it will upend the way he has always connected with others. Those in other generations can either help Derek transition to online calendaring or accept how he prefers to set up meetings.

Likewise, those in older generations should understand that their younger colleagues want automation to free them of minute tasks. Whether it is hesitation or the cost to switchover a process, organizations that do not embrace automation could end up deterring younger people from working there. Thus, organizations should invest in infrastructure, applications, platforms, and systems that integrate automation, along with adequate and ongoing training and support, so that employees across all cohorts can recognize their utility and feel confident in using them.

Connecting Work to Company's Larger Goals

It's not unusual for a company's mission statement to be posted on a wall where workers obliviously pass it every day, or having the 250-page strategic plan available on an internal company web page gathering digital cobwebs. According to research conducted by Achievers, an employee experience platform, a whopping 61 percent of employees don't even know the mission statement of their workplace.[38]

Further, when organizations don't spend sufficient time visiting and revisiting their values, mission, vision, and goals with their workers, it can be difficult for them to feel knowledgeable about and connected to the larger purpose. Only 40 percent of employees surveyed in Gallup's State of the American Workplace report believe the mission or purpose of their organization makes them feel important.[39] For the rest, they either don't feel important or simply don't know the mission or purpose. Gallup's report states, "Employees cannot energize themselves to do all they could do without knowing how their job helps to fulfill a higher purpose."

Generational Considerations and Strategies

Connecting work to the company's larger goals is only in the top three productivity needs for Generation Z, which comes as no surprise as many are motivated by a desire to make a difference or impact.[8] Thus, knowing how their work connects with the bigger organizational picture is fundamental for them in being productive. They may ask themselves, "What am I working toward?" or "How does my work matter?"

Helping Gen Zers see the bigger mission is of critical importance, even before hiring. Consider creating a job description that discusses the outcome of their work in addition to the duties. For example, "As a mechanic, you will use your expertise to fix vehicles that owners need to get to and from their places of employment, pick up their children, and go to the grocery store to buy food. You are impacting the lives of countless customers who depend on you for their livelihoods. What you do matters." While it might seem unconventional, it sure is inspiring!

And, once Gen Zers are hired, it can be beneficial to involve them in strategy sessions and company town halls to allow for open communication with organizational leaders about values, mission, vision, and goals. In addition, having them view the entire supply chain in action, rotate to different roles along that supply chain, and see the outcomes of their work can help them connect to the larger purpose of the organization.

Clearly Defined Accountability

Think about a situation when you served on a committee that had clear goals and milestones. It was probably easy for your group to know what to do with the allocated time, determine the metrics for knowing when a task is completed, and measure success. Having these accountability processes in place can make it easier to be productive. Instead of spending time trying to figure out what you should be doing, you can get right to the task at hand.

Generational Considerations and Strategies

While accountability is a universal concern across all cohorts, it's in the top three for those in Generation Z. This makes sense in that a majority of the Gen Zers don't enjoy working in groups because of the lack of follow-through from other members.[40] One participant in our Global Gen Z study captured this sentiment in saying, "Some members do most of the work while others do nothing."[40] Many also noted that having to worry about pulling the weight of another member makes them feel out of control, untrusting, and stressed out, specifically when they are evaluated equally on the outcome of the project rather than on their individual contributions. However, both their sense of responsibility and "Do It Yourself" nature mean that they may attempt to deal with group issues internally before involving a manager.[31] In one vein, this is resourceful if the problem ends up being effectively addressed. On the other hand, a complex situation that isn't resolved in a timely manner, perhaps with outside intervention, could end up being far more serious.

To infuse accountability into organizational culture, it's important as a manager to communicate clear goals and instructions, milestones and deadlines, anticipated outcomes, and team expectations from the onset. This may include incorporating a tracking tool where group members can see each person's task completion in real-time, which can also alleviate some of Gen Zers' fears. Second, conducting regular check-ins, providing resources and guidance along the way, and engaging in frequent communication can help Gen Zers feel more comfortable and confident that each person is getting their work done.

Conclusion

Ensuring productivity amid generational differences involves creating open lines of communication so everyone can better understand and appreciate the nuances across cohorts, especially as each might approach various aspects of productivity in unique ways. However, there are some proven strategies to enhance one's productivity that may be beneficial to learn, and each cohort has strengths that can help others leverage their potential to be more productive. This applies to organizations too, as they have a responsibility to provide guidance, support, and resources for all employees to be able to maximize their productivity in healthy and balanced ways.

Notes

1 Boyle, M. (2023). *Work shift: How Shopify culled 320,000 hours of meetings.* www.bloomberg.com/news/newsletters/2023-02-14/how-shopify-cut-320-000-hours-of-unnecessary-meetings

2 Adobe. (2021). *The future of time.* www.adobe.com/documentcloud/business/reports/the-future-of-time-confirmation.html?faas_unique_submission_id=66CEE6C4-3121-2D13-028E-FC86C06C1D9B

3 Dubois, D. (2023). *Saying no to meetings made my team more productive. Here's why.* www.fastcompany.com/90847963/saying-no-to-meetings-made-my-team-more-productive-heres-why

4 Gallup. (2023). The benefits of employee engagement. *Q12 meta-analysis.* www.gallup.com/workplace/236927/employee-engagement-drives-growth.aspx

5 Bureau of Labor Statistics. (2022). *Time use of Millennials and Generation X: Differences across time.* www.bls.gov/opub/mlr/2022/article/time-use-of-millennials-and-generation-x-differences-across-time.htm

6 Paczka, N. (2023). Different generations in the workplace – 2023 study. *LiveCareer.* www.livecareer.com/resources/careers/planning/generation-diversity-in-the-workplace

7 Seemiller, C., & Grace, M. (2023). *Generations in the workplace.* Unpublished dataset.

8 McKinsey & Company. (2012). *The state of human capital 2012: False summit.* www.mckinsey.com/capabilities/people-and-organizational-performance/our-insights/the-state-of-human-capital-2012-report#/

9 Kuvaas, B., Buch, R., Weibel, A., Dysvik, A., & Nerstad, C. G. L. (2017). Do intrinsic and extrinsic motivation relate differently to employee outcomes? *Journal of Economic Psychology, 61*, 244–258.

10 Vogels, E. A. (2019). *Millennials stand out for their technology use, but older generations also embrace digital life.* Pew Research Center. www.pewresearch.org/short-reads/2019/09/09/us-generations-technology-use/

11 Mark, G. (2023). *Attention span: A groundbreaking way to restore balance, happiness and productivity.* Hanover Square Press.

12 McKinsey & Company. (2022). *Mind the gap.* www.mckinsey.com/~/media/mckinsey/email/genz/2022/11/29/2022-11-29b.html

13 Jeong, S-H., & Hwang, Y. (2016). Media multitasking effects on cognitive vs. attitudinal outcomes: A meta-analysis. *Human Communication Research, 42*(4), 599–618.

14 Carrier, L. M., Rosen, L. D., Cheever, N. A., & Lim, A. F. (2015). Causes, effects, and practicalities of everyday multitasking. *Developmental Review, 35*, 64–78.

15 HomebyAmes. (2020). Battle of the generations: Who's more organized? *ClosetMaid.* https://inspire.homebyames.com/home-organization/battle-of-the-generations-whos-more-organized/

16 Bartolomea, J. (2023). Want to increase employee productivity? Start by defining it. *ClickUp.* https://clickup.com/blog/defining-employee-productivity/

17 Adobe. (2023). *Generational productivity: When are Gen Z, Millennial, Gen X, and Boomer workers most productive?* https://blog.adobe.com/en/publish/2023/04/18/generational-productivity-when-are-gen-z-millennial-gen-x-boomer-workers-most-productive#:~:text=When%20asked%20their%20most%20productive,9am%20—%20than%20any%20other%20generation

18 Wilkins, R. (2022). *8 reasons why many Baby Boomers fail at decluttering.* www.designservicesltd.com/2022/01/13/8-reasons-why-many-baby-boomers-fail-at-decluttering/

19 Weinbach, J. (Director). (2022). *The redeem team* [Film]. The Olympic channel, Kennedy/Marshall Company, and Mandalay Sports Media.

20 Ryan, R. M., & Deci, E. L. (2018). *Self-determination theory.* The Guilford Press.

21 Duckworth, A. (2013). *Grit: The power of passion and perseverance.* www.ted.com/talks/angela_lee_duckworth_grit_the_power_of_passion_and_perseverance?language=en

22 Sanders, S., Gedera, N. I. M., Walia, B., Boudreaux, C., & Silverstein, M. (2022). Does aging make us grittier? Disentangling the age and generation effect on passion and perseverance. *Journal of Data Science, 0*(0), 1–11.

23 Mannheim, K. (1952). The problem of generations. In P. Kecskemeti (Ed.), *Karl Mannheim: Essays*. Routledge.

24 Shatté, A., Perlman, A., Smith, B., & Lynch, W. D. (2017). The positive effect of resilience on stress and business outcomes in difficult work environments. *Journal of Occupational Environmental Medicine, 59*(2), 135–140.

25 Cartwright-Stroupe, & Shinners, J. (2021). Moving forward together: What hope, efficacy, optimism, and resilience tell us about Generation Z. *The Journal of Continuing Education in Nursing, 52*(4), 160–162.

26 Pearcy, A. (2023). *Gen Zers are shutting down accusations that they're 'lazy' by listing all the reasons why they don't want to work*. www.businessinsider.com/gen-z-respo nds-to-accusations-that-theyre-lazy-and-dont-want-to-work-2023-9

27 Cerullo, M. (2023). *With #Quittok, Gen Zers are "loud quitting" their jobs*. www. cbsnews.com/news/quittok-loud-quitting-tik-tok/

28 Kaplan, J. (2023). *Welcome to generation quit*. www.businessinsider.com/gen-z-jobs-generation-quiet-quitting-great-resignation-recession-economy-2023-2

29 Quiambao, L. (2021). Generations engagement survey. *Wrike*. www.wrike. com/blog/generations-engagement-survey/

30 Kane, G. C., Nanda, R., Nguyen Phillips, A., & Copulsky, J. R. (2021). *The transformation myth*. The MIT Press.

31 Seemiller, C., & Grace, M. (2019). *Generation Z: A century in the making*. Routledge.

32 Future Forum. (2022). *Future Forum pulse winter snapshot*. https://futureforum. com/wp-content/uploads/2023/02/Future-Forum-Pulse-Report-Winter-2022-2023.pdf

33 Target. (n.d.). *On demand*. https://jobs.target.com/job/reading/on-demand-guest-advocate-cashier-general-merchandise-fulfillment-food-and-beverage-style-t2529/1118/54718387728#:~:text=As%20an%20On%2DDemand%20 TM%20you%20will%20not%20be%20included,work%20best%20with%20y our%20schedule

34 Pinterest. (n.d.). *Introducing … PinFlex!* www.pinterestcareers.com/en/pinf lex/#:~:text=PinFlex%20promotes%20flexibility%20while%20prioritizing,off ice%2C%20or%20another%20virtual%20location

35 Salesforce. (2021). *New Salesforce research links lower stress levels and business automation*. www.salesforce.com/news/stories/new-salesforce-research-links-lower-stress-levels-and-business-automation/

36 UiPath. (2023). *Automation generation report*. www.uipath.com/assets/downlo ads/uipath-2023-automation-generation-report

37 Tsai, P. (2023). *The AI generation gap: Millennials embrace AI; Boomers are skeptical*. PC Magazine. www.pcmag.com/news/the-ai-generation-gap-millennials-embr ace-ai-boomers-are-skeptical

38 Achievers.com. (2015). *The greatness gap: The state of employee disengagement.* www.achievers.com/wp-content/uploads/2020/10/Greatness-report-FIN AL1.pdf

39 Gallup. (2017). *State of the American workplace.* www.gallup.com/workplace/238085/state-american-workplace-report-2017.aspx

40 Seemiller, C., & Grace, M. (2021). *Global Gen Z.* Unpublished dataset.

Interpersonal Dynamics   **8**

The experiences we have with people we work with can range from being productive and enriching to unproductive and damaging, which can affect both our day-to-day lives as well as our decision to stay or leave a particular job.

Interpersonal dynamics are those factors that "contribute to fulfilling social interactions between individuals and groups."[1] When there are positive dynamics at play, employees experience greater motivation, feel more connected to the organization, and have more intention to stay,[2] as well as have better job performance, satisfaction, and engagement.[3]

What Matters in Workplace Relationships

Sometimes when meeting a new person, things just "click," and an instant connection is formed. This can feel invigorating and enjoyable. Research has found that those who have at least one friend in their workplace are more satisfied, view their job as fulfilling and meaningful, are more excited about their work, and feel more appreciated by others than those who do not.[4] Workplace relationships present an added layer of sensitivity as their dynamics, positive or negative, can be impactful on job performance. Thus, it is helpful to understand what people look for in working with others to assess for compatibility and synergy.

DOI: 10.4324/9781003541035-8

Generational Considerations and Strategies
Friendships at work clearly provide many benefits. However, even if not yet risen to the level of friend, people look to have positive, productive, and collegial relationships. In our Generations in the Workplace study,[5] we found variation in the characteristics vital to cohorts when working with others. Of the seven choices, three were rated highest for "very important."

Table 8.1   *Relational Characteristics Sought by Generational Cohort*

	Baby Boomers	Gen Xers	Millennials	Gen Zers
1	Communication	Trust	Trust	Communication
2	Trust	Accountability	Accountability	Follow-Through* Accountability*
3	Accountability	Communication	Commitment	

*Indicates equal rating of importance.

Accountability

Being accountable includes taking responsibility for one's own actions and impact. It can involve apologizing for any negative outcomes one causes, rectifying a mistake, as well as holding oneself to a standard acceptable for the situation at hand.

Effectively practicing accountability is a way to build and foster trust, as it showcases the willingness to take responsibility and own up to one's mistakes or faults. It also contributes to a workplace free of unethical behavior and corruption.[6] A study of more than 40,000 workers across industries conducted by organizational consulting firm, Culture Partners, found that 82 percent of people try, yet fail at, or avoid altogether holding others accountable.[7] Thus, being able to work with colleagues who can manage their own behaviors takes the burden off of others to do just that.

Generational Considerations and Strategies
Being accountable is the only characteristic we found to be in the top three most important across all cohorts.[5] Given its significance in workplace functioning, it's no surprise. However, how each generation's practice of self-accountability may be born from other underlying characteristics and dispositions related to their cohorts.[5] For instance, Baby Boomers have

more of a need to strictly adhere to ethical standards, which may mean they rely less on external enforcement of policies and procedures. Gen Xers, in an effort to be trusted to do independent work, will likely hold themselves to their own high standards with little follow-up or redirection. Millennials feel a sense of responsibility to others and will want to rectify things after making a mistake, and Gen Zers strive to make a positive impact and will work to remedy any situations where that isn't the case.

Trust

As explored in prior chapters, trust plays a significant role in how people view work and their workplaces. Trust focuses on being able to rely on others and feel a sense of security that they have your best interests in mind.

Generational Considerations and Strategies

The propensity to trust others isn't universal. According to data from the Pew Research Center, 18- to 49-year-olds have lower rates who agree that "in general, most people can be trusted."[8] Thus, it makes sense that older generations need to be able to trust their coworkers. However, while more skeptical, still, 68 percent of Gen Zers indicated that trust is important when working with others.[5]

While workplace culture can model a trusting environment, building interpersonal trust is often an individual endeavor. Ken Blanchard and associates, in their book, *Trust Works!*, put forth the ABCD method for building trust in relationships.[9] He asserts that one must prove that they are Able (develop skills, solve problems, get experience, and help others), Believable (keep promises, admit mistakes, be respectful, and engage in honesty), Connected (listen, share about oneself, give praise, and show interest, empathy, and sensitivity for others), and Dependable (be responsive and accountable, follow through, follow up, and be consistent). Baby Boomers, given their other attributes and preferences previously discussed, may be drawn to using strategies in the Believable category, Gen Xers in the Dependable category, Millennials in the Connected category, and Gen Zers in the Able category. Given this differentiation, members from each cohort may demonstrate their trustworthiness in ways that are unique from how those in other generations might. Thus, it is important to be able to appreciate these differences and understand that while someone may not demonstrate it in the same way, they can still be trustworthy.

Communication

Being able to effectively communicate in the workplace is more critical than ever. So much so that research has found that jobs requiring social interaction grew at a rate of 12 percent between 1980 and 2012.[10] This growth, coupled with the more recent proliferation of additional communication modalities (such as texting, social media messaging, and video chat), has drawn attention to its importance.

Looking more specifically at communicating with coworkers, it's easy to see the benefits. For one, effective communication can lead to forming personal connections and enhancing collegiality, as discussed in the Mindsets chapter. Further, it can help in reducing mistakes, misunderstandings, and even conflict, making it easy to see why it plays such an important role in employee productivity and satisfaction.

Generational Considerations and Strategies

It's no surprise then that communication ranks in the top three for Baby Boomers, Gen Xers, and Gen Zers, and in the fourth spot for Millennials (still at a whopping 85 percent). Being able to communicate with others is a key aspect of interpersonal dynamics at work. But, a study published by The Economist found that the number one factor causing poor communication was having to contend with people's different styles.[11] So, while its importance is shared across generational cohorts, the execution of effective communication can vary.

The Economist study also found that setting meeting goals, providing clear instructions for task completion, offering firm-wide training on communication strategies, and integrating more communication tools could help people work across differences.[11]

Commitment and Follow-through

No one likes to be on the receiving end of someone not doing what they said they would do. That situation can lead to disappointment and an erosion of trust. Although commitment, which is a willingness to take something on or be responsible for something (i.e. a task, role, project), and follow-through, which is a tangible behavior or action that shows if someone has fulfilled a commitment they said they would do, are slightly different, they both foretell a person's ability and/or motivation to see something through.

Generational Considerations and Strategies

Millennials rank commitment as an important factor in workplace relationships, and Gen Zers rank follow through in their top three.[5] Why might this be? For one, both young generations have been plagued by societal systems that have let them down over time – Millennials trying to launch their careers post-recession, and Gen Zers trying to make ends meet during the COVID-19 pandemic. Despite any skepticism, they still want to be able to depend on others.

Perhaps the reason these characteristics did not emerge with the two oldest generations is because commitment and follow-through are simply essential to how work gets done. With Baby Boomers' focus on task orientation, coupled with their loyalty and desire for accomplishment,[5] and Gen Xers' high level of grit[12] and determination,[5] both cohorts may view these behaviors as general workplace expectations.

Building Relationships

There are several ways that people can go about building and fostering relationships with coworkers and colleagues. Some may take more casual approaches, like chatting between meetings or during breaks. Others may prefer to engage in more formal activities, like working on a project together or taking part in workplace gatherings.

Informal Conversations

For those who work onsite, it's nearly impossible to avoid chatting with others at some point throughout one's shift. While some of the talk may be about the job, the discussion may delve into more personal matters – like sharing about travels, family, or hobbies. Research has found that informal conversation in workplaces increases an employee's affective commitment to the organization, job satisfaction, feelings of being informed, and productivity.[13]

Generational Considerations and Strategies

So, which generations partake in informal conversations while working? All of them, with it being the primary way that Baby Boomers, Gen Xers, and Gen Zers, specifically, prefer to build relationships with colleagues. But, don't discount Millennials, as a sizeable number also like this practice.

Encouraging informal conversations at work is important but requires balance. This can be achieved by setting aside a few minutes at the beginning of meetings to catch up. Another strategy includes offering optional regularly scheduled coffee talks where employees gather to chat. Providing some fun questions to get discussions started can be a great way to encourage discussion, but be mindful not to structure the session too much to the point it feels forced or inauthentic.

Spending Time Together at Work

Consider this scenario: It's lunchtime. You grab your leftovers from the employee refrigerator and head to the break room. Do you sit in the corner and eat alone or join a boisterous group of coworkers dining with one another? Before taking that seat, you may want to know that there are actual empirical benefits for joining your colleagues. Having lunch together, for example, can foster a sense of community, belonging, and acceptance, along with helping elicit feelings of confidence and ease.[14] But, some folks just need some recovery time and a true break from their work and might be better served using that downtime in other ways.

Generational Considerations and Strategies
So, who is more likely to socialize at work with their colleagues? Millennials and Baby Boomers more so than Gen Xers and Gen Zers.[5] Given that social interaction between coworkers has its benefits, such as greater trust, cohesion, and collaboration, Millennials and Baby Boomers may want to reach out to others to invite them to join in for lunch. On the other hand, Gen Xers and Gen Zers might find it beneficial to sit with their peers on a periodic basis.

However, it is imperative that employees are given space to make independent choices about how they spend their break time. So, understanding that a quiet Gen Zer who hunkers down with their meal, scrolling their phone, and a Gen Xer, wolfing down food alone at their desk, are engaging in their free time in ways that work for them.

Spending Time Together Outside of Work

Building relationships outside of work allows those who want to foster connections with colleagues to do so while not having socializing interfere with their responsibilities during the workday. It also gives people the opportunity to be more present and focused on relationship building when they gather in an environment away from the day-to-day hustle of the workplace.

People, however, have different preferences for socializing outside of work. Some may enjoy going to dinner or happy hour, whereas others might gather to play in a community softball league or attend an event. Although doing so may seem commonplace, research conducted by the Survey Center on American Life found that more than half of workers in the United States seldomly socialize with coworkers outside of work.[3]

Generational Considerations and Strategies

Aligned with the previous study, we, too, found that the desire to spend time with colleagues was limited. For instance, fewer than half of each cohort indicated preferring to hang out after work or on weekends, leaving a sizeable group who want to reserve that time for other things. That number was considerably lower for Baby Boomers, specifically.

For those who do want to spend time together, when do they prefer to gather? Most would rather get together during the week. For example, tacking on a happy hour or pickleball game to the workday fits better into people's schedules, where they can afford to get home a little later without missing dinner and the evening routine. For those who work remotely, meeting up after the end of the day allows a break from the monotony of sitting for hours.

The weekends, however, are a different story. Meeting up on those days is far more appealing to Millennials and Gen Zers, likely due to their age. Those with no kids won't be pulled in multiple directions as they whisk them from dance and gymnastics to piano and tennis all weekend.

If outside-of-work activities are offered as opportunities to build relationships with coworkers, it is important to set the expectation that these experiences or gatherings are optional. And, if others decide to sit them out, they should be able to do so free from judgment, penalization, or pressure to attend.

Nuanced Relationship Building Strategies

While there is crossover in what people want in working with others, there are some slight nuances unique to different generational cohorts, which may provide insight for better interpersonal relations.

WORKING TOGETHER ON A PROJECT

Whether serving on a committee together, co-coordinating a process, or simply helping one another out with an assignment, there are multiple situations in which people can develop connections through shared task completion.

Generational Considerations and Strategies

Baby Boomers enjoy using project time to develop relationships, which makes sense in that 41 percent cited "being part of a collaborative team" as a factor most important to them when working with others.[5] Their desire for in-person interactions, coupled with their lesser interest in spending time with colleagues outside of work, creates a perfect setup for using projects as relationship builders.

While fewer people in other generations build relationships in this way, it is important that they understand this priority for Baby Boomers. By providing some dedicated social time at the beginning of a task, not only could this help Baby Boomers feel empowered and valued, but those in other generations might also be able to enhance their working relationships with them.

ENGAGING IN PROFESSIONAL DEVELOPMENT TOGETHER

Professional development experiences offer many benefits to participants – knowledge acquisition, upskilling, networking opportunities, and inspiration to refuel for the work ahead. However, attending with coworkers can also prove to be beneficial. For one, younger employees who may be more reluctant to attend can have company to go with. Further, though, being able to, for instance, take part in a multiple-day conference with colleagues can provide time and space to develop personal relationships with them. Perhaps while eating a meal with Susie, you learn that she doesn't like mushrooms. Traveling with Matt makes you realize that he can nap anywhere. And, while chatting with Barb before a session, you get to hear more about her son's upcoming baseball game. Regardless, seeing the more personal side of our coworkers can help us appreciate them more.

Generational Considerations and Strategies

Although Gen Xers often like to navigate their professional development experiences with a mission in mind, as discussed in the Learning and Development chapter, they do put a lot of stock in connecting with others, particularly during networking events and conferences. Thus, it isn't surprising that they want to engage in these types of experiences alongside others. This may be as informal as conversing with a colleague about non-work-related topics while attending a training or as formal as participating in activities that help foster relationships among coworkers, such as uncovering everyone's talent themes through the Gallup's CliftonStrengths program.[15]

To bond with Gen Xers, it may be useful to sign up for a professional development opportunity with them. Not only are there benefits in terms of learning new information for one's job, but it may be a great way to foster a connection with a Generation X coworker. For this cohort, though, it's important to remember that not everyone will want to use these experiences for personal connection. But, it could be helpful to try to engage anyway.

CONNECTING ON SOCIAL MEDIA

Research has found that one-third of employees do not like to connect with coworkers on social media, but for those who do, 50 percent said doing so enhanced their relationship; only 6 percent noting it made it worse.[16] But, the downsides of mixing personal and professional lives include having to censor one's posts or risk being reprimanded or fired for putting something online deemed workplace inappropriate.

Generational Considerations and Strategies
Some people, particularly Millennials and Gen Xers, are open to connecting on social media with colleagues, whereas others may prefer to keep more of a distance between their work and personal lives. To respect this preference, communicating with or following coworkers on social media should be determined by each individual based on their own comfort levels. This includes not pressuring people to connect, which seems to be more of an experience Gen Zers report than do those in other generations.[16]

Collaboration

The definition of collaboration is working with others to achieve a shared goal.[17] Many jobs require collaboration, such as project supervisors, health professionals, and teachers. But, even jobs that don't overtly call for it often need it in some way, whether simply to generate ideas, divvy up work, or launch a new product, service, or initiative.

Generational Considerations and Strategies

So, which generations are the most collaborative? It depends on who you ask. In surveying employees about whether they see themselves as collaborative, the rates vary with Baby Boomers at the lowest end (37 percent), Gen Zers (47 percent) and Gen Xers (54 percent) in the middle, and Millennials on the higher end (66 percent). However, if you ask people which generation they believe is the most collaborative, different answers emerge.[5]

Table 8.2   *Perspectives on Collaborative Generations*

	Baby Boomers	Gen Xers	Millennials	Gen Zers
How Baby Boomers see	89%	79%	55%	40%
How Gen Xers see	79%	92%	78%	65%
How Millennials see	82%	86%	90%	83%
How Gen Zers see	65%	75%	73%	73%

And those perspectives matter, particularly as individuals might not seek out opportunities or even agree to collaborate if they do not have a positive view of others' ability or effectiveness to do so.

The most noticeable trend is that each generation sees the one(s) adjacent to them as the most collaborative (outside of their own). This makes sense in that Baby Boomers, for instance, have worked longer with Gen Xers, and thus have more experience collaborating with them. The same is true in the opposite direction, where Gen Xers have spent their entire careers working alongside Baby Boomers. This adjacency phenomenon holds true for other cohorts as well, in that members of the generation prior often serve as supervisors, managers, and mentors who showcase what preferred team dynamics might look like. Thus, if you can't collaborate with members of your own generation, it's advantageous to do so with those in an adjacent one. The only exception to this observation of adjacency is with Gen Zers who see Gen Xers as slightly more collaborative than Millennials. This may stem from the fact that Generation X is the primary parental generation of Generation Z, and may be the closest adult cohort they know at their age.

On the other hand, it's apparent that the further one cohort is from another, the lower the number of people who believe that cohort is collaborative. For example, only 40 percent of Baby Boomers rate Gen Zers as collaborative. While this is likely due to having fewer opportunities to work together on projects, generational differences in communication preference or work styles can also play a role.

What is important to note is that if there is a perception that other people are as collaborative, it is likely that the group will work more effectively together to achieve shared goals. However, if others are perceived to be less collaborative, anticipation might bubble up at the thought of covering their work.

Trying to find places of collaborative synergy between non-adjacent generations is essential, both for effective organizational functioning as well as for fostering positive interpersonal dynamics. Without it, members of different cohorts might develop resentment or bias toward each other, which can lead to an unwillingness to consider others' perspectives or even diminish the efforts that others put forth. These implications can erode trust between colleagues over time. And while older generations may hold the belief that it is the responsibility of younger ones to adapt to them, not meeting each other in the middle can create a rift within organizations, leading to stalled progress and turnover. To enhance this synergy, it could be helpful to come together to talk about the definition and expectations each person has around collaboration in order to embrace the similarities, appreciate the differences, and agree on a process that works for everyone.

Why Collaborate?

Imagine coming together with a few coworkers to tackle a short-term project. The team sets up all the systems – milestones and progress tracking – as well as creates an agreement that lays out expectations around communication and conflict. Everything is set up for the project to be a success, especially since collaboration often results in enhanced quality, higher productivity, innovation, and greater overall employee satisfaction,[18] While all signs point to the positives of working together, is it even an enjoyable endeavor for everyone? For most people, it actually is.

Generational Considerations and Strategies
Our study uncovered that on the highest end, 91 percent of Millennials enjoy working with others on shared projects, and on the lowest end, 80 percent of Baby Boomers do, despite their desire to use collaboration for getting

to know their colleagues.[5] Let's explore, though, what makes collaboration enjoyable. To find out, we asked our survey participants to select their top three reasons out of ten choices.[5]

Table 8.3   *Top Reasons for Enjoying Collaboration*

	Baby Boomers	Gen Xers	Millennials	Gen Zers
1	Feeling a sense of camaraderie	Interacting with others	Feeling a sense of camaraderie	Interacting with others
2	Sharing the workload	Sharing the workload	Sharing the workload	Getting to hear new ideas and perspectives
3	Getting to hear new ideas and perspectives	Feeling a sense of camaraderie	Getting to hear new ideas and perspectives	Being motivated to get the work done

While there is similarity across generations for some, there was no one universal reason that aligns with members of all cohorts. Let's take a look at some of the more prominent reasons, though, more closely.

FEELING A SENSE OF CAMARADERIE

Camaraderie is "a sense of trust, mutual respect and friendship that exists among colleagues within an organization."[19] It is often fostered through open communication and mutual commitment, and is the result of either close ties for an extended period of time or having endured a specific experience together.[20] You might hear, "Remember that big storm we had that knocked the power out? We had to scramble to finish the project with no electricity!" Or, "That time, when we pitched our new product to the investors, we were so tired from pulling that all-nighter. But, we nailed it." Feelings elicited from camaraderie have the potential to be so strong that the loss of these bonds can be devastating, for example, with athletes after leaving their professional sport.[21]

Generational Considerations and Strategies
Feeling a sense of camaraderie is a primary reason the three oldest generations enjoy collaboration, with it being in the top spot for Baby Boomers and Millennials. By virtue of age, these three cohorts have had more time to work with one another, potentially even having endured

transformative experiences together, to build significant bonds. Because of this, it makes sense that Gen Zers, who have had fewer opportunities to develop camaraderie in the workplace, don't attribute it to being essential to their enjoyment. As these young folks get older and go through more camaraderie-building experiences, they may see its impact on their perspectives on collaboration.

SHARING THE WORKLOAD

The old phrase, "many hands make light work" has been around for centuries for a reason and speaks directly to the benefits of collaboration. Because groups can be more productive and achieve goals faster,[18] thus reducing the individual burden that one person might experience doing a project or task alone, it makes sense that sharing the workload could make collaboration more enjoyable.

Generational Considerations and Strategies

This shared responsibility for work tasks is a top reason that Baby Boomers, Gen Xers, and Millennials cite as to why they enjoy collaboration. Given these older generations likely have a higher number of tasks to accomplish in their more senior positions, being able to split up tasks can lighten their overall workload. This makes sense in that the primary reason all three of these generations indicated not liking group work was because others don't follow through.[5] But, when tasks can truly be distributed equitably, and each person completes their part, the collaborative experience can be positive.

While Baby Boomers, Gen Xers, and Millennials may find joy in the "divide and conquer" approach, it's not lost on Gen Zers, whose greatest concern in collaborating is also lack of follow-through. Perhaps after ample experience, they too will come to recognize the enjoyment that comes from divvying up work, especially when others actually fulfill their responsibilities.

INTERACTING WITH OTHERS

The first couple years of the COVID-19 pandemic threw organizations into frenzies as many had to continue operating either by using remote work or instituting isolating practices, like social distancing, for forward-facing occupations. This time in history elicited feelings of disconnection for many, particularly among young employees who were just entering the workforce. Remote work still has its challenges, specifically around interpersonal interaction. Statistics portal, Statista, reported the top struggles of remote employees being loneliness and difficulty with collaboration.[22] But, it isn't just those who work remotely who feel this. Research has found that 52 percent of employees "want more connection at work."[23]

Generational Considerations and Strategies
Collaborating with others, then, presents an ideal opportunity for interaction. And, that's likely why this reason topped the charts for two generations – Gen Xers and Gen Zers. Although, not exactly the same as camaraderie, which was in a lower spot-on Generation X's list and absent from the one from Generation Z, there is still a human interaction element with this option. Thus, between camaraderie and interaction with others, it's clear that spending time with others makes collaboration enjoyable for members across all generations.

GETTING TO HEAR NEW IDEAS AND PERSPECTIVES

Can you recall an instance when you came into a collaborative process knowing beforehand exactly what the group should do? Maybe you put together some notes or even primed some of the members ahead of time. But, before you got a chance to share your idea, someone else offered a perspective you hadn't considered, greatly impacting your impending suggestion. On the one hand, that experience might seem jarring, since you felt confident that once you shared your thoughts, the team would jump on board. But, there is another part of you that is more informed and enlightened, which would never have happened without being exposed to various new perspectives within a group. That is just one more benefit of collaboration.

Generational Considerations and Strategies
Who finds learning new perspectives enjoyable? Baby Boomers, Millennials, and Gen Zers. However, its absence from Generation X's list is not because they are resistant to new ideas, especially since the vast majority identify as open-minded.[5] Instead, it's simply not an enjoyable process for many of them because it can be time-consuming and stall progress.

Even though most employees want to exchange ideas, there isn't always an opportunity to do so. Thus, it's important that when leading or introducing a project, to create time and space for people to share their perspectives, both to enhance the outcome and because it will make the process more enjoyable for most. But, many Gen Xers don't want to stay in a state of idea generation for long periods, as doing so can make collaboration less gratifying for them. So, be sure to set a specific time block for this on the agenda and stay true to it.

BEING MOTIVATED TO GET THE WORK DONE

Psychological scientists from Stanford found that feeling like you are part of a team makes people more motivated to complete a task or project, leading to greater perseverance, engagement, and performance.[24] And in the event there is a positive outcome, a looping effect could take place where one becomes motivated to accomplish something because of the success of a previous task. So, whether working toward a common goal with others or running with a piece of a larger project, collaborating can be motivating.

Generational Considerations and Strategies
And, it is for Generation Z. Although many are motivated by intrinsic factors,[5] some welcome the pressure that is present with group accountability, driving them to complete their assigned tasks. This sentiment is evidence with words from a Gen Zer who said, "It's easier to motivate myself to do things when people are depending on me."[25]

Knowing this is a desire for Gen Zers, it might be useful for others to use the group process as a motivating experience designed to have a built-in mechanism for accountability for members of this cohort. This includes clarifying roles, tasks, and deadlines, as well as discussing the stakes of the project so that everyone is clear and accountable.

Communication

Whether swapping ideas at a team meeting, providing a weekly update to a supervisor, or interacting with a client or customer, employees must be adept at communicating. Not only can effective communication lead to better collaboration and more efficient processes, being able to communicate well can also enhance relationships and make the workplace more enjoyable. On the other hand, though, poor communication often has severe negative impacts, such as lower levels of productivity and job satisfaction, higher stress levels, and reduced trust with leaders and peers.[26] Thus, effective communication is critical for individual well-being, interpersonal connection, and productive organizational functioning.

Generational Considerations and Strategies

While universally communication is important, members of different generational cohorts have certain preferences in the modalities they like to use in the workplace.[5]

Table 8.4   *Professional Communication Modality Preferences*

	Baby Boomers	Gen Xers	Millennials	Gen Zers
1	In-Person	In-Person	In-Person	Text Messaging
2	Email	Phone	Video Chat*	In-Person*
			Phone*	Email*
3	Phone	Email		
4	Text Messaging	Text Messaging	Text Messaging	Video Chat*
				Phone*
5	Direct Messaging	Direct Messaging	Direct Messaging*	
			Email*	
6	Video Chat	Video Chat		Direct Messaging

*Indicates equal rating of importance.

The largest variance in preference comes with Baby Boomers, whose percentages span a range of 56 percent, highlighting strong partiality of some modalities over others. Conversely, the range for Millennials spans only 8 percent, indicating their relatively consistent preference for all forms of communication. Let's take a look at each, though, to get a better idea of its use in the workplace.

In-Person

In-person conversation is one of the oldest forms of human communication. And, it's clear why it is used so much in the workplace – it has been found to enhance one's mood, boost creativity, as well as stimulate a chemical response that triggers empathy, humor, and trust.[27] Overall, conversing with others is good for employees, and good for organizations.

Generational Considerations and Strategies

In-person conversations are the most preferred way to communicate in workplace environments for the three oldest generations, with rates decreasing with younger cohorts.[5] This makes sense in that many of the modalities we have today were not even around when Baby Boomers and Gen Xers entered into the workforce. There was the telephone, and later on, email. Thus, these two eldest generations have simply had more exposure to and experience in communicating face-to-face. Further, rates of remote work when they began their careers were very low, so much so that the concept of telecommuting was not even coined until 1973.[28] This meant that most employees when Baby Boomers and Gen Xers started out, regardless of duties, had to actually come in person to work.

While in-person conversation ranks higher than most other modalities for Gen Zers, the percentage who indicate it as a preference is considerably lower than it is for those in other cohorts. This may be attributed to several factors – the proliferation of technology, which has expanded choices for communication modalities, greater opportunities for remote work, and the impact of COVID-19 on their schooling and professional lives, which limited their ability to connect in-person. In addition, this generation has spent less time engaging face-to-face with others over their lifetimes, likely impacting their lower levels of confidence and competence related to interpersonal interaction.[29]

Providing opportunities for Gen Zers to develop their skills and comfort with face-to-face communication is critical. Consider offering social events, workplace buddies or mentors, and trainings on interpersonal communication. However, just calling them back to the office with the hope that doing so makes them better communicators misses the intentionality of skill development that could greatly benefit some in this generation. And, for those in older cohorts, it's essential to be aware of any communication issues Gen Zers are facing. Consider helping them develop skills by engaging them in practices that lead them to feel more competent and confident when speaking with others.

Further, with all generations, integrating in-person conversations into the fabric of the organizational culture should take a balanced approach. Not enough face-to-face interaction can lead to disconnection and miscommunication. However, too much can lead to distraction and decreased productivity, especially if some work activities require individual focus. And, studies have found that those with a greater number meetings per week experience more signs of burnout.[30] So, like with Gen Zers, the key is to create a culture that intentionally serves people's desire to communicate in-person while also acknowledging that not every interaction needs to be face-to-face.

Video Chat

Prior to the mid-1990s, video-based conferencing was only available in high-tech environments. It wasn't until platforms like Skype in 2005, Apple's FaceTime in 2010, and Zoom in 2011, emerged that video chat was available to everyday users. Since its launch, Zoom has become the most widely used video platform with over 640 million worldwide users[31] and makes up over half of the videoconferencing market share in the United States.[32]

Generational Considerations and Strategies

Of all cohorts, Millennials resonate most with video chat, followed by Gen Zers and then Gen Xers. Very few Baby Boomers prefer this modality. In thinking about when video platforms came about, it was right around the time many Millennials were entering the workforce. It was new, interesting, and novel. These young people were ready to jump right in and use it. And, they did. In 2016, 52 percent of 18–34-year-olds, who were mostly Millennials, were using the video features on their phones for chat.[33] Thus, this is a technology many are comfortable with and continue to use today.

While the rates are slightly lower for those in Generation Z, they are still noteworthy. This is a cohort that grew up FaceTiming their grandparents and watching and curating their own videos on YouTube. They, too, feel a sense of familiarity with this technology. Fast forward to the COVID-19 pandemic, which shifted much of their school and early professional experiences to remote settings. At the time, video chatting was the only means of communication people could use to see each other's faces. With these societal factors, it is not surprising that Millennials and Gen Zers are more likely to prefer video chat than older generations are.

However, the very low numbers of Baby Boomers who prefer this modality might create a stark contrast for Gen Zers and Millennials eager to jump on a video call. It's important, then, that younger workers appreciate that the majority of their older counterparts' careers did not involve talking into a webcam.

Aside from the technical learning that is necessary to adopt any new invention, utilizing a novel tool requires a mindset shift to embrace all that it has to offer. But, Baby Boomers who are using video chat are doing so to emulate the exact flow of an in-person conversation and not a dynamic virtual conference. For example, according to research collected by Zoom, Baby Boomers are the most likely to have their cameras on, thus emulating a familiar face-to-face environment.[34] They also don't like emojis, gifs, or waving goodbye with an interactive icon at the end of calls. So, when video chatting with a Baby Boomer, it might make them more comfortable if others refrained from using potentially distracting bells and whistles so that instead, the experience feels just like an in-person interaction for them.

Phone

Whether it was connecting through a party line, dialing on the rotary phone, chatting on the cordless, or reaching out through a smartphone, the concept of using the phone has never quite changed. You call someone and have a verbal conversation in real-time without having to be in the vicinity of the person you are talking with.

Just like phones have changed over the years, so has phone messaging systems. The advent of the answering machine made it possible to step out and not miss a call, listening to the recording once you return. And, today, voicemail can be checked from anywhere at any time, enhancing convenience.

However, the transition from landline office phones to work-issued cell phones has made it even more challenging to separate one's personal and professional lives. What once entailed leaving job-related duties at work now has shifted to employees essentially being on call 24 hours a day, tethered to their phones.

Generational Considerations and Strategies
Many Baby Boomers grew up with the one family rotary in the hallway, making calls more of a rarity than an everyday activity. Whereas, both middle generations spent their childhoods talking to friends late at night, using the phone as a lifeline to their social lives. Gen Zers, on the other hand, have had unprecedented access to their own devices, with their upbringing

inundated with calls. Thus, it's no surprise that Millennials, Gen Xers, and Gen Zers prefer phone calls more so than Baby Boomers. The telephone was a critical part of their formative years.

It's important to note that the difference in preference in using phone calls for work has the potential to create frustration if navigated improperly. For instance, Baby Boomers may feel a call is too impersonal and instead suggest a face-to-face option, which could make others annoyed if the outcome could have been achieved through a quick call. Knowing your audience and reaching out to them how they prefer can help ease any tension around communication expectations and get the information exchanged promptly.

But, the best approach may simply be to set expectations for the organization, unit, team, and even between coworkers and with supervisors. In what cases might a call be the most useful modality compared to a message? Perhaps for complex or emotional topics that couldn't otherwise be put in writing. However, voice memos, which allow people to leave short asynchronous audio updates for each other, providing a more convenient alternative for someone who may not be available to answer the phone at a specific time.[35]

Further, if you know someone won't answer their phone or check their voice mail but the conversation warrants more than a written message, simply text them and say, "Are you available for a quick call about this issue?" That way, when the phone rings, the person may just answer.

Email

Since it was first introduced in the late 1980s and early 1990s, email has become a mainstay in the workplace. Email, however, is not just a communication modality; it is also a way we do business. So much so, that research has found that most employees spend 15 percent of their work week emailing[36] and send an average of 112 emails per week.[37]

Generational Considerations and Strategies

Preferences for email are highest with Millennials and Gen Xers, dropping in popularity with Gen Zers and even more so with Baby Boomers. So, why do the middle generations like email? These are people, who as teens and young adults, watched Tom Hanks and Meg Ryan in *You've Got Mail*. Gen Xers had their AOL accounts, while Millennials were on Hotmail.

Both remember the buzzing dial-up as the precursor sound to accessing an inbox filled with messages from friends near and far. Thus, it was a standard "coming-of-age" technology that marked both generations' entrance into the workforce.

For Baby Boomers, on the other hand, learning how to use email required intentional effort as they were midway through their careers when this technology came about. While some jumped on board embracing it, others saw it as a necessary evil they had to master for survival in contemporary workplaces. And, that sentiment hasn't fully changed for some. For instance, research has found that nearly half of them view email as the top distraction during the workday.[38]

In regard to the youngest, Gen Zers have been privy to other modalities, like text, social media, and direct messaging, for much of their lives. With the speed and accessibility of those, email to them seems slow and clunky.

While preferences may vary, what's interesting is that across all generations, there is a higher percentage of those who report actually using email than those who prefer to use it.[5] Perhaps, in time, email will be phased out for lack of interest. For now, though, it is still very much embedded in our organizational cultures. And, given the variation in preference for using it, coupled with the notion that it isn't a modality that is one of the most preferred for any cohort, changing the dynamic around using email could help people be more embracing of it. Let's look at some strategies that might be beneficial. According to Colin Ellis from the Harvard Business Review, email should only be used for certain tasks – to communicate a decision, schedule or confirm meetings, document a conversation, or send a mass announcement.[39] Instead, he says that if you want to make a convincing argument, do so in person or on video chat. Quick check-ins should be conducted through messaging. And, for clarifying information, phone works best. Keeping these ideas in mind, regardless of preferences, could diffuse any confusion or tension that arises from the overabundance of emails.

Text Messaging

When T9 texting came on the scene in the mid-1990s, it was all the rage. Within a few years, people had their Motorola or Nokia flip phones and were pressing keys to send written messages through their phone lines. But, with the advent of the smart phone and its integration of a digital keypad on the screen, texting became faster and easier. This technology revolutionized the workforce. It was now possible to send a quick update from a device in your pocket, which meant that business could be done around the clock. And, with response rates being considerably higher for texts than emails,[40] it makes sense why so many people use messaging in their workplaces.

Generational Considerations and Strategies

Just around half of those in the three youngest generations like text messaging for work-related issues. But, numbers drop off with Baby Boomers, where fewer than one in four like it. Again, this may be explained by the fact that younger generations report having higher rates of adoption of new technology.[41] While texting isn't new to them, per se, those in older generations have had to make a conscious effort to learn how to do it and then embrace it as a workplace modality.

Those in Generation Z like texting above all other communication modalities. Why might that be? For one, as discussed earlier in the book, they see themselves as multi-taskers, which works well with texting – reply to their coworker's question about the location for the staff meeting, send a message to their supervisor letting her know the final report has been submitted, and then jump into a thread with the project team to ask for clarification on a deadline. All this can be accomplished while doing ten other things – at least that's what some try to do. In addition to helping with multitasking, text messaging allows Gen Zers to avoid uncomfortable or lengthy interpersonal interactions, since many report lacking the skills to have those types of conversations.[28]

However, using text messages to communicate about work-related matters can blur the line between one's personal life and professional life. And, most Baby Boomers are not interested in that. Even some younger employees aren't. So, it is important to be mindful to establish with everyone whether, and to what extent, texting is used for professional matters and if it is appropriate to text after hours. Unless it is required for the job, honoring each person's desire in using text messaging for work is critical to fostering a supportive and trusting team.

Direct Messaging

Direct messaging (DM), sometimes called Instant Messaging (IM), involves sending a short note to a recipient through a web-based platform such as

Google Chat (GChat), Microsoft Teams, or a project management tool such as Slack. People are "pinged" throughout the day as new messages come in, and entire conversations can be had as users type back and forth. There are great benefits of using DM in the workplace – real-time conversation, more informal channel to discuss issues, and quick response times.

While professional platforms are the primary place where work-related messaging occurs, DMs can also be sent through social media apps like Instagram, Facebook, TikTok, Snapchat, and WhatsApp. It may seem like these places should be reserved for personal use, however more companies today are actually using them to track down workers and send reminders.[42]

Generational Considerations and Strategies

DM is most preferred by Millennials, but Gen Xers and Gen Zers also welcome this method of communication. Given that Millennials grew up communicating through early IM platforms, such as AOL Instant Messenger, it is not surprising that they have continued to use messaging apps in their working years. And, many see them as valuable. For example, research has found that 42 percent of Millennials feel like their chat apps at work make them more productive, a greater number than those in other generations.[43]

Like email, there is a higher percentage across all four cohorts who use DMs in the workplace than actually would like to.[5] This may be particularly noteworthy in that if these DMs are coming through their personal social media accounts, there may be some hesitation or even resentment for this modality. On the other hand, DMs are quick and are often built into professional platforms that organizations are already using, making them convenient and easy to access and utilize. Thus, it is likely the usage rates will increase despite preferences.

If an option for direct messaging is not in place, organizational leaders should explore providing this to workers, especially younger ones who are more prone to use it. However, given that 34 percent of employees would like to disable their chat apps at work,[42] mostly due to how distracting they can be, one idea is to implement "ping" etiquette to reduce the most common pet peeves such as too many emojis, oversharing, looping more people in than need to be, sending irrelevant messages, and saturating a thread with chatter. Further, the sound of a notification going off every few seconds can be overwhelming and annoying.

Some tips to address these issues include having message-free work times to eliminate distractions, reducing the propensity to send off-topic messages, being intentional about only "looping in" only those who need to be, putting longer information-sharing pieces into email, and trying to find the answer to something first before pinging someone for it.

With these etiquette tips in mind, perhaps those more prone to use DMs will not overdo it or turn off others who aren't interested in communicating in this manner. On the other hand, DMs are here to stay. So, it might be useful for Baby Boomers, in particular, to learn a few strategies and jump into these platforms as well.

Social Media Use

Social media plays a prominent role in how people connect, presenting another option for interaction and communication among employees. Some, however, use work time to check their personal Facebook or Instagram accounts, pulling themselves away from their actual duties. Thus, many organizations have created policies that outline the use of social media during work hours as well as what can and cannot be shared online.

But, using social media at work does have its upsides. Employees can use it to network, recruit for open positions, showcase achievements, advertise events, get information about work-related issues, and bond with coworkers.[44]

Generational Considerations and Strategies

All generations utilize social media for professional purposes. However, Millennials and Gen Zers have the highest usage rates, whereas Baby Boomers have the lowest.[5] These patterns make sense due to younger cohorts' higher rates of technology adoption.[40] But, not all apps are equal, particularly across generations.[5] Let's look at what each cohort is using and for what purposes.

Table 8.5   *Professional Uses of Social Media*

	Baby Boomers	Gen Xers	Millennials	Gen Zers
To Share Personal Info	Facebook	Facebook	Facebook	Facebook
To Share Expertise	LinkedIn	Facebook	Facebook	Instagram
To Follow Others	Facebook	Facebook	Instagram	Instagram
To Learn	YouTube	YouTube	YouTube	YouTube

While Facebook is the go-to across all generations for sharing personal information and YouTube for learning, there is some variance in other categories, particularly in sharing expertise and following others.[5]

It's important, though, to point out that these trends are related to social media use for professional purposes rather than social ones. For personal reasons, Gen Zers, for example, are primarily on Snapchat and Instagram for sharing personal information and expertise as well as to follow others.[24]

While the idea of a social media policy may create tension in the workplace, having one could help employees identify what is appropriate to post. Further, though, it might be useful to come up with an organization-wide strategy for employees to use their personal social media accounts to advance the work of the company. This wouldn't be mandated, however, providing marketing templates for an upcoming event that employees could share out might help with branding and outreach for the organization as a whole.

Conclusion

Regardless of one's occupation, having to navigate interpersonal dynamics is a workplace reality. And, while there are similarities in how this is done, each cohort has its own unique views and approaches that necessitate broader understanding from others. Beyond appreciation, though, there are strategies that could be useful to build relationships, communicate more effectively, and maximize interactions across generations. Employing these can yield benefits, such as job satisfaction, productivity, and goal achievement, for organizations and individuals alike.

Notes

1 Beenen, G., Fiori, M., Pichler, S., & Riggio, R. (2023). Editorial: Interpersonal skills: individual, social, and technological implications. *Frontiers in Psychology*, *14*, 1–3.

2 Cameron, K., Mora, C., Leutscher, T., & Calarco, M. (2011). Effects of positive practices on organizational effectiveness. *The Journal of Applied Behavioral Science*, *47* (3), 266–308.

3 Braha, M., & Karabulut, A.T. (2023). Energizing workplace dynamics" Exploring the nexus of relational energy, humor, and PsyCap for enhanced engagement and performance. *Behavioral Sciences*, *14*(1), 23.

4 Orrell, B., Cox, D.A., & Wall, J. (2022). *The social workplace: Social capital, human dignity, and work in America*. www.americansurveycenter.org/research/the-soc ial-workplace-social-capital-human-dignity-and-work-in-america/

5 Seemiller, C., & Grace, M. (2023). *Generations in the workplace.* Unpublished dataset.

6 Ghanem, K. A. (2022). Leadership self-accountability to prevent corruption in the workplace. *Open Access Library Journal, 9*, 1–21.

7 Culture Partners, (2019). *Landmark workplace study reveals crisis of accountability.* https://culturepartners.com/insights/landmark-workplace-study-reveals-crisis-of-accountability/

8 Pew Research Center. (2020). *Younger people less likely to say most people can be trusted.* www.pewresearch.org/short-reads/2020/12/03/social-trust-in-advanced-economies-is-lower-among-young-people-and-those-with-less-education/ft_2020-12-03_internationaltrust_02-png/

9 Blanchard, K., Olmstead, C., & Lawrence, M. (2013). *Trust works! Four keys to building lasting relationships.* Polvera Publishing and Cynthia Olmstead.

10 Deming, D. (2017). The growing importance of social skills in the labor market. *Quarterly Journal of Economics, 132*(4), 1593–1640.

11 The Economist Intelligence Unit. (2018). Communication barriers in the modern workplace. *The Economist.* https://impact.economist.com/perspectives/sites/default/files/EIU_Lucidchart-Communication%20barriers%20in%20the%20modern%20workplace.pdf

12 Sanders, S., Gedera, N. I. M., Walia, B., Boudreaux, C., & Silverstein, M. (2022). Does aging make us grittier? Disentangling the age and generation effect on passion and perseverance. *Journal of Data Science, 20*(3), 401–411.

13 Koch, T., & Denner, N. (2022). Informal communication in organizations: work time wasted at the water-cooler or crucial exchange among co-workers? *Emerald Insight.* www.researchgate.net/publication/357971915_Informal_communication_in_organizations_work_time_wasted_at_the_water-cooler_or_crucial_exchange_among_co-workers

14 Bosch, C., Sonnentag, S., & Pinck, A. S. (2018). What makes for a good break? A diary study on recovery experiences during lunch break. *Journal of Occupational and Organizational Psychology, 91*, 134–157.

15 Gallup. (2019). *The CliftonStrengths movement continues to accelerate.* www.gallup.com/cliftonstrengths/en/253754/history-cliftonstrengths.aspx#:~:text=More%20than%2090%25%20of%20Fortune,development%20to%20their%20workplace%20culture

16 Koebert, J., & McNally, C. (2023). *Social media in the workplace: 1 out of 3 prefer not to connect with co-workers on social media.* allaboutcookies.org/social-media-in-the-workplace#bottom-line

17 Indeed. (2022). *Collaborate vs. cooperate: Definitions and differences.* www.indeed.com/career-advice/career-development/collaborate-vs-cooperate

18 Deloitte Access Economics. (2014). *The collaborative economy.* www.deloitte. com/content/dam/Deloitte/au/Documents/Economics/deloitte-au-econom ics-collaborative-economy-google-170614.pdf

19 Evotix. (2023). *7 ways camaraderie enhances workplace health and safety.* www.evo tix.com/resources/blog/7-ways-camaraderie-enhances-workplace-health-and-safety

20 Collins Dictionary. (n.d.). *Camaraderie.* www.collinsdictionary.com/us/diction ary/english/feeling-of-camaraderie#:~:text=Camaraderie%20is%20a%20feel ing%20of,some%20kind%20of%20experience%20together

21 Senecal, G. (2017). Solidarity and camaraderie – A psychosocial examination of contact sport athletes' career transitions. *Cogent Business & Management, 4*(1), 1–15.

22 Statista. (2024). *Struggles with working remotely worldwide from 2020–2023.* www. statista.com/statistics/1111316/biggest-struggles-to-remote-work/

23 BetterUp. (2022). Why community matters in the new world of work. https:// grow.betterup.com/resources/build-a-culture-of-connection-report

24 Carr, P. B., & Walton, G. M. (2014). Cues of working together fuel intrinsic motivation. *Journal of Experimental Social Psychology, 53,* 169–184.

25 Seemiller, C., & Grace, M. (2021). *Global Gen Z.* Unpublished dataset.

26 Hoory, L., & Main, K. (2023). *The state of workplace communication in 2024.* www. forbes.com/advisor/business/digital-communication-workplace/

27 Harter, J. (2023). How important is time in the office? *Gallup.* www.gallup.com/ workplace/468599/important-time-office.aspx

28 Gan, V., & CityLab. (2015). What telecommuting looked like in 1973. *The Atlantic.* www.theatlantic.com/technology/archive/2015/12/what-teleco mmuting-looked-like-in-1973/418473/

29 Seemiller, C., & Grace, M. (2019). *Generation Z: A century in the making.* Routledge.

30 Atlassian. (2022). *The state of teams.* www.atlassian.com/blog/state-of-teams-2022

31 Statista. (2023). *Total global visitor traffic to Zoom.us 2023.* www.statista.com/sta tistics/1259905/zoom-website-traffic/

32 Emailtooltester.com. (2023). *The most popular video call conferencing platforms worldwide.* www.emailtooltester.com/en/blog/video-conferencing-market-share/#Zoom_zooms_ahead_as_it_is_revealed_as_the_most_popular_vide o_call_platform

33 Circana. (2016). *52 percent of Millennial smartphone owners use their device for video calling, according to the NPD group.* https://connected-intelligence.com/about-us/press-releases/52-percent-millennial-smartphone-owners-use-their-device-video-calling

34 Zoom. (2023). *Here's how you used Zoom in 2022.* www.zoom.com/en/blog/ how-you-used-zoom-2022/

35 Zajechowski, M. (2024). *Voice notes may be the new phone call, according to 40% of Americans.* https://preply.com/en/blog/voice-notes-on-the-rise/

36 Microsoft. (2023). *Work trend index annual report.* www.microsoft.com/en-us/worklab/work-trend-index/will-ai-fix-work

37 Slack.com. (2023). *Swap email for Slack: How to save employees 11 hours a week.* slack.com/intl/en-gb/blog/productivity/save-employees-time

38 Vohra, R. (2021). *The state of your inbox in 2021: email burnout and browsing in bed.* blog.superhuman.com/the-state-of-your-inbox-in-2021/#METHODOLOGY

39 Ellis, C. (2021). Stop. Does that really need to be an email? *Harvard Business Review.* https://hbr.org/2021/03/stop-does-that-message-really-need-to-be-an-email

40 Pemberton, C. (2016). *Tap into the marketing power of SMS.* www.gartner.com/en/marketing/insights/articles/tap-into-the-marketing-power-of-sms

41 Vogels, E. A. (2019). *Millennials stand out for their technology use, but older generations also embrace digital life.* Pew Research Center. www.pewresearch.org/short-reads/2019/09/09/us-generations-technology-use/

42 Blum, S. (2021). *The companies sliding into workers' personal DMs.* www.bbc.com/worklife/article/20210715-the-companies-sliding-into-workers-personal-dms

43 Nulab Staff. (2023). *Do team chats make us more or less productive?* https://nulab.com/learn/collaboration/work-chat-distractions-do-work-instant-messengers-make-us-more-or-less-productive/

44 Ahmad, M. B., Hussain, A., & Ahmad, F. (2022). The use of social media at work place and its influence on the productivity of the employees in the era of COVID-19. *Springer Nature, 2*(10), 156.

Management and Supervision

9

Although the words are often used interchangeably, management and supervision offer two distinct functional purposes. Managers have an external focus on the direction of an organization and often oversee others who do different tasks than they do. Supervisors, on the other hand, usually do similar work as subordinates, directing their day-to-day duties and serve as "the link between higher management and the organization's workforce."[1] Both play significant roles in an employee's work life, with managers shaping the larger culture and supervisors influencing their everyday experiences.

Management

The study of management goes back decades, with early scholars putting forth theories to help explain how organizations function.[2] Classical theory, which reflects management practices common during the early 1900s, is centered on hierarchies, structures, incentives, standardization, and centralization. The idea is that processes and protocols ensure efficiency, productivity, and accuracy. Behavioral theory, which emerged in the mid-twentieth century, is all about people rather than strict standard operating procedures. It assumes that motivation, interpersonal relationships, communication, group dynamics, and mutual respect affect how efficient and productive workers are. Modern theory, which came about later on, incorporates both the structural focus from Classical theory, often through the use of technology, and the people approach from Behavioral theory,

DOI: 10.4324/9781003541035-9

which may include flexible scheduling, autonomy, benefits, and other employee perks.

Generational Considerations and Strategies

It makes sense that organizations would pay great attention to the human side of work, given the benefits like employee retention and productivity.[3] In order for workers to stay and maximize their efforts, they want to feel valued, invested in, and heard. But not everyone does.[4]

Table 9.1 *Personal Experiences in the Workplace by Generation*

	Baby Boomers	Gen Xers	Millennials	Gen Zers
The leadership in my organization is invested in my success.	22%	42%	47%	34%
I am valued for what I bring to my workplace.	31%	39%	46%	34%
I am encouraged to share my opinions with those in leadership roles.	22%	37%	46%	34%

These numbers can tell us a lot about how each generation experiences leadership in their organizations. For example, there is a clear lack when it comes to Baby Boomers on all measures. This is a cohort that values loyalty and has given nearly their entire lives to their industry, and for some, the same organization. So, when working with a Baby Boomer, it's critical to ensure that they are reminded of their value, appreciated for their contributions, and sought out for their years of experience. Not only can that be empowering to Baby Boomers, but their impact on the workplace could be even more monumental if they felt more support and engagement from management.

Gen Zers' rates on all measures were not much higher. This young cohort might lack the decades of wisdom to tap into, but they still want to feel like their contributions and voices matter. To assist them in better connecting to the organization, invite them to participate in visioning sessions, ask for their input, and help them create professional development plans that invest in their success now and in the future.

Overall, with low numbers across the board, managers may need to consider options that help support, value, and listen to all employees. Consider Target Corporation, which emerged in the number one spot on the 2022 PEOPLE® Companies That Care list from Great Place to Work.[5] Eighty-one percent of employees indicated feeling welcome at Target, 77 percent said they were given a lot of responsibility, and 76 percent felt they were treated as a full member, regardless of position. In addition, the company touts their high wages, tuition benefits, extensive physical and mental health coverage, time off policies, and discounts on fitness fees, pet insurance, and childcare.[6] The culture of this retail giant is to ensure that everyone feels cared for, valued, respected, and recognized.

Supervision

Similar to the historical trajectory of management theory, what constitutes effective supervision has evolved over time. In the early 1900s, supervisors would assign, direct, and monitor work. A century later, most rely on employees to serve as subject matter experts in areas they lack. Thus, the power dynamic has shifted in that subordinates with specialty knowledge crucial to the organization often have more say in where, when, and how they work, which changes the nature of the supervisory relationship.

Who Supervises Who?

While there is vast diversity in terms of what a supervisor looks like, some may think of Michael Scott from *The Office*, Miranda Priestly from *The Devil Wears Prada*, Dr. Richard Webber from *Grey's Anatomy*, or Bill Lumbergh from *Office Space* – all famous on-screen bosses who are older, experienced, and exude confidence.

Generational Considerations and Strategies
However, not all supervisors are the epitome of their TV and movie counterparts. For instance, 62 percent of Millennials and 49 percent of Gen Zers have direct reports,[7] making younger bosses more commonplace. And not all are self-assured. For example, Gen Zers are twice as likely as those in older generations to lack confidence in their leadership ability and are significantly more worried about failing as a supervisor.[8]

For both Millennials and Gen Zers who aren't in supervisory roles, their reluctance and disinterest in supervising others stems from a lack of trust in management, not wanting to take on more stress for a nominal increase in pay, and a desire to maintain work–life balance.[9] Through attrition of older employees, along with organizational succession planning efforts, even those younger workers not as keen on progressing toward supervisory positions eventually will.

Offering mentorship and training programs could be helpful in developing their skills, confidence, and comfort, even before they step into any oversight role. Some examples include Macy's Executive Development Program for recent college graduates, which is designed to help them learn about the retail industry and offers them mentorship from leaders within the organization.[10] Marriott, International's program offers training to enhance transferable skills for future leadership roles, along with opportunities to enhance work–life balance. Both are examples of how businesses are preparing their own employees for internal advancement.

In addition, being a supervisor must have its tangible benefits, or young employees simply won't be interested. Taking on a higher-level role warrants significant salary adjustments to compensate for the increased workload and stress, as well as an organizational commitment to support work–life balance. This may include more paid time off as well as ensuring limited overtime expectations to cover for absent subordinates.

Another issue born from the proliferation of young people in supervisory roles relates to who they oversee. With 43 percent of employees over 35 having a younger boss,[11] this age difference can create some discomfort for older individuals, particularly when a less experienced supervisor thinks they know more by virtue of their position. Further, when an older employee is bypassed by a younger one for a higher-level role, it can be a hit to the ego, which could elicit negative emotions, such as fear and anger.[12]

There are many actions that can help reduce the discomfort and negativity of older employees in this situation. First, Baby Boomers, as discussed earlier, want to feel valued and heard. In supervising a Baby Boomer, it's essential to validate the years of experience and wisdom they have by asking their opinion, learning about the context of decision-making made in the past, and inviting them to contribute ideas. Younger supervisors should avoid acting like they know more than them – especially if they don't and are only asserting power to establish authority.

And, with Gen Xers being independent, they have often done a specific task successfully for quite some time. Changing up a process on them, particularly without getting their feedback, can result in some resistance.

However, younger supervisors can also feel discomfort, fearing their older subordinates will create unnecessary obstacles, not take feedback well, or won't upskill when needed. So, Baby Boomers and Gen Xers reporting to those who are younger need to understand that their boss may have some good insight as well, even without the same years of experience, and that they had been elevated to the position due to their track record. In order for everyone in this situation to work together effectively, it's helpful to keep an open mind and put aside egos.

Roles of a Supervisor

While supervisors can and often engage in many roles in an organization, what is considered most essential varies – particularly by generational cohort.

Generational Considerations and Strategies

In our Generations in the Workplace study, participants were asked to select the three most important roles of a supervisor from 14 choices.[4]

Table 9.2 *Roles of a Supervisor by Generation*

	Baby Boomers	Gen Xers	Millennials	Gen Zers
1	Create a team atmosphere among employees	Set measurable goals for employees	Follow up on employee work	Follow up on employee work
2	Solve problems	Create a team atmosphere among employees	Set measurable goals for employees	Set measurable goals for employees
3	Listen to concerns and ideas	Follow up on employee work	Create a team atmosphere among employees	Create a team atmosphere among employees

Creating a team atmosphere appears in the top three most important roles for all four generations, indicating a need for employees across all cohorts to feel a sense of belonging, unity, and collaboration with others.

There are, however, some nuances, both in the ranking and presence of some of the other items. This disparity could potentially bring challenges to the supervisory relationship, as both the boss and employee hold their own views of what constitutes the most important roles of a supervisor.

Let's see this in action. Gen Zer, Jonah, might expect more follow-up than his boss, Gen Xer, Lisa, provides – especially since Gen Xers like follow-up as a way to get information and resources from their supervisors and not for their supervisors to consistently check in on the progress of a project. While Lisa may be trying to give autonomy and space for Jonah to take ownership of his work, the lack of checking in could be perceived by Jonah as an absence of support. Or, Millennial, Abby, may end up closely overseeing the day-to-day tasks of Baby Boomer, Ted, leading him to feel like he is being micromanaged when Abby's intention is to come across as supportive and invested in Ted's work.

Some ideas to help strengthen intergenerational supervisory relationships include establishing clear agreed-upon expectations, ensuring open lines of communication, and asking employees what roles they want their supervisors to fill and then responding accordingly.

Key Behaviors of an Effective Supervisor

In addition to roles, there are also key behaviors that effective supervisors employ to help employees thrive. Let's take a look at some of them and how they might play out between members of different generational cohorts.

DEVELOPING RELATIONSHIPS

Almost everyone is able to recall a time they had a boss who simply lacked interpersonal skills. Whether only causing disconnection and tension or resulting in a full-blown toxic workplace, the lack of a functional supervisor–supervisee relationship can create challenging dynamics for employees. On the other hand, a supportive, respectful supervisor can be the reason an employee stays and thrives in their job.

We can better understand this dynamic by looking at the Leader–Member Exchange (LMX) theory, which essentially asserts that leaders have different types of relationships depending on the follower.[13] With some, they have stronger bonds; with others, they have weaker ones or none at all. And, in some cases, bonds exist but are negative. Because of this, an in-group and out-group can form; those with stronger positive bonds find themselves in the in-group with the leader, often receiving more opportunities and resources than those in the out-group who have weaker, negative, or no bonds at all.

Let's examine who becomes a part of the in-group. After interviewing frontline supervisors and middle managers about LMX, researchers found it's those who demonstrate competence, can effectively communicate, and are in alignment with the supervisor's goals who most often become a part of the in-group.[14]

Generational Considerations and Strategies

However, LMX can be influenced by age.[15] For instance, in cases where the age gap between leaders and subordinates is smaller, the LMX relationship is stronger, at least from the perspective of the subordinate. On the contrary, the bigger the age gap, the lesser the quality of the LMX relationship. This makes sense in that the two cohorts may not have much in common due to their life and career stage differences. However, this disparity can also be attributed to the different communication preferences, motivations, and productivity approaches of each generation, as described in earlier chapters. For instance, if one generation is motivated one way, and another is motivated a different way, there is cause for disconnect between members.

There are ways, however, to enhance LMX relationships across age gaps. Finding commonalities, particularly outside of their jobs, may help connect the supervisor and supervisee. For example, Jared, a Gen Zer could stop by his boss's office to tell her about a new hike he went on that weekend, knowing that Kerry is an outdoor enthusiast. The two don't need to hike together after hours, but perhaps they form a bond around their common interest, which could bring them closer.

Supervisors also want displays of competence and open communication from their employees. In this case, Jared could make sure that he shows Kerry that he can be trusted to do good work while keeping her up-to-date on his projects.

Demonstrating Kindness

Think about how it feels to have another driver cut you off in traffic, only to glare at you after doing so. Or having a colleague make a rude comment about your work in a meeting. These behaviors don't help you be a better driver or a more productive team member. They just tend to bring down the mood. The alternative can have an opposite effect – someone who lets you in while merging lanes of traffic or a coworker complimenting your idea often results in a more uplifting attitude about the situation. That's why many employees note kindness as being a fundamental behavior for supervisors.[16] There are many benefits of kindness in the workplace – retention, engagement, and productivity.[17] That's because receiving kind words or gestures helps people feel more fulfilled, increases their self-esteem, and releases neurotransmitters in the brain that can lead to feeling good. Books such as Kindness in Leadership[18] and Kindness Mindset in Leadership,[19] highlight how important this topic is for organizational leaders.

Generational Considerations and Strategies
In 2015, hundreds of thousands of individuals had completed the VIA Survey of Strengths. From this data set, researchers found that kindness was one of the five highest-rated self-described strengths (of 24) for Baby Boomer, Generation X, and Millennial cohorts.[20] A follow-up dataset of more than 150,000 Gen Zers from 2018 showcased kindness in the top five for Gen Zers as well.[21] Thus, members across all generations see themselves as kind.

Being Likeable

Related to kindness, "likership" describes the extent to which people have positive feelings for and generally liking, enjoying working with, valuing the relationship with, and being happy with their supervisors.[22] It's been found that workers who experience factors related to greater likership for their bosses have higher levels of happiness, well-being, performance, and productivity, as well as associate them with more positive views of leadership.[21]

Generational Considerations and Strategies
The importance placed on the likeability of a supervisor, though, can vary by generation. For example, a greater number of Millennials and Gen Xers, compared to Baby Boomers and Gen Zers, note likeability as critical when working with others.[4]

What do you do if there is a disconnect between members of two different generations in terms of the importance they place on likeability – with the supervisee prioritizing it more so than the supervisor? One option involves the supervisee simply accepting and appreciating the differences. On the other hand, being friendly to the boss could elicit a similar response and shape the interaction into a more positive one.

Supervisors who don't prioritize likeability, however, may need to intentionally demonstrate it more in order to connect with and support their team members and direct reports who do value it. For instance, asking how someone's weekend was or looking at pictures of their latest trip could be useful to the relationship, both for the employee and supervisor.

Building Trust

Trust is also critical in a supervisor–supervisee relationship. Employees aren't going to go to great lengths to put in more effort than is required for an organization or boss they can't trust. Not only can a mistrusting culture reduce productivity and engagement, but it is also a surefire way to lose talented employees.

Generational Considerations and Strategies

Perspectives on the importance of trust with supervisors vary by generation, though. We found that a higher number of Gen Xers and Baby Boomers reported trust being very important when working with others, with that number declining with Millennials and Gen Zers.[4] This isn't surprising in that younger people are less likely to see trust-related issues as problematic compared to those who are older.[23]

Let's take a look at why that might be, particularly when it comes to Generation Z. During this cohort's adolescence and young adulthood, several transformative societal issues emerged, leading to skepticism of the world around them. For example, they came of age after the Great Recession and during the COVID-19 pandemic, where circumstances led to significant changes from the future they were promised – shifts to remote instruction, difficulty entering career fields even with a college degree, exploding housing markets, and layoffs from jobs. They have learned to navigate their lives without relying on or trusting the system they were assured would provide them a stable future. So, proving to them that the organization, their supervisor, and their coworkers can be trusted is essential in building their larger sense of faith in society, beyond the supervisory relationship.

While one might surmise that younger people are inherently less trusting in all aspects of their lives, there are some situations where they have higher levels of trust than their older counterparts. For example, those in older generations tend to have greater trust in business leaders, whereas those who are younger put more faith in experts, like scientists and professors.[23] To gain the trust of Gen Zers in organizations, leaders must show how the decisions made in the organization are backed by evidence, data, or expertise and not just their own vision.

Although older employees are more likely to report having a "great deal of trust" for their employers,[24] not all do. Interestingly, a far greater number of executives believe that their employees, in general, highly trust them compared to the number who actually do.[25] To enhance trust across the board, organizations need to ensure they demonstrate transparency in their decisions, address their mistakes, stay true to their word by not shifting policies or going back on promises, act in alignment with organizational values, foster two-way communication channels, offer opportunities for employees to provide feedback on supervisors, and hold management to the same standards as their workers.

Maintaining Open Communication

Communication is a critical skill for supervisors, which is not surprising because the inability to communicate effectively can result in misunderstandings, confusion, hurt feelings, and misdirection in tasks – none of which are productive in a work setting. Furthermore, effective supervisory communication has been found to increase motivation, satisfaction, and organizational commitment of employees.[26]

Generational Considerations and Strategies
And members across generations tend to agree. All four cohorts in our study rated communication as a top supervisory skill.[4] While important for everyone, each generation has differing expectations about what constitutes effective communication. For example, Baby Boomers desire loyalty and believe others should follow through on what they say they are going to do. They seek this from their employees and supervisors. Gen Xers often need specific information from their superiors as well as their direct reports in order to do their jobs, and thus, don't fare well with being held up by a gatekeeper. They want it quickly so they can move forward with their projects without delay. Millennials as supervisees desire feedback to stay on track but also as bosses to make sure they are doing their best to support

their employees. Gen Zers seek and provide transparency so they aren't caught off guard. They want their supervisors to keep them updated on any challenges or issues, and they prefer to be authentic and open with their bosses.

In working across generations, it is important to communicate in ways that work best for the other person. For instance, a Gen Xer who simply needs an answer to a question in order to proceed with a task might not welcome substantial feedback from a Millennial. Or a Gen Zer who wants to be open with their supervisor about an issue they are facing could fare better if they come with a solution in hand to a Baby Boomer to demonstrate an attempt at following through.

Delegating to Others

Delegation involves more than just giving employees duties; it's empowering them to take on significant responsibilities, make critical decisions, and execute tasks successfully. According to the Center for Creative Leadership, delegation is one of the most essential supervisory skills, as it fosters efficiency, trust, and skill development of subordinates.[16]

Generational Considerations and Strategies

But, its importance is not viewed consistently across generations. Research has found that 62 percent of supervisors in their 50s and 60s thought delegation was a key managerial skill, whereas only 30 percent of those in their 20s and 30s did.[27] Perhaps that is because nearly half of Gen Zers and a third of Millennials report having difficulty delegating to their employees.[7]

The general hesitance of Gen Zers, in particular, is evident in how they view certain factors related to delegation. For example, demonstrating commitment is very important for members of all generations, but more so for the three oldest.[4] The same is true of follow-through and accountability. For some in Generation Z, it may be a lack of skills, and for others, a lack of opportunity. But, considering earlier discussions about young people's ability to still thrive within systems and cultures they don't trust, it makes sense that their reliance on commitment, follow-through, and accountability from others is not as essential as it might be for older workers.

While mutual understanding across generations about varied perspectives on delegation is critical for collegiality and team functioning, a larger goal could include developing Gen Zers' competence and confidence. For one, offering trainings, resources, and mentorship to quell concerns they have around delegation may help them develop their skill sets and enhance their comfort levels. In addition, if their supervisor models effective delegation, young employees might adopt practices they can use with others. Most importantly, though, building a trusting organizational culture can help Gen Zers feel more assured that those they delegate to will get the work done.

On the other hand, when delegating to members of each generation, it's important to keep in mind how they prefer to be delegated to. Baby Boomers want to be included in the decision-making process. Doing so can motivate them to work harder and contribute at greater levels.[28] While they like traditional hierarchy, involvement in "participative" leadership is critical for them. So, as much as possible, invite them to the table at the beginning of a task so they can have input in, or at least an understanding of, the larger goal. And, since Baby Boomers place great value on finishing strong before retirement, helping them see their contributions as part of their legacy will help them feel empowered and engaged.

With Gen Xers' desire for independence and autonomy, they prefer to be given a task and then left on their own to do it. But, members of this generation like to know the reasoning behind why they are being asked to do something.[27] So, simply delegating a task with little explanation doesn't work well for them. Gen Xers also prefer having straightforward communication from their supervisors. Just tell them about how the task fits into the bigger picture, give it to them, and leave them to work on it in a way that makes sense to them. While no generation particularly likes being micromanaged, Gen Xers, in particular, can feel trapped and untrusted. Thus, a micromanaging boss could impact their employee's productivity as well as the supervisor–supervisee relationship.

Unlike Gen Xers who prefer autonomy, Millennials like more involvement, defined instructions, deadlines, follow-up, and praise.[27] This means anyone delegating to a Millennial might want to incorporate both formal and informal check-in processes to reinforce expectations, as well as provide support, guidance, feedback, and an opportunity to ask questions. In addition, because Millennials enjoy collaboration, group accountability methods can work well when delegating tasks to them, as their follow-through can hinge on the notion that others are dependent on the quality and timeliness of their work. For example, holding periodic check-ins during a group meeting about task progress or having accountability partners for day-to-day follow-up can be useful.

Gen Zers have a different perspective when it comes to being delegated to. They prefer to draw clear boundaries, often not taking on anything beyond what they are contracted to do.[29] While those in older generations may decry this behavior as them not being team players, Gen Zers, for the most part, would still choose that than martyrdom. Thus, giving them tasks that could keep them working after hours or during their time off will be unwelcome for many in this generation. When delegating to them, it can be helpful to re-prioritize their other work or remove existing tasks from their to-do lists to make room for any new ones. In addition, Gen Zers like to know how their effort contributes to making a positive impact (e.g. "your part in this is crucial to solving this larger issue"). Being sure to tell them both the why and how behind delegated tasks can go a long way in enhancing their commitment, follow-through, and accountability.

Let's take a look at a scenario to see generational differences at play when it comes to delegation. Rhonda is a Generation X supervisor who has been in her organization for more than ten years. She oversees Lacey, a Gen Zer, who is relatively new, but impressive in her work thus far. Rhonda has been tasked with completing a large-scale project to present to the organization's executive team, delegating portions of it to Lacey. But, right before the project is due, Lacey tells Rhonda she is unable to finish. Although she profusely apologizes, Rhonda is still upset that she'll have to take on Lacey's parts with little time to spare.

What could Lacey have done beforehand to demonstrate her commitment, follow-through, and accountability to Rhonda? For one, if she foresaw any challenges and knew there was a possibility something could get in the way of completing her tasks, she should have communicated with Rhonda earlier to reallocate the work or come up with a Plan B. Further, if Lacey had been progressing all along, she would have had at least a portion of the tasks complete to share with Rhonda. Without communication or preparation, Rhonda is left in a tight spot, and Lacey appears to be unreliable.

We can also consider what Rhonda could have done. For example, it might have been beneficial for her to have shared more details about the project and its impact with Lacey before starting. That way, Lacey would know the stakes ahead of time. In addition, tracking Lacey's progress by having her turn in small pieces along the way could have resonated with Gen Zers' desire for milestones while keeping Lacey accountable to the larger task.[30] Rhonda could also have considered that her "get down to business" approach might be off-putting to the supervisory relationship, making it difficult for Lacey to seek guidance or admit she is struggling. Having Rhonda clearly outline the experience and then provide ongoing support, empathy, and patience could have encouraged both her and Lacey to engage in a positive working dynamic with open lines of communication.

Giving Feedback

Giving feedback is also an important supervisory skill, according to the Center for Creative Leadership.[16] Positive validation can inspire employees and give them purpose, while critical information can help redirect them. Feedback isn't just useful to the employee to enhance performance; it is also an essential part of relationship-building between supervisor and supervisee, as it fosters a sense of care and trust between the two.

Several types of feedback can be deployed by a supervisor to an employee – through formal processes, often in writing at the end of a performance cycle, like an annual review, or informal ones, typically given verbally and in real time when a behavior occurs. Regardless of its delivery, the information shared can be positive or critical, depending on the situation.

Generational Considerations and Strategies
People have differing thoughts and behaviors when it comes to giving feedback, though, that vary by generational cohort.[4]

Table 9.3   *Perspectives on Giving Feedback by Generation*

	Baby Boomers	Gen Xers	Millennials	Gen Zers
I regularly give feedback to others.	66%	75%	87%	63%
I believe my feedback is often helpful for others.	71%	83%	89%	51%
I avoid giving feedback as much as possible, unless it is positive.	28%	54%	76%	51%
Giving feedback makes me nervous.	31%	51%	66%	60%
I give feedback in the moment, when something occurs that warrants it.	66%	77%	84%	70%
I listen to the perspective of the person I'm giving feedback to about any feedback that person may disagree with.	71%	82%	89%	63%

Let's take a closer look at what these numbers mean for each generation. For one, most Baby Boomers say they are not nervous about providing feedback and thus, don't avoid it. Many utilize a direct approach, absent of any sugarcoating, but combine it with listening. So, those supervised by Baby Boomers may find it useful to first consider the information they are receiving, as it likely comes from a helpful place, and then afterwards, provide their own thoughts in a non-defensive manner.

Because many Gen Xers give feedback in the moment and are often direct in their communication, some may end up expressing thoughts they later wish they had more time to think through. Thus, it could be useful for Gen Xers to schedule dedicated check-in meetings, where they can thoughtfully prepare and deliver feedback in an intentional and meaningful way. If receiving feedback from a Gen Xer, it's important to note that, despite their direct demeanor, they are typically willing to listen, so the conversation won't be just one-sided. And, if they happen to give feedback in the moment, make sure to schedule a follow-up time with them to gain more depth and clarity.

While Millennials may be reluctant to give feedback, they still often do it. But, more than three quarters avoid saying anything critical, perhaps due to their own desire for praise.[27] Similar to Gen Xers, Millennials would do well with dedicated time in order to prepare their thoughts, especially if they have to deliver negative information. Being supervised by a Millennial, one could expect to receive a great deal of accolades, recognition, and appreciation, which for other Millennials works well. However, those in other generations, particularly independent Gen Xers, may instead prefer to get right to the details and move on.

In terms of Gen Zers, many don't give feedback regularly, think what they have to say is helpful, or listen to those who may disagree. Further, most get nervous to share anything critical. So, it wouldn't be surprising if this cohort avoided providing feedback altogether, which might necessitate others to ask for it. When they do share, though, it would likely reflect how one's actions or choices impacts others, which is reflective of one of their main motivations as discussed in the Getting Things Done chapter. For example, a Generation Z supervisor might say, "This project is going to make a difference in the lives of so many people. Here are a few ways I think you could build on what you've been doing, so the impact is even stronger ..." While that could resonate with other Gen Zers, most in older cohorts, like Gen Xers and Baby Boomers, will look to cut to the chase to learn the details of what needs to be done. Thus, Gen Zers may need to be more straightforward with them than they might be inclined to be.

RECEIVING FEEDBACK

Research from Gallup found that employees who receive clear expectations, along with frequent feedback, are more engaged than those who do not.[3] However, members in different generational cohorts have varied perspectives about the specifics.[4]

Table 9.4   *Perspectives on Receiving Feedback by Generation*

	Baby Boomers	Gen Xers	Millennials	Gen Zers
I regularly ask for feedback.	46%	65%	82%	62%
I appreciate getting critical feedback so I can improve my performance.	67%	78%	86%	67%
I appreciate getting positive feedback so I know I am on the right track.	77%	85%	87%	67%
Getting feedback makes me nervous.	25%	57%	72%	62%
I often debate critical feedback I receive.	21%	57%	79%	49%

Generational Considerations and Strategies

While the majority of members across all age groups appreciate getting both positive and critical feedback, the generational nuances around other factors offer insight that might be helpful to supervisors when delivering it.

For one, many Baby Boomers are not likely going to ask for regular feedback, although most are grateful and aren't nervous or prone to push back when receiving it. But, Baby Boomers don't want any drawn-out explanations or beating around the bush.[31] Their supervisors should be straightforward with them. For example, "Stuart, let's talk about ways to accentuate section two of the report you've been writing. I have a few ideas."

Gen Xers need autonomy, trust from supervisors, and the ability to engage in self-directed work.[31] As a hands-off generation, they won't want a lot of intervention and unsolicited feedback, unless they deem the information is crucial and timely. For instance, "I know you're working on that report now, so I'm glad we're able to connect right away before you get too far along. Can you expand on the second section more to highlight the data and then do that for the rest of the sections when you start writing them?"

Millennials have higher rates of asking for and appreciating feedback. But, the majority get nervous and may experience difficulty in hearing anything negative. Because of this, praise must be frequent, and critical thoughts must be delivered with empathy and compassion, focusing on areas of improvement rather than missteps and mistakes. The feedback should also be framed in a way that the employee will understand its present or future benefits.[32] Even with delicate delivery, supervisors should be prepared for pushback from their Millennial employees. Thus, having tangible and observable evidence is essential. A supervisor might say, "I know you've been working hard on this report and have a lot on your plate. I wanted to see if you could expand on the second section, like you did on the first. We need at least two justifications to support our argument, and right now, there is only one."

Two-thirds of Gen Zers say they need feedback at least every few weeks to find out how they are progressing, where their areas of improvement are, and what they should be focusing on more.[33] But, most won't ask for it regularly, thus necessitating consistent outreach by the supervisor.[3] Further, for the majority, hearing about their performance makes them nervous. Add to that, they have the lowest levels of happiness at work[31] and higher numbers rating their mental and emotional well-being as poor.[34] Supervisors must be aware that providing feedback is more than just offering a few tips or redirecting an employee's energy to different priorities. Instead, it is part of an important guidance and support system for Generation Z employees to thrive at work, in general. To align with their needs, a supervisor might say, "Great job so far on that report. Here are a few ideas as you start drafting the next section. Let's meet in a week to talk about your progress and see how you are feeling."

In looking across all four generations, though, there is one similarity – the majority find more value in receiving feedback in-the-moment rather than through formal processes, especially performance reviews. And, organizations are finding great utility in making that shift. For instance, companies such as Netflix and Apple have eliminated annual performance reviews in favor of ongoing forms of feedback that are not a "waste of time."[35] Thus, consider providing any guidance or redirection when something occurs instead of waiting to do so during their annual evaluation. However, keep in mind that a continued barrage of in-the-moment feedback can be overwhelming. If the feedback is time-sensitive, it will likely be better-received by the employee right when something occurs. If it can wait, though, even just a short time, utilizing a "parking lot" approach where future fixes and ideas are captured on a document and visited at an upcoming one-on-one meeting might be the best strategy.

Conclusion

Being in tune with the needs of varying generational cohorts can help enhance organizational success. At the management level, shaping policies, culture, and processes to best align with the diversity of employees can lead to them feeling valued and heard, resulting in greater engagement and retention of talented workers.

Much of an employee's work experience, though, is also fundamentally impacted by the behaviors of their direct supervisor, which can and should be informed by generational differences. Being able to adapt one's style can result in stronger supervisor–supervisee relationships, better communication, and higher levels of employee engagement – all of which can lead to happy, productive employees and thriving organizations.

Notes

1 Rothwell, W. J., Bakhshandeh, B., & Zaballero, A. G. (2023). *Successful supervisory leadership: Exerting positive influence while leading people.* CRC Press.

2 Villanova University. (2022). *An overview of management theories: Classical, behavioral, and modern approaches.* www.villanovau.com/articles/leadership/an-overview-of-management-theories/

3 Gallup. (2017). *State of the American workplace.* www.gallup.com/workplace/285818/state-american-workplace-report-2017.aspx

4 Seemiller, C., & Grace, M. (2023). *Generations in the workplace.* Unpublished dataset.

5 Great Place to Work. (2022). *2022 PEOPLE® Companies that care*. www.greatplac etowork.com/best-workplaces/companies-that-care/2022

6 Target. (2024). *Culture*. https://corporate.target.com/careers/culture#:~:text= A%20rewarding%20career%20begins%20in,certificates%20in%20busin ess%2Daligned%20areas

7 Zapier Editorial Team. (2020). *Millennials are managers now*. https://zapier. com/blog/millennial-managers-report/

8 Visier. (2023). *A looming succession problem: New research shows individual contributors shun management in favor of free time*. www.visier.com/blog/new-research-individual-contributors-shun-management/

9 Dodgson, L. (2023). *A career influencer says millennials and Gen Z don't want to be managers anymore – Here's why*. www.insider.com/why-millennials-and-gen-z-dont-want-to-be-managers-2023-11

10 Indeed. (2023). *25 of the best training programs companies offer*. www.indeed.com/career-advice/career-development/best-training-programs-companies

11 CareerBuilder. (2009). *More than four-in-ten workers over the age of 35 currently work for a younger boss, finds new CareerBuilder survey*. https://press.careerbuilder. com/2010-02-17-More-Than-Four-in-Ten-Workers-Over-the-Age-of-35-Curren tly-Work-for-a-Younger-Boss-Finds-New-CareerBuilder-Survey

12 Kunze, F., & Menges, J. I. (2017). Younger supervisors, older subordinates: An organizational-level study of age differences, emotions, and performance. *Journal of Organizational Behavior, 38*(4), 461–486.

13 Dansereau, F., Jr., Graen, G. B., & Haga, W. J. (1975). A vertical dyad linkage approach to leadership within formal organizations: A longitudinal investigation of the role making process. *Organizational Behavior and Human Performance, 13*, 46–78.

14 Uhl-Bien, M., Carsten, M., Huang, L., & Maslyn, J. (2022). What do managers value in the leader member exchange (LMX) relationship? Identification and measurement of the manager's perspective of LMX (MLMX). *Journal of Business Research, 148*, 225–240.

15 Gupta, M., Bhal, K. T., & Ansari, M. A. (2020). Relational age and leader-member exchange: Mediating role of perceived trust. *Journal of Indian Business Research, 12*(4), 563–576.

16 Center for Creative Leadership. (2021). *Building relationship skills at work*. www. ccl.org/articles/leading-effectively-articles/building-relationship-skills/

17 Swinand, A. (2023). Why kindness at work pays off. *Harvard Business Review*. https://hbr.org/2023/07/why-kindness-at-work-pays-off

18 Haskins, G., Thomas, M., & Johri, L. (2018). *Kindness in leadership*. Routledge.

19 Taylor, R. (2023). *Kindness mindset in leadership: Discover why kindness matters for effectiveness in leadership*. Relmnt.

20 Niemiec, R. M. (2015). *Baby Boomers, Gen X, Millennials: Are strengths decreasing?* VIA Institute on Character. www.psychologytoday.com/us/blog/what-matt ers-most/201508/baby-boomers-gen-x-millennials-are-strengths-decreasing

21 VIA Institute on Character. (2018). *The VIA Survey of character strengths: United States Gen Z.* Data prepared by The VIA Institute on Character.

22 McAllister, C., Moss, S., & Martinko, M. J. (2019). Why likable leaders seem more effective. *Harvard Business Review.* https://hbr.org/2019/10/why-likable-leaders-seem-more-effective

23 Pew Research Center. (2019). *Young Americans are less trusting of other people – And key institutions – Than their elders.* www.pewresearch.org/short-reads/2019/ 08/06/young-americans-are-less-trusting-of-other-people-and-key-institutions-than-their-elders/

24 EY. (2016). *EY research reveals less than half of full-time workers surveyed globally trust their employer, boss or colleagues a great deal.* www.prnewswire.com/news-releases/ey-research-reveals-less-than-half-of-full-time-workers-surveyed-globa lly-trust-their-employer-boss-or-colleagues-a-great-deal-300287869.html

25 PwC. (2023). *PwC's 2023 trust survey.* www.pwc.com/us/en/library/trust-in-business-survey-2023.html

26 Mikkelson, A. C., York, J. A., & Arritola, J. (2015). Communication competence, leadership behaviors, and employee outcomes in supervisor-employee relationships. *Business and Professional Communication Quarterly, 78*(3), 336–354.

27 Birkenshaw, J., Manktelow, J., D'Amato, V., Tosca, E., & Macchi, F. (2019). Older and wiser? How management style varies with age. *MIT Sloan Management Review, 60*(4), 75–83.

28 Al-Asfour, A., & Lettau, L. (2014). Strategies for leadership styles for multi-generational workforce. *Journal of Leadership, Accountability and Ethics, 11*(2), 58–69.

29 Jewell, H. (2022). *Gen Z workers should be proud of being 'snowflakes' rather than martyrs.* www.theguardian.com/commentisfree/2022/jan/27/gen-z-workers-snowflakes-bad-treatment-bad-pay

30 Seemiller, C., & Grace, M. (2017). *Generation Z goes to college.* Jossey-Bass.

31 Cangrade. (2023). *Happiness at work in 2023.* www.cangrade.com/blog/hr-strategy/what-you-should-know-about-generational-happiness-at-work-research/

32 Anderson, E., Buchko, A. A., & Buchko, K. J. (2016). Giving negative feedback to Millennials. *Management Research Review, 39*(6), 692–705.

33 GenHQ (Center for Generational Kinetics). (2018). *The state of Gen Z 2018.* https://genhq.com/generation-z-research-2018/

34 Gallup and Walton Family Foundation. (2023). *Voices on Gen Z: Perspectives on U.S. education, wellbeing and the future.* www.gallup.com/analytics/506663/american-youth-research.aspx#ite-544721

35 Tabrizi, B. (2023). *Why the performance review is dying out – Including at companies like Apple and Microsoft.* www.fastcompany.com/90943074/why-the-performance-review-is-dying-out-including-at-companies-like-apple-and-microsoft

Leadership 10

Your company just hired a new CEO, and you are at her welcome speech in a room full of anticipatory coworkers. Rodney, a Baby Boomer, says he has faith in this leader because of her track record with her previous company. Brad, a Gen Xer, comments about how he hopes she'll fix the things that don't work but not touch those that do. Carly, a Millennial, chimes in by sharing how she wants the CEO bring people together and create far better morale than the last leader. And, Twyla, a Gen Zer, says she hopes the organization stays true to its values because that's why she chose to work there. What they're seeking in a leader is quite different, yet all important, and certainly informed by their generational preferences and perspectives.

Before jumping into generational nuances about leadership, we need to define the term. But, that isn't easy. Scholars, Warren Bennis and Burt Nanus, in their seminal book, Leaders, assert that there are more than 850 definitions of leadership.[1] And, that was in 1997, back when most Gen Zers weren't even born yet. Today, the number is likely considerably higher. While there is no universal definition of leadership, most have similar attributes: they involve motivating, inspiring, persuading, or influencing people to reach a larger goal, advance a cause, or create change. Peter Northouse, acclaimed leadership professor, sums up the definition as, "a process whereby an individual influences a group or individuals to achieve a common goal."[2]

Generational Considerations and Strategies

There are three main leadership styles: autocratic (telling people what to do), participative (asking the group what they want to do), and laissez-faire

DOI: 10.4324/9781003541035-10

(leaving it up to the group to make their own decisions). In a study of Baby Boomers, Gen Xers, and Millennials around these styles, researchers found that all three cohorts prefer participative, then laissez-faire, and then autocratic, in that order.

However, when comparing generations, there were some unique findings. For one, Baby Boomers had higher preference rates for laissez-faire compared to the other two generations. Their need for consensual and shared responsibility as well as mutual respect[3] aligns more with a laid-back, group consensus approach. Gen Xers had higher rates for democratic, which isn't surprising in that they prefer egalitarian relationships, fairness, and honesty.[5] Millennials had the highest rates for autocratic.[4] They are more likely to respond to position power than personal power,[5] as well as find rewards to be important,[6] which can be doled out by those in charge. And, a different study found the Gen Zers resonate with democratic leadership,[7] which aligns with their need for authenticity and having a voice.[8]

Given the definition of leadership as "a process whereby an individual influences a group or individuals to achieve a common goal,"[2] let's take a look at some skill-based behaviors associated with leadership within the domains of strategic thinking, executing, influencing, and relationship-building.[9]

Strategic Thinking

As defined by Gallup, strategic thinking involves analyzing situations and information in order to make good decisions.[8] The Center for Creative Leadership asserts that having a strategic perspective to analyze challenging problems is one of the most important leadership competencies for organizational leaders.[10]

Developing a Vision

Consider the vision statement of video communications site, Zoom: "One platform delivering limitless human connection."[11] Or, Lego: "A global force for Learning-Through-Play."[12] While these words might seem vague, they can provide inspiration and clarity to employees as they aim to create more opportunities for limitless connection (Zoom) or make more products that foster both learning and play (Lego).

A great example of making a vision a reality occurred with eBay, the world's largest online reseller. Their founder, Pierre Omidyar, wanted to create a platform to facilitate large-scale retailing and did that by developing a process in which buying and selling goods would be easily accessible. So, big ideas can lead to big actions.

Being visionary is a critical skill for effective leadership.[13] And, it is not solely associated with one specific generation, as many of the most innovative organizational leaders span different cohorts: Baby Boomers (Bill Gates with Microsoft), Gen Xers (Sara Blakely with Spanx), Millennials (Whitney Wolfe Herd with Bumble), and Gen Zers (Sydney Keys III with Books N Bros).

Generational Considerations and Strategies

However, one generation stands out in terms of vision – Millennials. They have higher rates of believing that creating a strategic vision is important for a leader to do[7] and prefer visionary leadership to other types.[14] But, the Millennial cohort doesn't just seek this from others. They have the highest rates when it comes to describing themselves as visionary and are tied with Gen Xers in being able to "imagine future possibilities for an organization."[7]

In addition, approaching the visioning process may be unique depending on the generation. For instance, Baby Boomers like to be valued for their experience and wisdom. Combine that with their desire to be included in major organizational decision-making, and you will see a Baby Boomer far more invested in the process when they can either lead it or have a heavy consultative role in it.

Gen Xers enjoy developing a vision but often prefer expediency. So, a long-drawn-out visioning exercise might not resonate with them. If they are the ones leading it, they might ask everyone to come prepared to the session with ideas in hand. Or, if they are the participant, they may offer a streamlined process for idea generation and suggest some independent work in order to finalize the vision.

Given Millennials' strong preference for and desire to be visionary, many seek opportunities in their organizations to create and deploy a vision, asking questions like, "Where do we really see this organization in ten years?" or "How does this idea align with our vision?" They are often energized by the visioning process, especially in doing so collaboratively, whether as a leader or employee.

Being a values-driven generation, Gen Zers need alignment and impact. Thus, the visioning process is right up their alley. As a leader and an employee, they want to be involved in setting the course. However, they will be the first to question whether the vision statement is simply just a collection of words on paper or a guiding beacon to the impactful work of the company. If they think the organization is straying from the vision, don't be surprised if they leave.

Solving Problems

The World Economic Forum's Future of Jobs Report 2023 indicated that employers believe the ability to solve problems is rising in importance as a critical workforce skill.[15] And, there is no leadership role in which problem-solving isn't a nearly daily function.

Generational Considerations and Strategies
All four generations rank problem-solving in their top skill sets[16] and believe they have strong competencies in this area.[7] However, with the varied ways in which people can approach solving problems, there are bound to be generational nuances. In our workplace study, we asked participants to rate the frequency with which they deployed six different problem-solving approaches. Let's take a look at the three most and one least used approaches by generation.[7]

Table 10.1   *Problem-Solving Approaches by Generation*

	Baby Boomers	Gen Xers	Millennials	Gen Zers
1	Investigate an array of possible solutions	Explore how things have been done before	Investigate an array of possible solutions	Investigate an array of possible solutions
2	Deconstruct the problem	Investigate an array of possible solutions	Deconstruct the problem	Deconstruct the problem
3	Go with your gut	Deconstruct the problem	Explore how things have been done before	Ask for input or guidance
Least Used	Use trial and error	Go with your gut	Use trial and error	Go with your gut

Members across all generations deconstruct the problem and consider multiple solutions, which isn't surprising in that these two approaches are the essence of problem-solving. Gen Xers and Millennials are more likely to look to the past, which makes sense in that they both have ample career experience to reflect on for ideas, yet enough time left in their occupational journeys to invest in finding the right answer for the future. Gen Zers are the only cohort to ask for guidance, which typically comes from newer employees.

One of the more interesting findings, though, is the role of intuitive decision-making, particularly with Baby Boomers ranking it in their top three and Gen Xers and Gen Zers in their bottom slots. Why might this be so? Gen Xers, on the one hand, need proof, which contradicts the notion of intuition. Consider this quote: "In contrast to the axiom 'Trust, but verify,' as the president of their childhood, Ronald Reagan, famously coined, Gen Xers believe in 'Don't trust, validate.'"[17] Gen Zers, on the other hand, being the newest employee cohort, likely wouldn't have enough experience to "go with their gut" quite yet.

In working across generations, Baby Boomers, in particular, will need to appreciate the value of data-driven decisions that Gen Xers, in particular, desire. However, the three youngest cohorts might also have to learn to trust Baby Boomers' intuitive wisdom, as there is a likelihood of accuracy in it. According to research shared by Connson Chou Locke in the *Harvard Business Review*, it takes about ten years of expertise to be able to deploy "accurate intuitive judgments," which is most useful when the situation lacks objective or clear rules.[18] However, what might be helpful when Baby Boomers are working with those from other generations is to blend data with intuition to come up with decisions that marry the two, validating the strength of their idea.

Generating Big Ideas

What does it take to come up with big ideas to execute a vision or solve a problem? Several skills, like curiosity, creativity, and determination to discover unconventional paths. One must be interested in alternative ways of looking at a situation as well as moving away from the status quo. Further, there is some element of risk involved, in which there is no guarantee that the idea is going to work. But, leaders take bold steps anyway. Consider Whole Foods, for example, an organic specialty grocery store that took a risk, hoping people would want to pay a higher price for natural food. And, it paid off.[19]

Generational Considerations and Strategies

Let's take a look at these skill sets with members across generations. Compared to those in other generations, more Gen Zers rate themselves high in being curious, Millennials in being creative, Gen Xers in being determined.[7] Gen Zers might then be prone to ask more questions, which can help uncover new approaches, whereas Millennials might be able to deploy unconventional solutions. Further, Gen Xers can stick with a problem for an extended duration, implementing various options until one works. Despite having the very lowest rates in all three categories, Baby Boomers have years of accumulated wisdom that can also be helpful in idea generation.

Having an open mind is also useful in generating ideas, as it allows one to consider a variety of options, sometimes outlandish, that spur creative thinking. Research has found that people 49 years old and under are the most open-minded, with rates declining as individuals age, that is, until 62–70 years old, when curiosity piques again right around retirement age.[20]

Open-mindedness can show up in many different ways. For instance, while far more Gen Zers are generally open-minded compared to their older counterparts, they have the lowest rates of being willing to listen to others' perspectives.[7] In a world that has become so politically polarized, many Gen Zers have been bombarded with ideas and opinions that don't align with their values, particularly manifesting into policies and actions that restrict people's rights. So, although this cohort may be open to a new customer service protocol being bantered about in a meeting, they may not be as on board to consider an organizational policy limiting or scaling back efforts around diversity, equity, and inclusion in the workplace.

Not all ideas are generated individually; some are born from working with others. The two youngest cohorts like group idea generation because it creates a wide selection of viable options, in which they can pick the most optimal idea from among those that emerge. Gen Xers like that it offers the ability to integrate the best elements of each idea into a wholly unique one. And, Baby Boomers enjoy partaking in a process that empowers everyone to share their insight.[7]

On the other hand, across all generations, many are concerned that some voices are louder than others, and those people's opinions are given more attention regardless of merit.[7] Baby Boomers and Gen Xers believe some may be reluctant to share innovative, off-the-wall suggestions for fear of negative feedback. Millennials do not like that ideas can be scrutinized or critiqued in a semi-public setting. And, Gen Zers worry that if the idea derived in the group is not the one implemented, members can feel disempowered.

So, with each cohort, idea generation could look different, with Gen Zers asking a lot of questions, Millennials building out someone else's idea, Gen Xers digging into the data-driven details, and Boomers' past experience providing wisdom to help re-conceptualize an old problem in new ways. Thus, crafting any idea generating experience that embraces these preferences could be empowering and beneficial.

In addition, it might be useful to develop a formalized decision-making process that everyone can agree to. This could include submitting anonymous ideas into a hat, using a talking stick to give each person the opportunity to speak without interruption, brainstorming only pros (versus cons) to an idea, or asking people to come to the meeting with three options. It is less important what the exact process looks like and more so about making sure all members are on board.

Executing

Imagine coming up with a brilliant idea, the solution to that one pressing problem. The excitement you have to get started, make the change, and see the impact of the implementation can hardly be harnessed. Thus, leadership involves taking action, even in the face of adversity.

Taking Initiative

While making things happen requires drive, focus, determination, and all the skills discussed earlier about productivity, it also takes initiative to get an idea off the ground.

Generational Considerations and Strategies
Perspectives of initiative, though, vary by generation. The three youngest believe that taking initiative is an important skill for effective leadership, more so than Baby Boomers. However, it is the eldest that rank themselves highest in possessing that competency, with that rate declining with each younger cohort.[7] Part of this may be explained by the Lifecycle Effect, in which those who are older have acquired enough experience and political capital within their organizations to garner more support and have greater

levels of self-assuredness to launch new ideas. It's important to remember, though, that younger individuals may be reluctant to take initiative for fear that their idea lacks merit, they will be judged by others, or they just don't have the confidence or ability to take action.

Despite the variance by generation, each cohort has unique attributes that can impact the way they go about taking initiative. With Baby Boomers describing themselves as responsible,[7] they may be mobilized by their sense of accountability for the outcome of a situation or loyalty to the people impacted by it. Gen Xers are practical and sensible,[7] which may result in only wanting to move forward after feeling confident in the implementation plan. Millennials are spontaneous,[7] wanting to take advantage of opportunities and rewards that arise from taking action. Because Gen Zers are the consummate DIYers, in nearly every industry, being a part of the development of the idea is key for them in actually implementing it.[21]

To foster personal initiative across all generations, it's important to support doing so at a larger level. For example, research has found if an organizational climate is supportive of initiative-taking, employees will have higher rates of self-efficacy, an ultimately personal initiative behavior.[22] Thus, members of all generations could benefit from being given the latitude to take action.

However, given that Gen Zers have the lowest levels of self-ascribed initiative, there may be more that can be done to assist them. For one, it is critical that they are provided guidance and support to take initiative, even if with smaller, lower-stakes projects at first. The way to build their confidence is to create the circumstances that leverage the capacity of employees to do their best. So, setting them up with opportunities for success can help them develop their efficacy to move forward in the future.

Managing Change

Laws and policies, variability in resources and supply chains, innovative ideas, employment trends, and competition can spur leaders to create change in their organizations. These may be as monumental as a car manufacturer having to adapt their automotive technology in order to meet new federal emissions standards or as small as a non-profit instituting an updated travel protocol. Whatever the change, the implementation can be challenging as employees aren't always on board, especially if they hadn't been consulted or effectively communicated with along the way. That's why it's no surprise that 63 percent of the nearly 14,000 global leaders across sectors who were surveyed by the global consulting firm Development Dimensions International say managing successful change is a critical leadership skill.[23]

Generational Considerations and Strategies

There are some generational nuances when looking at change management. In our study, Baby Boomers ranked implementing change lower than the three other generations when it comes to skills for effective leadership; they also indicated innovation and flexibility to be less important factors essential to a workplace.[7] In addition to their perspectives on the importance of being able to implement change, research has found that Baby Boomers are also more change-resistant than Gen Xers and Millennials.[24] This may be attributed to their longevity in the workforce and being less interested in altering what they've grown accustomed to, particularly anything they had a hand in establishing in the first place.[24]

Baby Boomers' desire for the status quo may result in younger generations feeling stifled, though. While it's important for these cohorts to appreciate organizational history, Baby Boomers could benefit greatly from their younger employees' excitement for change. As older members of leadership tend to hold onto paradigms that have become obsolete, it is recommended to invite newer, younger members to the executive team who will bring in diversity, curiosity, and "bold exploration."[25] And, if it isn't feasible to engage them on the leadership team, having formal ways for them to have a voice to share their ideas, such as through committee work and feedback processes, is key.

Handling Adversity

Even the best laid plans don't always go smoothly. Sometimes, we are missing critical information needed to make a timely decision, we continue to face hurdles making us question our decisions, we tire from the stamina necessary for moving forward, or we must adapt quickly to avoid failure altogether. Being able to handle adversity is not just an important leadership skill; the ability to confront obstacles can have dire effects on entire organizations.

Have you heard of Google Reader, a once-promising online newsfeed? It was outdone by Facebook and became obsolete. What about Colgate Kitchen Entrees? The food line never took off because of Colgate's nearly

200-year history of making toothpaste and other cleaning products. However, both companies dealt with the setbacks and continued to persist. Other organizations, when confronted with obstacles, though, were not as successful. Consider Borders Books and Music, which didn't enter into the e-reader business and lost out to other companies, or Sears department store, whose archaic infrastructure couldn't keep up with the fast-paced digital economy. Behind all of these companies are leaders, making critical decisions, either finding ways to bounce back or costing them their entire company.

Generational Considerations and Strategies

In looking at four adversity-related competencies, including ambiguity, persistence, adaptability, and resilience, we can get a better idea of how each cohort rates their proficiency in handling obstacles and setbacks. The following are the percentages of those who indicated that they strongly agree they possess each of these competencies.[26]

Table 10.2 *Leadership Competencies Related to Handling Adversity*

	Baby Boomers	Gen Xers	Millennials	Gen Zers
Ambiguity	36%	26%	25%	18%
Persistence	68%	56%	49%	39%
Adaptability	43%	38%	36%	27%
Resilience	59%	52%	51%	44%

Given the roles that age and life experience play, it makes sense that Baby Boomers have the highest proficiency levels across every competency, with rates declining for each subsequent generation. However, what is interesting is that Baby Boomers and Gen Xers rank persistence higher compared to other competencies, whereas Millennials and Gen Zers instead rank resilience. But, despite that being their highest percentages, they are still lower than those of their two older counterparts.

Why might Baby Boomers and Gen Xers have higher levels of persistence? For one, Gen Xers have a propensity to keep going even when others are ready to cut their losses, as they are relentlessly determined.[7] However, they like data, clear answers, and to move forward with expediency, which doesn't bode well for being in ambiguous situations requiring adaptation. As for Baby Boomers, they may be prone to persist due to their prioritization of loyalty and follow-through.[7] They, too, don't fare as well in having to deal with ambiguity or adaptability, likely because they have been found to be more change-resistant than those in other generations.[24]

Given the lower scores in all four competencies across the board, how then can younger generations develop higher capacities for handling adversity? For one, it could be helpful for them to see setbacks as a part of taking on a project or initiative, meaning that if one believes that obstacles will likely arise, they may be less distressed when they do. They also may find it useful to develop a persistence timeline, in which they vow to stay the course for a set period of time regardless of what emerges. Doing so could help them stick with something longer than they might otherwise. In addition, those in other generations play an important role in skill-development with younger cohorts – they can model the way, encourage them to persist, and provide support and guidance during challenging times.

Although differences in both perceptions and actions around handling adversity could create some tension between cohorts, the sentiments of "persist at all costs" along with "cut bait when things get tough" can be powerful. Integrating both allows the team to exert efforts toward those projects and ideas that have a greater potential of coming to fruition, without wasting time and resources on those that might lead to a dead end.

Influencing

In today's world of leadership, influence is not about exerting power to get someone to behave or act in a certain way, but instead about persuasion, inspiration, and empowerment to leverage the strengths of others to do their best. Employees want to feel excited about the work they do and look to their leaders to light that fire. It's no surprise then that influence is a critical leadership skill, according to 61 percent of global leaders.[20] Let's take a closer look at what it takes to be influential and each generation's perceptions of their own skills.

Being Charismatic

One element of influence is charisma, which is a kind of charm – one that elicits an emotional response in others by virtue of the leader's ability to communicate and share a vision, typically with energy and enthusiasm. Although the notion of charisma may invoke thoughts of potential manipulation and unwavering loyalty from followers, researchers have found that it is positively associated with strategic behavior and greater levels of effectiveness.[27]

Generational Considerations and Strategies

When looking at charisma by generation, the numbers tell a unique story. Eighty-four percent of Millennials agree or strongly agree that they are charismatic, whereas only 34 percent of Baby Boomers do.[7] This isn't unexpected in that as people age, they tend to be less charismatic,[28] which might help explain the lower rates for Baby Boomers, reflecting a decline in charisma over their lifetimes.

Gen Xers and Gen Zers fall in between in the upper 60th percentile. While rates are lower for both groups compared to Millennials, the majority still see themselves as charismatic. And, Gen Zers, in particular, really resonate with the concept. So much so that Oxford added "rizz," Generation Z's word for charisma, to their dictionary in 2023.

While Baby Boomers might have had higher levels of charisma earlier in their careers or simply have always had lower levels, there are real ramifications in leading, especially with those who are younger, like failing to inspire or engage them in their work. But, with intention, charisma can be developed and deployed. Strategies such as using an animated voice, sharing similes and metaphors to explain ideas, engaging in strong nonverbal gestures, asking rhetorical questions, and demonstrating confidence about the potential of reaching lofty goals, can help one appear more charismatic.[29] Research has found that executives who trained in these skills had their charisma ratings from observers rise by 60 percent. Thus, charisma can be learned (or re-learned) – and Baby Boomers are prime candidates for it.

Inspiring Others

Think back to a time when you felt inspired because of someone else's words or actions. Maybe it was the coach who believed in you, pushing you to want to be the best athlete you could be. Or, perhaps it was the teacher who helped develop your love for science by simply modeling her passion for it.

While charisma can be associated with vigorous and energetic communication, inspiration is often achieved through telling a story, showing empathy, and living one's values and beliefs. Being able to inspire others can motivate employees to strive toward greatness, set grandiose ambitions, and innovate. One study found that ranking in the top ten percent of one's peers on just one of 33 inspirational leadership traits, such as humility, expressiveness, and harmony, doubles the chances that others see that person as an inspirational leader.[30]

Generational Considerations and Strategies

In looking at inspiration in the workplace, there are varying perspectives by generational cohort.[7,22]

Table 10.3   *Perspectives on Inspiration by Generation*

	Baby Boomers	Gen Xers	Millennials	Gen Zers
Inspiring others is one of the three most important skills for effective leadership.	46%	42%	48%	43%
My coworkers from this generation are inspiring. (Highest rate other than their own generation.)	Generation X	Baby Boomer	Generation X	Millennial
I can easily inspire others.	57%	76%	87%	59%
Inspiring: Greatly describes me	23%	56%	64%	48%

It's clear that members across all generations find inspiring others to be an important leadership skill, with the majority believing they can easily do so. But, there are some nuances between cohorts that might provide some specific insight.

For one, Baby Boomers are inspired by leaders who take a stand and were the only generation in our study to list decisiveness in the top three skills they think leaders should have.[7] They are eager to give their loyalty to someone who they believe in, as 78 percent see themselves as loyal. Baby Boomers also have the highest rates of self-described confidence when expressing opinions and beliefs.[22]

Gen Xers value practical, sensible, and intellectual ideas and believe that authenticity, compassion, and communication are essential skills in the workplace.[7] Eighty-six percent saying they often speak up when they have a thought or idea.[7] Thus, if they believe in something, they can rally around it, serving as the biggest champions. Further, they are held in high esteem by other generations, specifically Baby Boomers and Millennials, as being the most inspiring generation.

Millennials see themselves as inspirational on every measure, which isn't surprising in that they identify as courageous and confident.[7] And, they want leaders to show up with strength and take initiative. However, as self-described team players and the generation that most wants collaboration in the workplace, they look to be inspired with others rather than by others.

Gen Zers look to their leaders to inspire them to be the best they can be so they can make a difference for others. They are motivated by the opportunity to gain experience and advance through their careers,[7] seeking ways to develop themselves so they can move into roles that have more decision-making power, agency, and chance to create larger impacts.

It is key to remember that what might inspire one person, doesn't necessarily inspire another, and this holds true across generational differences.

Table 10.4   *How Generations Are Inspired*

	Inspired by...	Leader says...
Baby Boomers	Their leader	"I've got this."
Gen Xers	Ideas	"Here's my vision."
Millennials	The process	"Let's do this together."
Gen Zers	The potential for impact	"You can make a difference, and I'll help you."

Baby Boomers are looking for confident leaders who don't second-guess themselves,[1] meaning others should be sure to deliver their ideas with conviction and assuredness. With Generation X, it's imperative to put forth a solid, viable idea they can resonate with. For Millennials, it's essential to convey the message of camaraderie. And, Gen Zers want to be inspired to better themselves in order to enhance the lives of others.

Relationship-Building

No matter the job, leaders must be able to build relationships. Even seemingly autonomous occupations like park rangers in remote areas often need to report back to their teams and scientists with lab assistants working during various hours. And, given the array of people in the workplace, it is all but certain that leaders across industries will work across generational lines.

Displaying Emotional Intelligence

We all know what it looks like when someone doesn't exhibit emotional intelligence. That person gets triggered and says or does something that is rash, disrespectful, blunt, or even hurtful. Consider a scenario in which it could be easy to respond hastily or even unproductively: a coworker makes a flippant comment, criticizing your work at a meeting in front of your supervisor. A common response would be to snap back with either an insult or a defensive comment. However, neither contributes to a positive interaction. An emotionally intelligent reply might be, "Thank you for the feedback. I want this to be the best project it can be. I'll be sure to follow up with you later to get more details about how I can improve it." Not only would this diffuse the situation and demonstrate professionalism, but responding in that manner might also preserve the relationship.

According to Emotional Intelligence 2.0, a key to building productive relationships is being proficient in competencies associated with the following four quadrants[31]:

- Self-Awareness: understanding your strengths, weaknesses, values, motivations, and triggers
- Self-Management: managing stress, maintaining self-control, and fostering an optimistic outlook
- Social Awareness: being aware of others, respecting others' needs, and paying attention to body language
- Relationship Management: effectively communicating, handling conflict appropriately, and demonstrating empathy

Engaging in each of these has the power to influence our behaviors so we can be more thoughtful and intentional about acting in healthy, productive ways with others.

Generational Considerations and Strategies

Let's take a look at emotional intelligence across generations. According to findings from a survey on emotional intelligence, 70 percent of Gen Zers indicated that emotional intelligence (how you act) was more important that cognitive intelligence (what you know), a higher rate than that of other generations, particularly the 36 percent of Baby Boomers who indicated the same.[32]

Despite the youngest generation's view on its importance, research has found that this cohort actually has lower rates of emotional intelligence than their older counterparts.[33] This is evident nearly any way you look at the research. For example, when narrowing in on the four specific quadrants, Gen Zers, in data collected using the Student Leadership Competencies Inventory, reported lower proficiency scores for competencies related to self-awareness (understanding their strengths and weaknesses),[26] which is corroborated by findings from another study that found members of this cohort are less able to navigate emotions and manage volatility.[29] It's important to remember, though, that many young people are still learning about themselves and may need to be given some latitude as they clarify their values, uncover their strengths, and contend with weaknesses they may not have been aware of. So, offering professional development opportunities and peer feedback experiences that aid in expanding their self-awareness could be useful.

In addition, Gen Zers' scores fall behind those in other generations when it comes to self-management (behaving in an ethical manner).[26] We found this to be true in our workplace study as well, with their slightly lower levels of proficiency in being able to recognize and manage emotions.[7] To enhance the competencies in this quadrant, consider having them participate in training sessions on identifying and mitigating triggers, case studies and role plays around challenging scenarios, mind-mapping exercises to pre-identify obstacles, as well as stress-reduction workshops.

Gen Zers also had lower scores for social awareness (assessing a situation to determine socially acceptable behavior).[26] This isn't surprising in that hiring managers have noted Gen Zers struggling with professionalism, particularly with their inappropriate language use, lack of appropriate dress, and inability to make eye contact when talking.[34] But, it's important to consider that Gen Zers have been in the workforce for far less time than their older counterparts and may not be used to the more formal professional culture, especially since much of the early years of their careers were spent isolated during the pandemic, stripping them of opportunities to interact with others. Thus, high schools, colleges, and even workplaces may want to offer more training for Gen Zers to learn what professionalism looks like, for instance, appropriate dress code for certain tasks (like differentiating what one might wear to meet with the company CEO versus what to wear for day-to-day work). On the other hand, those in older generations might need to be more open to redefining professionalism to embrace the authenticity of Gen Zers. For instance, Air New Zealand removed their employee tattoo ban, and General Motors replaced their ten-page dress code policy with the words, "dress appropriately."

In terms of relationship management, members across all generations equally believe they develop healthy, trusting, and respectful relationships.[26] However, what they are looking for can vary. Baby Boomers want to feel valued and appreciated[7] and seek out people they can trust and are loyal. Gen Xers are reliant on relationships that foster independence, accountability, and with whom they share values. Millennials enjoy collaboration and open-mindedness and want to connect with those who are cooperative and value them for who they are. Gen Zers' desire for authenticity and inclusion allows them to easily reach out to others, especially across differences.

Leading Teams

Research has found that employees are spending 50 percent more time engaged in collaborative activities than two decades ago. That's a lot of team time! However, not everyone loves working in groups, likely because 20 to 35 percent of the tasks being undertaken are done by only 3 to 5 percent of the members.[35] Thus, having a good team leader can make all the difference, ensuring the purpose is well-defined, time is used wisely, and the distribution of work makes sense.

Generational Considerations and Strategies

While team orientation is a critical component of leadership across all generations, it is especially pronounced among the two youngest cohorts. For instance, knowing the members of their teams, leveraging their strengths, working alongside them, and looking out for their best interests have been identified by Millennials and Gen Zers as the qualities and behaviors most associated with an effective leader.[35]

So, which generation more often leads when on a team? Millennials by far, with 80 percent indicating they regularly take on the leading role in their groups.[7] On the other hand, only 45 percent of Baby Boomers noted the same. This may be due to them taking more of a backseat, relinquishing their seniority to younger generations, or simply out of less interest in needing to take on roles that might position oneself for career advancement.

In addition to how individuals engage in leadership roles can be instrumental to the functioning of the team. Let's take a look at two types of leadership approaches – task-orientation, which involves prioritizing the completion of the task over the relationships of team members, and relationship-orientation, which involves prioritizing relationships over the task. All four cohorts noted the importance of finishing a task at or above expectations (task-orientation). However, the other factor deemed most critical differed, with Baby Boomers prioritizing meeting deadlines (task-oriented), whereas those in the other three generations, want to ensure others involved in the task felt included (relationship-oriented).[7]

Let's say you have been tasked with leading an intergenerational ad hoc committee to plan the upcoming all-staff retreat. One of your members, Steve, is a Boomer who has worked for the organization for over two decades. So, he's been to his fair share of retreats. As discussed earlier, Baby Boomers are drawn to opportunities for critical thinking. Thus, Steve will likely want to look at past retreats to see what worked and what didn't, making those evaluations based on his personal experience. He will need the other team members to offer appreciation for the wisdom he brings as well as build on ideas rather than throw out something that might have worked in the past. To best lead Steve in this context, it's important to recognize his value and experience and perhaps lean on him to help the team explore various angles that could enhance the retreat rather than rebuild it entirely.

Katrina, a Gen Xer, is excited to be on the committee. She's attended three previous retreats and has some ideas for improvement. Being part of an expedient generation, she will likely want to use the team's scheduled meeting time to complete work so that there is less to do in between sessions. This may be challenging for Steve, in particular, as Baby Boomers would rather use the time together to brainstorm and solve problems than do work that could be completed outside of the meeting. Because of this, having a clear agenda about how much time is allocated to brainstorming versus task completion could be useful for everyone. Further, Katrina will want whatever tasks that aren't finished during the meeting to be divided equitably, with the expectation that all members follow through on their assigned parts.

Layla, a Millennial, is looking forward to serving on a team, as doing so offers a built-in mechanism for collaboration and feedback. As a relationship-builder, she will likely want everyone to get along and feel heard in the group process. Because of this, Layla may have a hard time focusing on the actual tasks if there is any outstanding tension. Team leaders will need to make sure to tend to the group processes by fostering teambuilding as well as addressing conflict quickly when it arises. Too much attention to this, however, could result in some task-oriented older employees wanting to check out.

Connor is a Gen Zer, new to the organization. He is ready to participate on the committee but is a bit anxious as he's never even been to a staff retreat before. Connor, like other Gen Zers, wants everyone to feel included, but he may lack some of the interpersonal skills needed to bring the group together. That's because greater amounts of screen time and less social interaction, along with the isolation of COVID, set some Gen Zers back in their interpersonal skill development. Thus, Connor may be inclined to relinquish any relationship-building roles to other members of the team. In leading Connor, it's important to seek his input, both to help him feel included and to validate that his opinion, which he may not readily give without encouragement, is valuable to the group. He, like Layla, would benefit from relationship-oriented activities that contribute to everyone getting to know each other and feel more comfortable in the team environment.

Leadership Development

With the high numbers of Baby Boomer retirements already in progress, there will continue to be a growing leadership gap. However, Development Dimensions International's study of global leaders reported that only 12 percent of organizations say they have a strong "bench" to draw from after their leaders move on.[23] And, the bench they do have might not be eager to stay the course.

Generational Considerations and Strategies

A global study of 7,700 Millennial full-time employees conducted by Deloitte found that the vast majority of those who were looking to leave their roles say that their leadership skills are not being fully developed in their current organizations.[36] Young employees crave leadership development opportunities, and providing them might help prepare and encourage Millennials and even Gen Zers to step into higher-level positions, ready to lead.

With the U.S. market for leadership development programs valued at $81.9 billion in 2024, with growth expected to reach $216.9 billion in

2034,[37] the time is now. And, some corporations are heeding the call. Take, for instance, the streaming music platform, Spotify. In 2023, the company offered 58 leadership programs for employees at all levels. And, the federal government's Office of Personnel Management provides dozens of leadership courses for aspiring to senior-level employees, along with offering certificate and coaching opportunities. Furthermore, higher education is responding as the number of leadership majors at colleges and universities tripled between 2000 and 2018.[38] Leadership development is critical for the functioning of and succession planning for organizations, and leveraging training opportunities can help ensure that those on the bench are ready and willing to play when called upon.

Conclusion

Billions of dollars are spent each year on developing and cultivating effective leaders who can empower employees and drive organizations toward success. While many factors are at play, generational characteristics, perspectives, and preferences shape how both leaders and followers show up. To best leverage the potential of both, it is important to consider these nuances to deploy the most effective, empowering, and engaging leadership for today, as well as for the future.

Notes

1 Bennis, W., & Nanus, B. (1997). *Leaders: Strategies for taking charge*. HarperBusiness.

2 Northouse, P. G. (2016). *Leadership: Theory and practice* (7th ed.). SAGE.

3 Arsenault, P. (2004). Validating generational differences: A legitimate diversity and leadership issue. *Leadership & Organization Development Journal, 25*(2), 124–141.

4 Bertsch, A., Saeed, M., Ondracek, J., Abdullah, ABM., Pizzo, J., Dahl, J., Scheschuk, S., Moore, W., & Youngren, D. (2022). Variation in preferred leadership styles across generations. *Journal of Leadership in Organizations, 4*(1), 1–16.

5 Anderson, H., Baur, J. E., Griffith, J. A., & Buckley, M. R. (2017). What works for you may not work for (Gen)Me: Limitations of present leadership theories for the new generation. *The Leadership Quarterly, 28*, 245–260.

6 Seemiller, C., & Grace, M. (2023). *Generations in the workplace*. Unpublished dataset.

7 Agustia, A. S., & Pandin, M. G. R. (2021). *Leadership style for Z generation.* https://doi.org/10.31219/osf. io/68mh9

8 Seemiller, C., & Grace, M. (2019). *Generation Z: A century in the making.* Routledge.

9 Gallup. (n.d.). *What are the four domains of CliftonStrengths?* www.gallup.com/cliftonstrengths/en/253736/cliftonstrengths-domains.aspx

10 Center for Creative Leadership. (2022). *The most important leadership competencies.* www.ccl.org/articles/leading-effectively-articles/most-important-leadership-competencies/

11 Zoom. (n.d.). *The heart of human connection.* www.zoom.com/en/about/

12 Lego. (n.d.). *About us.* www.lego.com/en-us/aboutus/lego-group/the-lego-brand?locale=en-us

13 Ancona, D., Malone, T. W., Orlikowski, W. J., & Senge, P. M. (2007). *In praise of the incomplete leader.* Harvard Business Review. https://hbr.org/2007/02/in-praise-of-the-incomplete-leader

14 Kraus, M. (2017). Comparing Generation X and Generation Y on their preferred emotional leadership style. *Journal of Applied Leadership and Management, 5,* 62–75.

15 World Economic Forum. (2023). *The future of jobs report 2023.* www.weforum.org/reports/the-future-of-jobs-report-2023/

16 Paczka, N. (2023). Different generations in the workplace – 2023 study. *LiveCareer.* www.livecareer.com/resources/careers/planning/generation-diversity-in-the-workplace

17 Mellan, O., & Christie, S. (2017). *Thinking Gen X: An overdue look at an overlooked generation.* www.thinkadvisor.com/2017/05/01/thinking-gen-x-an-overdue-look-at-an-overlooked-generation/

18 Locke, C. C. (2015). When it's safe to rely on intuition (and when it's not). *Harvard Business Review.* https://hbr.org/2015/04/when-its-safe-to-rely-on-intuition-and-when-its-not

19 Whole Foods. (2024). *Whole foods market history.* www.wholefoodsmarket.com/company-info/whole-foods-market-history#

20 Caballero-García, P. A., & Ruiz, S. S. (2024). The influence of gender and age on the open-mindedness of university students. *Education Sciences, 14*(1), 62.

21 Horizon Media. (2022). *The Gen Z field guide.* https://horizoncatalyst.com/the-2022-gen-z-field-guide

22 Hong, Y., Liao, H., Raub, S., & Han, J. H. (2016). What it takes to get proactive: An integrative multi-level model of the antecedents of personal initiative. *Journal of Applied Psychology, 101*(5), 687–701.

23 Development Dimensions International. (2023). *Global leadership forecast 2023.* www.ddiworld.com/global-leadership-forecast-2023

24 Bourne, B. (2015). Phenomenological study of generational response to organizational change. *Journal of Managerial Issues, 27*(1–4), 141–159.

25 Reeves, M., Rüdiger, F., Boulenger, A., & Job, A. (2023). Businesses need to bring younger employees into their leadership ranks. *Harvard Business Review.* https://hbr.org/2023/10/businesses-need-to-bring-younger-employees-into-their-leadership-ranks

26 Seemiller, C. (2024). *Student Leadership Competencies dataset.* Unpublished data set.

27 Vergauwe, J., Wille, B., Hofmans, J., Kaiser, R. B., & De Fruyt, P. (2017). Too much charisma can make leaders look less effective. *Harvard Business Review.* https://hbr.org/2017/09/too-much-charisma-can-make-leaders-look-less-effective

28 Rosing, K., & Jungmann, F. (2015). Leadership and Aging. In N. Pachana (Eds.), *Encyclopedia of Geropsychology.* Springer.

29 Antonakis, J., Fenley, M., & Liechti, S. (2012). Learning charisma. *Harvard Business Review.* https://hbr.org/2012/06/learning-charisma-2

30 Horwitch, M., & Whipple Callahan, M. (2016). *How leaders inspire: Cracking the code.* Bain & Company. www.bain.com/insights/how-leaders-inspire-cracking-the-code

31 Bradberry, T., & Greaves, J. (2009). *Emotional intelligence 2.0.* TalentSmart.

32 Machová, R., Zsigmond, T., Lazányi, K., & Krepszová, V. (2020). *Generations and emotional intelligence: A pilot study.* www.researchgate.net/publication/341363435_Generations_and_Emotional_Intelligence_A_Pilot_Study

33 Six Seconds. (2023). *State of the heart 2023.* https://eq.6seconds.org/soh23

34 Intelligent.com. (2023). *Nearly 4 in 10 employers avoid hiring recent college grads in favor of older workers.* www.intelligent.com/nearly-4-in-10-employers-avoid-hiring-recent-college-grads-in-favor-of-older-workers/

35 Aguas, M. J. (2019). Millennials and Generation Z's perspectives on effective leadership. *Emerging Leadership Journeys, 1*(13), 1–23.

36 Deloitte. (2016). *The 2016 Deloitte Millennial survey.* www2.deloitte.com/content/dam/Deloitte/global/Documents/About-Deloitte/gx-millenial-survey-2016-exec-summary.pdf

37 Future Market Insights. (2024). *Leadership development program market outlook from 2024 to 2034.* www.futuremarketinsights.com/reports/leadership-development-program-market

38 Lichtenwalner, B. (2020). *New study: Only 15% of schools offer leadership programs.* Radiant Forest, LLC. https://modernservantleader.com/resources/new-study-only-15-of-schools-offer-leadership-programs/

Putting Ideas into Action   **11**

This book has provided a deep dive into the perspectives, preferences, and behaviors of members of the four working generations and how those impact the way they navigate the world of work. By understanding generational nuances, organizational leaders, supervisors, and coworkers can deploy strategies for positive engagement and leverage the capacity of members of each cohort so that everyone can thrive together.

Baby Boomers

Baby Boomers entered their careers when landline phones, typewriters, and carbon copy machines were all the rage. As young employees, few saw women in the workforce, with more in teaching or secretarial roles, while their male supervisors made critical decisions behind closed doors in smoke-filled offices. The 1960s era was marked by the Civil Rights Movement, drawing attention to racism and discrimination in and out of the workplace. By the end of that decade and into the early 1970s, anti-war protests, environmentalism, and women's rights were hot topics. And Baby Boomers were witness to it all.

Today, some are retired; some are still working in their careers; and, some have moved into a golden career where they have changed industries or become entrepreneurs to focus more on their passions. Their presence in the workforce is strong and continues to shape the culture of the world of work for future generations.

DOI: 10.4324/9781003541035-11

Outreach and Recruitment

Whether switching workplaces, upskilling to new jobs, or starting their golden careers, Baby Boomers are still looking for work opportunities. Thus, knowing what is important to them in is paramount to recruiting them. For one, they are seeking organizations that will appreciate their skills and expertise and treat them as valuable and irreplaceable members. They want to feel like a part of the workplace family, where each individual matters.

In being recruited, they want to see demonstrable actions that show-case the organization's loyalty to employees (i.e. pensions, benefits, flexible scheduling, and trust). These should be evident in the recruitment materials, interactions with prospective coworkers and leaders, as well as during the interview. Essentially, what can Company X do for the Baby Boomer? Remember, they are interviewing the organization as much as the organization is interviewing them. And, many are willing to return to a former employer if the benefits are a better match.

While most Baby Boomers care about the pay, they also believe that work should help elicit in them a sense of purpose – doing something that matters. And, they want to know how their skills align with what the organization needs as well as how they can upskill in the job. Hiring managers and leaders need to do their homework to better understand what each Baby Boomer employee brings to the table and articulate a connection between the role and what the candidate offers.

In addition, they seek out places that demonstrate integrity. As the interviewee, Baby Boomers want to know about all the downsides and missteps of the organization upfront and what has been done to rectify those. Being honest and transparent is necessary to recruit this cohort.

In terms of recruitment tactics, most Baby Boomers enjoy face-to-face interactions and informal conversations, as authenticity and interpersonal connection are essential for them. Set up a coffee or lunch interview, if possible, as well as opportunities for them to engage with current employees and leaders to see if there is a fit.

Training and Development

Like all new employees, Baby Boomers will go through onboarding, but they are also seeking ongoing training and skill development. There want ample opportunities to participate in additional training sessions and professional development. While their preference is to do so in-person and in-house, they also enjoy conferences where they can meet and connect with people in their networks.

Although they prefer in-person trainings, Baby Boomers find webinars, online courses, and certificates valuable. Two caveats, though. They don't want all the bells and whistles of a complex tech platform, and they enjoy receiving paper or even digital copies of materials to refer to later. While they like intrapersonal learning, where they can self-pace or simply acquire new information on their own (particularly from YouTube), they aren't huge fans of social learning. This means that bringing them together in a conference room to complete individual online modules is not a good use of time for them.

Outside of events, Baby Boomers seek out mentors for skill development, meaning that they want to learn actual technical or leadership competencies from others directly. Given they might be some of the most experienced people in their industry or workplace, pairing two Baby Boomer employees together could help them learn from one another.

Job Structure

It's one thing to recruit an employee into a promising organization, and another to deliver all that was promised. What do Baby Boomers want in their workplaces to keep them there? For one, this is a generation that finds benefit in both on-site and remote work, thus a hybrid structure works well for many of them. Ideally, they want at least some control over their schedules. Perhaps this means being onsite two days per week and working at home the rest of the time. The flexibility is not just about scheduling for them, though; it's about balance and, most importantly, trust. They want to feel as though they are seen as competent and loyal enough to get their work done and be trusted to make decisions about when and where they work.

Consistent with other generations, they are productive, with the 9 am–6 pm workday being their preferred time block. They enjoy having dedicated space to work. Even in a hybrid situation, they want to come to their workplace and have their personal items and paper copies of important documents.

An essential consideration in retaining Baby Boomers, though, is that many aren't excited about change. Thus, any alterations to the workspace, scheduling, duties, or other aspects of their day-to-day work might not be met with open arms – unless either they helped conceive and implement the change or see a tremendous value in doing so.

Employee Engagement

Many Baby Boomers have worked in the same organization for a good portion of their careers and want it to be reiterated by their bosses and organizational leaders that they are an integral part of the larger landscape of the organization, and not just a number. Their main drivers of engagement are intrinsic. They thrive when their values align with their work, are excited about their duties, and feel a sense of commitment to the outcome. It's important to make sure that they know that their work matters.

Baby Boomers, more so than those in other generations, tend to trust their leaders, and excel in situations where they are trusted in return. This reciprocal relationship, built on loyalty and integrity, is critical for them to be engaged in the workplace.

Members of this generation also have a desire to feel productive and accomplished. They like to direct their own work and get things checked off their lists, particularly those tasks that fulfill an important purpose for the organization. In doing so, they are keen to deploy their critical thinking skills to tackle problems. And, with their initiative and persistence, they often won't give up until they've found an answer to a challenging question. In turn, they want their supervisors to listen, follow through, and solve problems, thriving most when they can work together to make a difference.

Well-being

Baby Boomers crave intellectual stimulation and seek out work that challenges them. It can be valuable to ask them for assistance with complex tasks, which not only serves the purpose of finding a solution but also says to them, "I value your insight."

Their spiritual well-being is also of utmost importance, emphasizing the role values alignment, purpose, and meaning have in their lives. Their strong focus on this underscores why they trust their gut when making decisions.

While they believe employers should be focusing on intellectual well-being, they also think workplaces have a responsibility to help foster emotional well-being. They want to work for people who value and appreciate them as well as are likable, kind, and can exercise appropriate emotional management. Interpersonal relationships play a significant role for many, and offering support aids in their ability to feel connected.

Working with Others

While Baby Boomers are typically task-oriented, their true focus is on building trusting, responsible relationships with others. They like to get to know their coworkers by collaborating on projects and even spending breaks with them. Their desire for face-to-face communication and camaraderie is evident in how they tend to want to utilize their time at work – chatting with colleagues, establishing personal connections, and learning more about others' ideas and perspectives.

Baby Boomers prefer in-person conversations but are open to using emails and phone calls to connect about work matters. Many resonate more with less automated tasks, as they are a way to preserve interpersonal relationships. This may include stopping by someone's workspace to ask a question rather than sending a direct message or email.

They want to work with others who are responsible and loyal and who hold themselves accountable. Perhaps based on how seasoned they are in the workplace, many have developed great levels of emotional intelligence and embrace a high standard of professionalism. This may take some young generations aback in that this is a generation that may put more emphasis on formal writing, professional dress, and appropriate interactions.

This is a generation that has grown through their careers with formal feedback mechanisms, like the annual performance evaluation. While they are used to this and, in many cases, deploy it with their subordinates, they would prefer others' opinions in the moment. They also want direct and straightforward feedback, without it being sandwiched between positive accolades.

Overall, Baby Boomers are hardworking, loyal employees with wisdom that can enhance organizations. It's important to appreciate and value them for the years of experience they bring and their conscientiousness to building positive, trusting relationships with those they work with.

Gen Xers

Many Gen Xers remember a time when you dropped off your application in-person at a job site – no emails, uploads, or video resumes. And, sometimes, you were even hired on the spot. Life seemed simpler; less red tape and bureaucratic processes. Stories of working your way up from the mailroom to the boardroom underscored the promise of "persistence and loyalty pay off." But, this access wasn't necessarily available to everyone. Although many of their moms were in the workforce, these kids were witness to disproportionate numbers of women in feminized professions, like teaching, nursing, and administrative support work, which garnered lower wages. While the inequity was discouraging, it also provided a motivation for some young girls to forge their way into higher-level, higher-status positions when they got older.

As Gen Xers aged, computers became commonplace, and they embraced technology, like the Internet, social media, and smartphones, as each was invented. Today, many Gen Xers are hard at work, trying to make ends meet to pay off their debt and cover caregiving expenses for their children and aging parents, all while saving for retirement, which seems further away every year.

Outreach and Recruitment

With work–life balance at the center for many of them, Gen Xers are prime for finding new roles to finish out their careers. They are seeking workplaces that offer flexibility and independence, particularly around scheduling, location, and work duties, as well as work that fills a purpose and where they can use their skills. If this information is not offered through the recruitment process, Gen Xers will ask. They have been in the workforce long enough to know what they are looking for.

Many members of this cohort identify as responsible and loyal and want to work for people who demonstrate those qualities. Thus, when being recruited, having a good fit with their future supervisor is paramount for them in making career decisions. Including a potential boss in the interview will be important for helping Gen Xers determine if the organization is the right place to be.

In addition to balance, pay is critical. Gen Xers hold the highest percentage of the overall student debt nationally and feel the pressure to bring in enough revenue to cover caretaking expenses of both their parents and children. But, they also want to work in roles that foster a sense of purpose and where they can utilize their skills to their utmost potential.

Like Baby Boomers, Gen Xers like informal conversations to build relationships and would likely welcome the opportunity to interact with potential coworkers as part of the interview process. This has to be a purposeful meeting as many are get-down-to-business type folks who won't want to participate in a long, drawn-out selection. Typically, though, Gen Xers are often recruited because they know someone already in the field. Thus, using personal networks, both online and offline, might help attract excellent Gen X candidates for the position.

Training and Development

Most Gen Xers' tenure in the workplace has allowed them the ability to soak up opportunities for professional development along the way. Thus, many seek out events and trainings as a means to re-skill and upskill, as well as foster meaningful, mentoring relationships with others.

For instance, most enjoy conferences, especially when there is a set purpose and clear agenda laid out so they can align their goals with those of the event to maximize their learning. Gen Xers, however, also use that time to connect with others, either catching up with old friends or seeking out new networks, particularly mentors who may help them clarify and leverage their passions as they reflect post-pandemic and mid-career.

Many Gen Xers, though, also find digital learning useful and valuable, including webinars, online courses, and certificates. In particular, they enjoy the interactive components available in these settings. While they like acquiring new information through videos, especially from YouTube, they aren't as keen on social learning, where they would be gathered with others to complete individual training in a group setting. Again, this is an independent, expedient generation who is interested in being responsible for their own experiences. When designing digital learning, consider that Gen Xers will want a clearly stated purpose, interactivity, and then to be left to do it on their own.

Job Structure

The COVID-19 pandemic set in motion a reflection and revisitation of values for many Gen Xers. Some have moved along to different jobs, and others into entirely new careers. There is one main reason for that – flexibility. In terms of location, more Gen Xers want to work remotely than are actually doing so. Many have not been eager to come back to the office, as they see remote work as a perk that has been taken from them. Aside from this impacting balance, the call-back move, in their minds, is also reflective of a lack of trust by organizational leaders. This is an autonomous, driven generation, with many feeling they don't need close supervision or micromanagement (and would fare better without it). Too much oversight can feel suffocating for them. If organizations want to keep talented Generation X employees, they must be flexible with them in terms of work location.

Unsurprisingly, Gen Xers prefer the 9 am–6 pm workday. Some like full control over their schedules, and others are fine with their employers setting their shifts. The vast majority, though, want whatever those schedules are to be flexible and balanced.

Gen Xers, more so than Baby Boomers, welcome change – as long as it makes sense. They are taken aback if a new protocol or process, for example, is implemented without consulting those who it affects the most. If they can't see the value in the change or their concerns have gone unwelcomed, they may become resistant and find it to be a reason to leave their workplaces. If an organization is planning changes, it is helpful to at least run it by Gen Xers to allow an opportunity for review and feedback before full implementation.

Employee Engagement

Gen Xers can be highly engaged in their organizations, a lot of which is driven by the conditions that allow them to leverage their passions and potential. Generally, they are motivated by setting their own goals and determining their own workflow. And it is clear that they need autonomy, independence, and trust. Just accomplishing a task at a high caliber is drive enough for many of them to do so, especially if the process is absent from micromanaging. This is a practical, sensible, and industrious generation. Others view them as determined, and it's true. They are persistent and gritty. Oftentimes, Gen Xers won't stop until they figure out the problem or fix the issue. Be aware, though, that some might focus on something too long, trying to salvage an idea that has run its course.

While trust is an important component for retaining Generation X, it is also imperative for engagement. When Gen Xers feel trusted by their supervisors, many rise to the challenge, putting forth their best and most creative work. Without it, not only might they feel disconnected from their duties and potentially lack in their performance, some may opt for a different career opportunity altogether.

Gen Xers crave challenging work where they can gain a sense of accomplishment while simultaneously developing their capacities. Their desire to feel productive and get business done quickly shows up as them needing ample information, clear, data-driven solutions, organized workspaces, and expedient meetings. Even their visioning process moves with purpose, as many desire to get started on a project right away even if they won't reap the benefits until later.

Well-being

This is a generation that rates themselves higher in intellectual, emotional, and occupational well-being. In summation, they feel they are cognitively stimulated, emotionally in tune with themselves, and in a good place when it comes to their careers. Their own views of themselves align with what they believe is important in the workplace – particularly working in an environment that is supportive of emotional well-being.

Further, many think that employers should focus on financial well-being to ensure workers are provided ample salaries and benefits, along with resources, advising, and opportunities to manage their money better. This is of critical importance, as financial well-being is rated the lowest among Gen Xers in terms of their own lives.

Many in this cohort also think that organizations should have a greater focus on intellectual well-being and should offer duties and tasks that stimulate one's mind as well as provide opportunities for workers to enhance their expertise.

Working with Others

Even though they like independent work and efficient processes, Gen Xers always have time to create collegial relationships. They enjoy engaging in professional development experiences, particularly conferences, with coworkers as well as hanging out after work. Some even add their colleagues on social media. But, know that Gen Xers identify as responsible and loyal and look to their connections to be the same, wanting relationships to embody open communication and trust.

Gen Xers like to see themselves as collaborative and enjoy interacting with others through group work, as long as the workload is distributed fairly and everyone is accountable. But, with many desiring to operate at a speedier clip, they may have high standards for their teammates.

Similar to Baby Boomers, this cohort believes communication is a critical workforce skill. They strive to be adept at this and expect others to be as well. Through informal conversations and relationship-building outside of work, Gen Xers invest in personal connections, both for social fulfillment, as well as to have greater ease in being able to discuss ideas and make decisions together in the workplace.

While they like to make decisions in conjunction with others, most have been in the workforce long enough to feel confident and support their own ideas. Given members of other cohorts regard them as the most inspirational generation, don't be surprised if they are wholeheartedly convincing with the ability to mobilize others.

In terms of supervision, this is a generation that wants timely and direct feedback, often in a more informal manner. Most are not interested in waiting until their annual evaluation to hear about an issue they could have rectified months earlier. And, many don't appreciate receiving unsolicited feedback unless it's crucial and contains information they need to know. Despite their desire for straightforward communication, they do value kindness and likeability from those they work with and work for.

Aside from face-to-face communication, Gen Xers like using the phone, email, and texting. This makes it easy for them to be able to speak multiple digital languages with those from other generations.

Many Gen Xers, by virtue of their stage in the career lifecycle and their generational attributes, can serve as the backbone and lifeblood of many organizations. They are keepers of institutional knowledge, yet open to sensible change. Others can often depend on them to work hard, persist when things get difficult, rise from failure, and move forward.

Millennials

Millennials were promised an amazing future with stability and prosperity, especially for those with a college degree. But, their entry into the workforce, burdened by the 2008–2009 Great Recession, provided anything but that. These T-9 texting, MySpace users were instead saddled with student debt and low wages as they embarked on their newfound occupations. It's no surprise then that this cohort has been playing career catchup most of their professional lives. For many, this has meant taking advantage of any advancement opportunities within or even outside of their organizations. For others, it has involved asking for a raise or promotion perhaps, prematurely – at least in the eyes of those in older cohorts. But, that doesn't hold them back. Parents of this generation infused in their Millennial children a sense of positivity, great self-worth, and an "ask for what you want" mentality, which has served them well during their careers.

Outreach and Recruitment

As a responsible, loyal, and confident generation, Millennials know that what they bring to their workplaces is immensely valuable. Thus, they have high expectations for what organizations will provide them – in particular, in the form of good salaries, advancement opportunities, and accolades.

Because of this, many in this cohort believe people should be rewarded for their hard work rather than experience and are not shy to apply for roles they may not be fully qualified for, in the hopes they can demonstrate their competencies once on the job. This aligns with the notion that their primary reasons for working include to earn an income and use their skills. With a significant number of them having student debt, many are prone to advance outside the organization, especially if the compensation is better. However, the majority also want to engage in work that gives them a sense of purpose. It's important, then, to highlight both the potential opportunities for growth within the organization, along with the meaningfulness of the day-to-day work.

In addition, many in this generation care deeply about DEI and seek out organizations that support policies and initiatives that create fair and inclusive workplaces. Highlighting employee resource groups, programs, and other efforts will give Millennials a more holistic picture of the organization.

From knowing someone in the field to seeing a job portrayed in the media, Millennials come into their career fields through a variety of pathways. The key for organizations is to diversify recruitment strategies so that there are several channels to reach this prospective employee population.

Millennials entered the workforce when computers, the Internet, and email were widely used, making online job search platforms commonplace.

They could upload one resume and select any number of positions to apply for simultaneously. Thus, they are comfortable and confident in a broad and comprehensive job search process. Once they are in the interview stage, many enjoy informal conversations to build relationships. Like their older counterparts, it might be useful to have opportunities for Millennials to get to know their potential colleagues and have meaningful interpersonal interactions as part of the selection process. Given that they are highly collaborative, they want to know how they will be a part of a team and what their interpersonal connections within an organization will be like.

Training and Development

This is a generation that finds webinars, online courses, and certificates valuable, with many posting their attendance on social media, highlighting the content they learned or the certificate they earned. While they like these digital modalities, many do not resonate as much with social learning, where they gather with others to engage in development opportunities side-by-side, minus any interaction.

Millennials see their professional development experiences as more holistic. They participate to learn and develop for their careers but aim to also fuel their own personal goals and desires. Many will select conferences to attend that are located in destinations they want to visit and read inspirational biographies that provide life lessons. In addition, because inclusive workplaces matter to them, both for their personal and professional well-being, they believe training around these subjects is essential, so everyone gains the knowledge and skills necessary to create welcoming environments.

An important note about training this generation is that they benefit from demonstrated learning. Many of them would like to see a task completed or a skill executed in front of them first before being asked to do the same. A supervisor, in particular, then might need to take a Millennial through a task from start to finish before delegating work. Demonstrations, like a checklist with screenshots or a quick video tutorial, can provide Millennials even more confidence to complete their work without having to seek out their supervisors to ask questions. Further, this is a generation that takes advantage of mentoring opportunities, always looking for additional networks to help develop their skills and connect them with others for career advancement.

Job Structure

Many Millennials grew quite comfortable doing remote work during the height of the COVID-19 pandemic. As they, along with those in other generations, have gotten called back on-site either full-time or in a hybrid capacity, many have been reluctant to go. They crave flexibility and want to determine the best location for their productivity and engagement – not have it determined by management. Given their desire for advancement and lack of hesitation in applying for other roles, an office callback may be short-lived for those Millennials who want to work remotely. They will simply leave and find flexibility in other places.

The same could be said of scheduling, where they, too, have a desire for flexibility. While most enjoy working 9 am–6 pm work, they want to be able to flex those times on occasion. But most aren't in situations where they can. For instance, fewer Millennials who prefer full or even some control over their schedules believe they have it. As it is with location, some Millennials may simply opt to leave places that are inflexible in search of greater balance and more autonomy over their work conditions.

Employee Engagement

This is a generation that sees themselves as visionary, and in turn, wants to be inspired with others and not by others. They are generally optimistic, spontaneous, and driven by accomplishment. Essentially, they want to do big things. And, many are confident, courageous, and determined. Workplaces that capitalize on their visionary, bold convictions are likely going to maximize the potential of this cohort.

Many Millennials are also drawn to opportunities for creativity, and utilize their entrepreneurial spirit to get there. They want to be tapped to do higher-level, complex work, and welcome automation and artificial intelligence as a means to streamline their jobs. However, if they are asked to do rote tasks that could easily be digitized or automated, they may feel their talents and creativity are being underutilized.

For some, though, it takes more than a courageous vision, meaningful work, and creative latitude; they also need ample accolades, rewards, and incentives. Providing opportunities for them to exact their innovative skills, and then recognizing them for their efforts, can help this generation bring their visions to life.

Well-being

Many Millennials rate themselves high in intellectual well-being, likely given their ability to be creative and entrepreneurial in their workplaces. However, they also believe their physical well-being is strong, which involves healthy eating, exercise, and an attention to their health, in general. Despite this, a large number want their employers to focus even more so on this. This makes sense in that the image of the Millennial startup in the mid-2000s often involved a workout room, fitness area, recreational spaces with pool tables and other games, food and beverage buffets open all day, and even nap pods. Although some more established workplaces may not be able to institute all of those amenities, there is a value for Millennials in offering at least some.

Many in this cohort, though, believe their social well-being is low, and that employers have a responsibility for increasing it. This may mean offering more networking events, teambuilding activities, formal lunches, and organized gatherings around specific interests, like a book club or hiking group.

Working with Others

Millennials tend to be a collaborative, collegial generation. And, as much as they want to foster social connection with their coworkers in the workplace through formal activities, they also like more informal out-of-work experiences. They enjoy spending time together after hours and on weekends, connecting with them on social media, and even chatting over lunches and breaks during their shifts. But they don't just want friends to hang out with; they seek trust, accountability, and commitment in all of their relationships. If they are going to open themselves up, they expect the same in return.

This highly collaborative generation enjoys the sense of camaraderie that is formed when working with others. They like to distribute the workload and consider new ideas and perspectives, although they try to ensure that those expressed are acknowledged as valuable contributions rather than scrutinized. Many take on the leading role in groups, liking to set the direction for the team.

While generally identifying as confident and charismatic, some may still suffer from the imposter syndrome, striving to prove their legitimacy to those they work with. Because they may apply for and even obtain positions that are more aspirational in terms of their knowledge and skills, the conditions are in place for imposter syndrome to take effect. It's important, then, for there to be strong mentoring and a trusting culture so that Millennials can express any insecurities they may have and receive support, guidance, and further training.

There is consistency among Millennials in terms of their preferences for using different communication methods for work. While in-person conversations are rated highest among this cohort, the gap between their preferences for other forms of communication is small. They are also fairly forthcoming on social media, sharing personal information and expertise with their connections. And, given that they like to add colleagues as connections on social media, it wouldn't be unusual for coworkers to know their business.

While the majority of Millennials have direct reports, most are not in senior management roles and thus report to their own supervisors. It is important for them to make sure they are on the right path, prompting them to ask for instructions, deadlines, follow-up, frequent feedback, and praise. And, they like it in real-time – no waiting until a formal meeting to go over details of a project or an end-of-the-year performance evaluation. Unlike Baby Boomers and Gen Xers who prefer direct, cut-to-the-chase feedback, Millennials like theirs delivered with empathy and compassion from their "likeable" supervisors.

Gen Zers

Recession babies, Zoomers, digital natives – call them what you will. Generation Z has entered the workforce and brings with them perspectives and experiences shaped by the events that took place during their adolescence and young adulthood. Growing up during an era marked by post-Recession recovery, political hyper-partisanship, the proliferation of social media, and the COVID-19 pandemic, this cohort has come face-to-face with issues that have challenged their interpersonal development, trust in institutions, financial mindset, and perceptions of well-being. Thus, we have a generation of young people with very distinct expectations. These authenticity-seeking, meaning-making, boundary-setting individuals are in the workforce to make their impact – in their own unique way.

Outreach and Recruitment

Like other generations, Gen Zers want a salary where they won't have to struggle to make ends meet, a place where they can develop and then utilize their skills, and engage in work that has purpose and meaning, connecting their duties to the larger goals of the organization. Being able to convey that to prospective Generation Z employees is critical for recruiting them.

However, some Gen Zers might be prone to take jobs that have less than livable salaries or work in less appealing geographic areas at the onset of their careers to get their foot in the door. But, given high numbers engage in 1099 contract work, it isn't surprising that some may supplement their primary roles with side hustles and either balance the two or ultimately leave their full-time jobs to invest more time in these gigs. Thus, flexibility in scheduling to accommodate these side jobs as well as a clear path to increased compensation is paramount for these young employees to stay and thrive in their organizations.

Further, as a highly loyal generation, many are seeking organizations that are loyal in return and value their uniqueness and authenticity, particularly around diversity. They want to work in places that embrace inclusive dress codes, offer employee resource groups, as well as have a culture that is compassionate towards all employees. Mentoring is also key for this generation. They want to know they have access to people who can aid in their professional growth. Thus, if they feel compensated, connected, supported, and valued, they have a likelihood of staying in their organizations for the long term.

Gen Zers often find their careers through more informal means, like knowing someone in the field, already having a related hobby, seeing it on TV, or reading about it. Thus, it is their personal connections and experiences that are more likely to propel them into their future careers.

Training and Development

Gen Zers seek out opportunities for development, particularly in that being adequately trained helps them feel more prepared for and engaged in their work. But, they don't just participate in any opportunity. They want to know the value proposition ahead of time. If they are going to invest, what is expected of them, and what they will get out of it? They are most drawn to experiential learning, where they can apply their knowledge in practice settings, with others, and not simply just next to them. This means that being called together in person must have a reason other than account-ability for attendance. Further, many aren't keen on participating in an event where they don't know anyone. Helping connect them to others in attendance can help reduce any hesitance on their part.

With the right value proposition and others to accompany them, in-person events can be beneficial for this cohort. However, many prefer online options like webinars, courses, and certificates, and are even more interested in tuning into a pre-recorded TED Talk than watching a speaker present live. What is key for many of them is utilizing any digital modality to its fullest capacity, rather than giving an analog presentation in a virtual setting. Thus, they are most engaged when hand-raising, polls, and quizzes are integrated.

Further, their interest in self-help books, as well as mentoring, can assist them in capitalizing on their passions and link them to career opportunities in a more personalized and tailored fashion.

Job Structure

This is a generation that enjoys remote work. However, a hybrid situation may be advantageous for those who like the social and supportive nature of onsite work. Thus, going into the office a few days a week guarantees they have an adequate workspace, given some don't have a distraction-free one at home. But, being onsite the entire time is too confining for some of them. They like the flexibility that comes with remote work, less because their spaces are ideal and more because they can control their location, giving them a greater ability to be mobile.

Like those in other cohorts, Gen Zers prefer the typical 9 am–6 pm day. Outside of that, though, many thrive better at night. For those doing shift work, this may be beneficial in that being open to a wide variety of schedules can expand their possibilities for employment. For others in an office setting, flexibility in their schedules is important. If they get a surge to work from 10 pm to midnight, perhaps they don't start the next day until later than usual. But, the pressures of presenteeism are real. There is a burden of having to be "seen" during regular hours when their supervisors take note, giving them little incentive to press on later at night as additional, not substitutive, hours. Removing this pressure may help empower Gen Zers to maximize their productivity by working hours that align better with their strengths.

Employee Engagement

This cohort is primarily intrinsically engaged, meaning they are excited to come to work and committed to doing a good job when they feel their tasks and roles align with their values and what they are doing is meaningful. Because of this, they want to know why their work matters – not just an overall sentiment of its importance but also why and how each duty they engage in makes a difference.

While many are flexible, adaptable, open-minded, and curious, they also have clear boundaries about what they are willing to do. It would not be surprising to hear a Gen Zer say "no" to a task outside their job duties, unless it was adequately compensated, in lieu of another assigned duty, or clearly articulated to them as to its positive impact.

When Gen Zers feel connected to their work, they put in great effort. Many are DIYers, always looking for creative and entrepreneurial ways to innovate; they thrive on feeling accomplished. Some, though, might give up easily, as they have been known to be the least gritty generation. This may stem from the notion that fewer of them compared to those in other generations believe demonstrating commitment, follow-through, and accountability are important workplace skills. Likely shaped by their upbringing post-Recession and during the COVID-19 pandemic, they saw what staying the course looks like, even in times when it isn't healthy to do so. Some of what might appear as low resilience could also be reflective of their lack of desire to remain in a toxic or bad situation – especially in that many exhibit lower levels of optimism which can manifest as over-worrying, distrusting others, or not taking risks, ultimately prompting them to leave. Thus, trust-building is key for Gen Zers to feel safe and stable in their jobs. And, providing support and guidance to stick through challenging times can help model for them ways to enhance their resilience in a healthy way.

This is a generation that likes challenging work and opportunities for growth, couched within a trusting organizational culture that mitigates stress and has clearly defined systems and protocols. Essentially, they want to work somewhere that has clear expectations, pathways and resources for meeting those, and are free from stress as much as possible. Like Millennials, many support AI and automation, making them worried less about losing their jobs and more interested in utilizing technology to aid in their success.

Well-being

The early years of the COVID-19 pandemic made a great impact on Generation Z young adults entering the workforce. Many faced educational challenges, having to take time off from college or mustering their way through a last-minute adapted online educational experience. However, the largest setback, involved their interpersonal development, which began even pre-COVID due to the proliferation of social media and other technology. Many were not taught or even witnessed how to effectively interact with others. Then, with COVID, the opportunity and ability to have in-person conversations during their pivotal social development years became limited, reducing the time one spent honing those skills. And, those who entered the workforce during the height of the pandemic were often quite distanced from their coworkers and supervisors, making relationship-building a bit more challenging. While they rate their social well-being the lowest, some believe that the responsibility of enhancing employee social well-being falls, at least in part, on employers. Opportunities for connection in the workplace are critical to helping this generation feel healthy and engaged.

Their higher levels of intellectual and spiritual well-being, though, indicate what these young employees lean on to persist and thrive. Being cognitively challenged in the job can make one feel utilized and help to pass the time by being in a flow state. Gen Zers may also find solace in their spiritual beliefs and sense of purpose, helping them cope with a world that has been relatively unstable since their emergence into adolescence.

It's no surprise that Gen Zers want employers to focus on financial well-being, given that they tend to be the least tenured, and thus lowest paid, generation. And, their desire to have employers focus more on this makes sense – their organizations are the gatekeepers of their salaries and benefits. However, there is even more that can be done aside from raising wages, such as holding financial literacy workshops, offering financial advising and mentoring, and providing options for preparing for retirement.

Working with Others

Gen Zers like building relationships with coworkers – as long as those can be authentic, welcoming, and compassionate. They are looking to connect with people who share their values rather than are simply housed in adjacent workspaces. And, many enjoy connecting after work and on weekends.

However, some lack high levels of emotional intelligence to be able to understand themselves, manage emotions, and act in a professional manner. This is likely due to a combination of spending more time on technology, and less in-person, as well as not having been taught these skills, given many grew up in a standardized testing era where classes with social components, like physical education, music, and art, were replaced with math and science. Thus, employers may have to play a more significant role in the development of emotional intelligence skills with Generation Z professionals.

Many of them, like their Millennial counterparts, have had imposter syndrome. Yet, as their confidence grows with experience and time, this may fade. Given they want authentic environments, it is likely that they will let their supervisors or even peers know when they are struggling. Making sure to check in with them, though, is critical, as some might wait too long before speaking up.

Many Gen Zers like working in groups because it offers them the opportunity to interact with others, hear new perspectives, and gain motivation to get work done. However, there are particular conditions that are important for Gen Zers when engaging on teams. For one, they want an inclusive space where all ideas are welcome, especially since some wait to be invited before sharing their thoughts in groups. In addition, an explicit means for measuring contribution is essential as they don't like having to worry about doing other people's tasks or having their performance negatively impacted by others.

For Gen Zers, communication is a critical workforce skill and one that is important for developing productive workplace relationships. Although some struggle with interpersonal skills, they do see the value of being able to communicate effectively across multiple channels. Gen Zers report using video chat, telephone calls, and emailing at higher rates than they indicate liking these methods. They also prefer text messaging, followed by in-person conversation, email, video chat, and phone, with direct messaging slightly lower. They have the ability to toggle between modalities, yet are the only generation to prefer a digital method over a face-to-face one. In addition, social media is intertwined in their lives, where they also move between platforms, engaging in specific tasks on each.

While 49 percent have direct reports, there isn't an overwhelming sentiment for many to move into supervisory roles. Some lack confidence, others don't like giving feedback, and even others want to avoid the stress and feel it's not worth the measly pay bump. Just as they may be sure about their supervisory aspirations, they have clear expectations of what they want. They are looking for their bosses to follow up with them, give frequent and in-the-moment feedback, and provide support to maximize their strengths and mitigate their weaknesses.

Many in this cohort have learned to work around systems they don't trust. But, in an ideal world, they want to be in trustworthy environments, one where bosses are transparent and managers base decisions on data. Thus, creating this type of culture is imperative for helping to restore their faith in organizations, institutions, and their leaders.

Conclusion

As the world of work continues to change, so too do the employees within it. Understanding, appreciating, and maximizing interactions with members across generational cohorts can help create and sustain optimal conditions in which everyone has the opportunity to thrive in authentic and meaningful ways.

Index

Printed in the United States
by Baker & Taylor Publisher Services